ISBN 978-1-331-42445-1
PIBN 10188282

For support please visit www.forgottenbooks.com

1 MONTH OF
FREE
READING

at

www.ForgottenBooks.com

By purchasing this book you are eligible for one month membership to ForgottenBooks.com, giving you unlimited access to our entire collection of over 1,000,000 titles via our web site and mobile apps.

To claim your free month visit:

www.forgottenbooks.com/free188282

English Worthies

EDITED BY ANDREW LANG

RICHARD STEELE

BY

AUSTIN DOBSON

LONDON
LONGMANS, GREEN, AND CO.
1886

PREFATORY NOTE.

As the authorities upon which the following memoir is based are generally indicated in its pages, and any new facts which it contains are sufficiently announced in the text, it is unnecessary to do more here than make one or two indispensable acknowledgments. My sincere thanks are due to the Duke of Marlborough for his kindness in granting me access to those MSS. at Blenheim which relate to Steele; and to the Earl of Egmont for permission to transcribe the valuable letters of Bishop Berkeley to Sir John Perceval, quoted in Chapter VI. Among many friends who have aided me with advice or suggestion I must specially record my obligations to the late Mr. Edward Solly, who not only placed his unique eighteenth-century library at my service, but also gave me the benefit of his own indefatigable research and scrupulous accuracy.

CONTENTS.

RICHARD STEELE.

---◆---

CHAPTER I.

SCHOOLBOY AND SOLDIER.

'I AM an *Englishman* born in the City of *Dublin*,' says Steele, in one of his political papers. It would have saved his biographers some misconception, and no little perplexity, had he carried his confidences further, and added the date of his birth. In the *Biographia Britannica*, that event is said to have occurred 'probably about the year 1676,' while Nathan Drake, who did so much for the essayists of the eighteenth century, places it about 1675. This is the date adopted by Steele's most fervent apologist, Mr. John Forster. Yet, not very long after Drake's sketch first appeared, Nichols the antiquary published a certificate from the register of St. Bridget's, Dublin, to the effect that Steele's baptism took place on the 12th of March, 1671. This, supposing him to have been baptized like his friend Addison on the day of his birth, should, one might think, have sufficed to settle the question, especially as a copy of the certificate is preserved among Steele's

B

loose papers in the British Museum. Unfortunately, this date is at variance with those given in two other records which have equal claims to authenticity. One is the entry of his nomination to the Charterhouse, where he is described in November, 1684, as aged thirteen on the 12th of March next, which would make him to have been born in March, 1672. The other is the entry of his matriculation at Christ Church, Oxford, in March, 1690, which gives his age as sixteen. This entry, no doubt, is answerable for the date chosen by Drake and the *Biographia Britannica*; and it is, in all probability, an error. The Charterhouse entry has the greatest look of accuracy, and was most likely supplied by Steele himself, or by some one connected with him, who was properly informed. Moreover, if we assume March, 1671, in the register of St. Bridget's, to have been March 'Old Style,' instead of March 'New Style,' the year may be read as 1672. In March, 1672, then, Richard Steele was born. He was consequently by some weeks the senior of the famous writer with whom he is so often associated—the friend who was his schoolmate at the Charterhouse and his contemporary at college. For Joseph Addison entered the world—and there is luckily no doubt about the date of that occurrence—on the 1st of May, 1672.

Of Steele's parentage little is known.[1] By his

---

[1] The late Dr. W. E. Steele, of Dublin, in a communication made to *Notes and Queries* in July, 1861, asserted that Steele's father was the son of William Steele (d. 1680), Lord Chancellor of Ireland under the Cromwells. But from pedigrees printed by Mr. R. S. Boddington in Howard's *Miscellanea Genealogica et Heraldica* (New Series), 1877, pp. 36–38, the connection between Richard Steele, Steele's father, and Richard Steele, William Steele's son, is not clearly made

earlier biographers his father, also Richard Steele, was
described as a Counsellor at Law and private secretary
to James Butler, first Duke of Ormond, Lord Lieutenant
of Ireland, and this statement was industriously repeated. But, as recently as 1868, Mr. W. H. Wills,
making some preliminary researches for a biography of
the great essayist, which, to the less of literature, he
never lived to complete, speedily discovered that no
such name as Steele appears in the lists of counsel in
the Four Courts of Dublin for the period required,
although a Richard Steele was admitted a member of
the King's-Inns, as an attorney, in 1667. Neither—so
Mr. Wills assured himself—did any gentleman named
Steele hold the office of private secretary to the first
Duke of Ormond, though, as will presently appear, that
post was filled by one of Richard Steele's relatives. It
is, therefore, possible that he may, in some way or other,
have been employed in his legal capacity by the Duke;
and that thus colour was given to the story of his more
confidential relations with Ormond. His son, as far as
we can remember, alludes to him on two occasions only.
In one of these (*Tatler*, No. 22), speaking of the actor,
Cave Underhill, then in his decline, he says (not indeed
with perfect lucidity): 'My Father admir'd him extremely when he was a Boy.'[1] Steele could scarcely
have learnt this from his father himself, as another
famous *Tatler*, No. 181, informs us that that father
died in his son's childhood. 'The first Sense of Sorrow

out. It seems also highly improbable that Steele, always tenacious
about his being 'a Gentleman born,' would have suppressed the
fact that his grandfather had been a Lord Chancellor.

[1] In the original *folio* it is 'my Grandfather,' so that the phrase
has no particular autobiographical value.

I ever knew,' he says, in one of his most beautiful and pathetic passages, ' was upon the Death of my Father, at which Time I was not quite Five Years of Age; but was rather amazed at what all the House meant, than possessed with a real Understanding why no Body was willing to play with me. I remember I went into the Room where his Body lay, and my Mother sat weeping alone by it. I had my Battledore in my Hand, and fell a beating the Coffin, and calling Papa, for I know not how I had some slight Idea that he was locked up there. My Mother catched me in her Arms, and transported beyond all Patience of the silent Grief she was before in, she almost smothered me in her Embrace, and told me in a Flood of Tears, Papa could not hear me, and would play with me no more, for they were going to put him under Ground, whence he could never come to us again. She was a very beautiful Woman, of a noble Spirit, and there was a Dignity in her Grief amidst all the Wildness of her Transport, which, methought, struck me with an Instinct of Sorrow, which, before I was sensible of what it was to grieve, seized my very Soul, and has made Pity the Weakness of my Heart ever since.' Beyond the above reference to his mother, nothing further is recorded of her; and it must be assumed that she did not long survive her husband,—at all events, that she was dead when Steele wrote the foregoing *Tatler*. Tradition affirms that she was Irish; and that she came of a Wexford family. It has also been stated that her maiden name was Gascoigne,[1] but the statement requires confirmation.

[1] Nichols, *Epistolary Correspondence of Sir Richard Steele*, 1809, i. 204, infers this from the fact that Gascoigne was the name of Steele's

In any case the name of Gascoigne must have been familiar enough to Steele, in his earlier days. In 1674, the Duke of Ormond's secretary, Sir George Lane, was succeeded by one Henry Gascoigne, who was Steele's uncle. It is probable that he early began to interest himself in the fatherless boy, since, in a letter that we shall presently quote, his nephew says 'to his goodness I humbly acknowledge my being.' It is also only reasonable to suppose that, through Gascoigne's interest with the Duke, who was one of the Governors of Charterhouse, Steele was nominated to that school on the 17th of November, 1684, being then, according to the entry in the register, which the kindness of the Head Master has permitted us to verify, between twelve and thirteen. Here is the record :—' Richard Steel admitted for the Duke of Ormond, in the room of Phillip Burrell—aged 13 years 12th March next.'

Of Steele's school-days nothing is known with certainty ; indeed, there are few traditions respecting them, beyond the fact that he then made the acquaintance of Addison, who, as already stated, was his junior. The Head Master of that time was Dr. Thomas Walker, ' a man of high character and extensive learning' to whom incidental reference is supposed to be made in *Spectator*

uncle. But in *Notes and Queries* for the 3rd of August, 1861, it is stated upon the authority of a 'Mr. Wm. Steele, of Dublin,' that ' Sir R. Steele's mother was a Miss Devereux, of the County of Wexford.' To complicate matters further, according to Howard's *Miscellanea Genealogica et Heraldica* (New Series), 1877, ii. 36, there is an entry in the Consistorial Court, Dublin, of a licence dated 1670 ' for the marriage of Richard Steele, of Mountain, co. Dublin, gent., and Eleanor Symes, of St. Bridget's Parish, Dublin, widow, and daughter of —— Sheyles.'

No. 488, and it is pleasant to think that the old gentleman, fifty-four years of whose long life were spent in
Thomas Sutton's school at Smithfield, continued to
take an interest in his distinguished pupils. 'The
ingenious *T. W.*,' says Addison, *à propos* of the increased
price of the paper in consequence of the Stamp Tax,
'tells me, that I have deprived him of the best Part of
his Breakfast, for that, since the Rise of my Paper, he
is forced every Morning to drink his Dish of Coffee by
it self, without the Addition of the *Spectator*, that used
to be better than Lace to it.' The Usher was an undistinguished John Stacey,—Tooke of the *Pantheon*,
whose 'fair humanities of old religion' still interchange
their quaint dialogues in the four-penny box, belonging
to a decade later. But of Steele's dealings with either
Usher or Master, Time has left no trace, although it
may safely be assumed that the rites connected with the
whipping-block sometimes brought them into intimate
relations. 'In my Twelfth Year,'—says Mr. Bickerstaff,—'I suffer'd very much for Two or Three false
Concords.' Elsewhere he tells us pleasantly that the
stripes he endured about *Digito male pertinaci* are the
cause of his irreconcilable aversion to Coquettes; and
when, later, he wrote in the *Spectator*[1] a noble paper
about the barbarity of flogging at school it is only
reasonable to suppose that his indignation was stimu-
lated by his memories. But whether he was or was not,
to use Gay's phrase—'lash'd into *Latin* by the tingling
rod,' he must, judging by his after proficiency in 'Tully'
and Terence, have been fairly grounded in the classics
before he went up to Christ Church, to which place he

[1] *Spectator*, No. 157.

was 'elected' on the 1st of November, 1689, obtaining a small exhibition. Concerning the prompt and early payment of this, in one of the much-mutilated MSS. at Kilkenny Castle, he is characteristically anxious. ['No one living'] says he, writing to his uncle Gascoigne, 'can live upon lesse than I' [a phrase in which one hardly recognises the future prodigal] 'and I would not have mentioned this businesse if I had thought it would not lessen your charges.' Another letter, also undated and addressed to Gascoigne's wife, was probably written from Charterhouse. It has never hitherto been printed in any life of Steele, and as it is one of the earliest examples of what Nichols pleonastically calls his 'epistolary correspondence,' it is here reproduced :—

'HONOURED MADAM,—Out of a deep sense of y^r la^{sps} Goodnesse Towards me, I could not forbear accusing myselfe of Ingratitude in omitting my duty, by not acknowledging y^r lad^{ships} favours by frequent letters; but how to excuse myself as to that point I know not, but most humbly hope y^t as you have been alwaies soe bountiful to me as to encourage my endeavours, so y^u will be soe mercifull to me as to pardon my faults and neglects. but, Madam, should I expresse my gratitude for every benefit y^t I receive at y^r lad^{shps} and my good Vnkle, I should never sit down to meat but I must write a letter when I rise from table; for to his goodnesse I humbly acknowledge my being. but, Mada^m, not to be too tedious, I shall only subscribe myself Mada^m, y^r la^{ships} Humble servant and obedient though unworthy nephew   R. STEELE.

'Pray mada^m give my duty to my uukle and my good Ant, and my Ingenious Cousin and humble service to good Mrs Dwight.'

Whether this was written by the Charterhouse boy or the Oxford man, it is clear that the writer was already no mean master of that art of effusive laudation of which his subsequent prefaces and dedications afford so many examples.

On the 13th of March, 1690, in Hilary Term, Steele matriculated at Christ Church, Oxford, being described in the register as the son of Richard Steele, of Dublin, Gentleman, a fact which, as Mr. Wills points out, may be held to confirm the statement that the elder Steele was not a barrister, since, in that case, he would have been styled 'Esquire.' Addison, who had left Charterhouse two years earlier, was now at Magdalen, having obtained a demyship there in 1689. In the same year the famous Dean Aldrich, sometime Tutor to the second Duke of Ormond, had been appointed to Christ Church, and Steele's letters to his uncle contain more than one reference to that learned and glee-loving divine. In one of them, among the Ormonde MSS., he announces that he has been much indisposed by 'a bile' over his left eye; and another records that a certain Mr. Horne has invited him to a tavern and treated him with 'Claret and Oysters.' But it is characteristic that these letters are already largely occupied with questions of money and preferment. His Charterhouse exhibition was small, his uncle's expenses consequently heavy, and he is laudably anxious to obtain a studentship, either by favour of the Duke of Ormond, who was Chancellor of the University, or directly from the new Dean, who had two in his own gift. The following letter on the subject is dated May 14 [1690] :—

'S^r,—I have received the Bundle My Lady sent to me And do most humbly thank ye for that and all the rest of y^r favours, but my request to you now is that you would compleat all the rest by solliciting the Dean who is now in London in my behalfe for a student's place here; I am satisfied that I stand very fair in his favour. He saw one of my Exercises in the House and commended it very much and said y^t if I went on in me Study he did not question but I should make something more than ordinary. I had this from my Tutour. I have I think a good character through the whole Coll; I speake not this f^r out of any vanity or affectation but to let you know that I have not been altogether negligent on my part : these places are not given by merit but acquired by friends, though I question not but so generous a man as our Dean would rather prefer one that was a Scholar before another. I have had so great advantage in being . . . . [excellent school[1]] . . . my own abilities are so very mean I believe there are very few of the Gown in the Coll. so good scholars as I am. My Tutour before told me that if you should be pleased to use your interest for me, or p^t my lord's letter or word in my behalfe; it would certainly do my businesse. And y^r Friend Dr Hough

[1] This letter is printed from Mr. W. H. Wills's transcript in *All the Year Round* for the 5th of December, 1868. The words in brackets are added from the copy printed in the Appendix to the Seventh Report of the Hist. Manuscripts Commission, 1879, pp. 753-4 (Ormonde MSS.).

the new Bishop of Oxon, I believe may doe much now, for Dr Aldrich is, as it were, his Dean. Perhaps, Sir, you may be modest in solliciting him, because you may think others trouble him for the same thing; But pray, S^r, don't let that hinder you for it will be the same case next Election, and if we misse this opportunity 'tis ten to one whether we ever have such another; besides the Dean won't have such a place this three year; therefore I beseech you S^r as you have been always heretofore very good to me to use your utmost Endeavour now in my behalfe And assure y^{r}self that whatever preferment I ever attain to shall never make me ingratefully forget, and not acknowledge the authour of all my advancement but I shall ever be proud of writing myself Your most obliged and

Hum : Ser^{vt}

Rich : Steele.

The application was made, apparently without success. Among Henry Gascoigne's papers is a note to remind him to ask the duke,—*i.e.* the second duke, the first having died in 1688,—to ' be pleased to befriend Dick Steele, who is now entered at Ch. Ch., by getting him a student's place there, or something else, to Exse : mee of charges besides what is allowed him by the Charter House.' But ' Dick Steele's ' desire was compassed in another way, though probably by the same agency. He was made a postmaster of Merton. In those days the postmasterships, as distinguished from fellowships, were not entered in the College Records, and the precise day of his election cannot be ascertained.

His name appears for the first time in the Postmasters' Buttery Book on the 27th of August, 1691.

Beyond the indications given by himself in the foregoing letter, little has been preserved as to his college career. His 'Tutour'—as he styles him—was Mr., afterwards Dr., Welbore Ellis, later Bishop of Kildare and Meath. Mr. Forster and others, probably misled by a note in the earlier editions of the *Tatler*, call him Steele's Master at the Charterhouse. But that master was Dr. Walker, and there was never an Ellis master there at all. On the other hand, Welbore Ellis was elected from Westminster to Christ Church in 1680, becoming an M.A. of that college in 1687 (when, from a reference in the *Ellis Correspondence*, i. 217–8, he was still resident at Oxford), and D.D. by diploma in 1697, four years before Steele speaks of him in the Preface to the *Christian Hero* as 'the Rev. Dr. *Ellis*, my Ever-Honour'd Tutor.' If it be added that when he was made Bishop of Kildare he was acting as chaplain to the Duke of Ormond, and that his eldest brother John had been secretary to the Duke's father, the gallant and high-minded Ossory, it is manifest that no other Ellis can be referred to. There is a portrait of him in the hall at Christ Church, but though Steele speaks of his works, his biography makes no mention of them. He was, however, a thoroughly estimable man.

Another name with which Steele's is connected in the scant chronicle of his academic life is that of Mr. Parker of Merton, who afterwards became Vicar of Embleton in Northumberland, and is supposed to have been a casual contributor to the *Tatler*. To Mr. Parker belongs the distinction of condemning Steele's first attempt at dramatic art. He had planned and completed an entire comedy, the name of which has not been preserved. But the inexorable Mr. Parker thought so poorly of his friend's performance that it was incontinently committed to the flames. Whether Addison stood by and consented to this literary sacrifice, or whether he was even consulted, historians have not related. Indeed, were it not for Steele's express statement that they had known each other from boyhood, one might almost suppose that the connection which undoubtedly existed between them had been exaggerated, and belongs rather to the maturer years of the *Spectator* and *Tatler* than to the early days of Smithfield and Oxford. But that they had been always friends is sufficiently plain from Steele's own letter to Congreve, prefixed in 1722 to the second edition of the *Drummer*, in which place, writing of Addison's father, he says : ' Were things of this nature to be exposed to public view, I could shew under the Dean's own hand, in the warmest terms, his blessing on the friendship between his son and me ; nor had he a child who did not prefer me in the first place of kindness and esteem, as their father loved me like one of them : and I can with pleasure say, I never omitted any opportunity of shewing that zeal for their persons and Interests as became a Gentleman and a Friend.' It is also clear that while at the University or the Charterhouse, and perhaps while at both places, Steele was in the habit of visiting at Addison's Lichfield home. The charmingly touched portrait which is drawn in *Tatler* No. 235, of a father at once judicious and affectionate, has always been supposed to have been intended for

Lancelot Addison, and it could only have been executed by some one who had opportunities of studying his model in the freedom of that model's own fireside.

While Dean Addison's son was decorously pursuing his university career, that of Richard Steele came to a premature conclusion. Wars and rumours of wars had been rife during his residence at Oxford. In 1690, when he was yet but a student at Christ Church, the battle of the Boyne had been fought, to be followed in due time by the reduction of Ireland, the victory of La Hogue, and the defeats of Steenkirk and Landen. At Landen, Steele's own patron, Ormond, charging gallantly at the head of a squadron, had been wounded and taken prisoner—an event which had been duly celebrated, with fitting metaphor, in the facile couplets of Prior. Both by his family traditions and his personal tendencies the young postmaster of Merton was on the side of the Revolution ; and he seems to have become incurably infected with the desire for a military life. Failing to induce his friends to procure him a commission, he boldly enlisted in the army as a private gentleman. There is no reason for suspecting that any other cause than his own inclination prompted this abrupt cancelling of his college prospects. On the contrary, we are assured by the writer of his life in the *Biographia Britannica* that he was ' well-beloved and respected by the whole Society, and had a good interest with them after he left.' That his relatives did not approve his act is perhaps intelligible. ' When,' he wrote years afterwards in the *Theatre*, speaking of himself—' he mounted a War-horse, with a great sword in his hand, and planted himself behind King WILLIAM the Third against LEWIS the Fourteenth, he lost the succession to a very good estate in the county of Wexford in Ireland, from the same humour which he has pursued ever since, of preferring the state of his mind to that of his fortune.' From this it would seem that he was a trooper. In what regiment, is not easy to guess, but from his further reference to his 'cocking his hat' and 'donning broad sword, jack-boots and shoulder-belt, under the command of the unfortunate Duke of Ormond,' it is most likely that it was the second troop of Life Guards, which Ormond about this time commanded. In this case, the enormity of his offence is greatly diminished. The 'Gentlemen of the Guard,' as they were called, had many cadets of good families in their ranks; they had special privileges, a splendid uniform, and a pay far better than that of any regiment of our day. Though Steele's services as a 'common Trooper' were afterwards seized upon by his enemies, there is, therefore, nothing to show that he sustained any social degradation. Indeed, many of his fellow-soldiers—as Macaulay points out in his famous third chapter—had held commissions during the civil war.

Steele's name ceases to appear in the college records after 1694, but the exact date of his entry into the army is unknown. That it had taken place before March, 1695, is demonstrable. In December, 1694, Queen Mary died of small-pox. In March following she was buried with great pomp in Westminster Abbey—a funeral, says Macaulay, 'the saddest and most august that Westminster had ever seen.' Steele was apparently present at this ceremony—it may be that he was even a part of it in his military capacity;

and, like many other faithful Whigs, he threw his impressions into the conventional elegiacs of the day. His verses, familiar enough in his own reprint of some years later, are more interesting in their original *folio* form of 1695. The title is *The Procession. A Poem on Her Majesties Funeral. By a Gentleman of the Army*,—thus proving distinctly that the author was already a soldier. For the couplets themselves, the best praise that can be given to them is that they are loyal. Probably they were as good as any of the hundred and one effusions evoked by ' Dread MARIA'S *Universal* Fall ' —not excepting Mr. Congreve's *Mourning Muse of Alexis*. The acknowledged grief of William, who was not present on this occasion, is deftly touched upon; and there are judicious compliments to Ormond and Lord Somers. There is even—in the true spirit of the tormented poetical models of the time—a horse, that ' heaves into big *Sighs* when he would *Neigh.*' But the chief passage deals with the late Queen's impartial benevolence, a feature of her character, which, whatever its defects may have been, can scarcely be contested. ' She never enquir'd of what opinion persons were, who were objects of charity,' says Evelyn; and Steele rightly dwells upon this side of her memory :—

From distant homes the *Pitying Nations* come,
A Mourning World t'attend her to her Tomb :
The Poor, Her First and Deepest Mourner's are,
First in Her *Thoughts*, and Earliest in Her care ;
All hand in hand with common Friendly Woe,
In Poverty, our *Native* State, they go :
Some whom unstable Errors did engage,
By Luxury in Youth, to need in Age :

Some who had Virgin Vows for Wedlock broke,
And where, they help expected, found a *Yoke* ;
Others who labour with the double Weight
Of Want, and Mem'ry of a *Plenteous* State ;
There Mothers Walk wh' have oft despairing stood,
Pierc'd with their Infants deafning sobs for Food.
Then to a Dagger ran, with threat'ning Eyes
To stab their Bosoms, and to hush their Cries ;
But in the thought they stopp'd, their Locks they tore,
Threw down the Steel and *Cruelly* forbore :
The Innocents their Parent's Love *forgive*,
Smile at their Fate nor know they are to *live* :
These modest wants had ne'er been understood,
But by MARIA's *Cunning* to be good ;—

and so forth. One line—'Pleasure it self has something
that's *severe*'—is all that deserves preservation in this
ingenuous performance, and the author seems to have
acknowledged its unique character by afterwards incor-
porating it in the Prologue to the play of the *Lying
Lover*.

With an appreciation of the main chance which
never deserted him, Steele dedicated *The Procession* to
another 'Gentleman of the Army'—John, Lord Cutts.
Until its recent publication by the late Mr. Edward Solly
in *Notes and Queries*, this dedication, which is almost as
long as the poem, was little known—indeed it does not
seem to have been known at all to Steele's biographers.
There was much discernment, and even propriety, in
the poet's choice of his patron ; and it is possible that
he had a disinterested veneration for the man whose
'Most Passionate Admirer And Most Devoted Humble
Servant' he (with an unusual ‾profusion of capitals)
declared himself to be. The name of Cutts, although,

as Prior says, 'in Meeter something harsh to read,' was legible enough in the military annals of the time. His exploits at Buda had been celebrated in Latin verse by Addison; he had fought gallantly at Limerick and Namur; he had been wounded at Steenkirk. Swift, who later lampooned him as the 'Salamander,' a name which he had earned by his reckless daring under fire, called him 'the vainest old fool alive,' but then Swift was on the other side. Steele was probably attracted to him by three things:—he was a Whig; he was a man of education, who had published a thin volume of *Poetical Exercises*, dedicated to the late Queen, when Princess of Orange; and, last but not least, he had recently (October, 1694) been made Colonel of the Coldstream Guards. The immediate effect of Steele's compliment was that Lord Cutts sought out the unnamed author of *The Procession*—whose anonymity was doubtless easily penetrable, invited him into his household, and ultimately obtained for him a commission in the regiment under his command.

This connection of the Dedication of *The Procession* with Steele's military advancement would be in any case a justifiable inference from the facts. But it is curiously confirmed from an unexpected quarter. Some fourteen years later the notorious Mrs. De la Rivière Manley put forth the first instalment of that lavish 'cornucopia of scandal'—as Swift called it—the *New Atalantis*. She had been wronged, or imagined she had been wronged, by Steele; and she drew his portrait in her book with all the rancour of an angry woman. After an uncomplimentary description of his personal appearance, she goes on to say: 'I remember him

C

almost t'other Day, but a wretched common Trooper :
he had the Luck to write a small Poem, and dedicates
it to a Person whom he never saw, a Lord that's since
dead, who had a sparkling Genius, much of Humanity,
lov'd the Muses, and was a very good Soldier. He
encourag'd his Performance, took him into his Family,
and gave him a Standard in his Regiment.'

There is no reason for supposing that this account
is not substantially correct. It is certainly true of
Lord Cutts that he was dead in May, 1709, when Mrs.
Manley's book was published; it is also true that he
generally corresponds to her—in this instance not un-
flattering—account of him. It is true, besides, that
Steele was a trooper, without the decorative adjectives;
and that he was afterwards an Ensign in Lord Cutts's
regiment. This being so, there is no reason for supposing that the 'small Poem' was not *The Procession.*
The only doubtful point is the allegation that he had
never seen the man to whom he inscribed it. But in
one, at least, of the numerous editions of the *Atalantis*
this passage was withdrawn.

The date of the dedication to *The Procession* is the
19th of March, 1695. Allowing a certain time for publication, and the establishment of his relations with his
patron, it may fairly be concluded that he entered Lord
Cutts's service in the same year. There is, in fact,
evidence that he was acting as his confidential agent
or secretary in 1696 and 1697, as there are several
receipts among the Marlborough MSS. at Blenheim for
payments made by Mr. Steele on his Lordship's behalf,
and it is probable that his commission as Ensign was
not long deferred. But of his movements and means

from this time until the *Christian Hero* was published in April, 1701, we know little with certainty. We do know, however, that in the interval he became a Captain, for the advertisement of that book calls him 'Captain Richard Steel,' and the earlier accounts concur in stating that this captaincy was in Lord Lucas's regiment of Fusileers. An incident, which gives us our first certain glimpse of him as a recognised wit and friend of Addison, also enables us to fix the date of his second promotion more precisely.

In 1699 Dryden's 'quack Maurus,' Sir Richard Blackmore, resenting in his contemporaries a quality with which he himself was apparently but imperfectly equipped, published his *Satyr against Wit.*[1] It was directed mainly at the frequenters of Will's Coffee-House in Russell Street, Covent Garden, where, according to Sir Richard, 'first this Plague [of Wit] begun;' and with the aid of liberal dashes and initial letters, he managed to include a good many of the *literati* of the day in his general impeachment. Among the other couplets was this one:—

In G[arth] the Wit the Doctor has undone,
In S[malwood] the Divine, Heav'ns guard poor Ad—son.

Such an indiscriminate challenge was not likely to remain unanswered. Under the editorship of Tom Brown,—'Tom Brown of facetious memory' as Addison afterwards calls him,—a reply was promptly issued by the gentlemen of Will's. It bore the title of *Commendatory Verses on the Author of the Two Arthurs* [i.e.

---

[1] The *Satyr against Wit* was dated 1700. But it was published late in 1699.

Blackmore's Epics of the Prince and King] and included
contributions from Vanbrugh, Garth, Boyle, Sir Charles
Sedley, Smalwood, Arthur Maynwaring, Welsh, Lord
Anglesey, Lady Sandwich and a number of others.
Among the rest are some verses by Steele on the above
reference to Addison, who was then studying the French
language at Blois. They conclude thus :—

> Well may'st thou think an useless Talent Wit,
> Thou who without it hast three Poems Writ :
> Impenetrably dull, secure thou'rt found,
> And cans't receive no more, than give a Wound ;
> Then, scorn'd by all, to some dark Corner fly,
> And in Lethargic Trance expiring lie,
> Till thou from injur'd G[a]rth thy cure receive
> And S[malwoo]d only Absolution give.

In Brown's *Works* these lines are openly ascribed to
Steele; and from the rejoinder which Blackmore presently issued under the title of *Discommendatory Verses*,
etc. there can be no doubt they were his. Blackmore,
whose position was much that of a bear who has over-
turned a beehive, answers his assailants *seriatim*, and
when he comes to Steele he heads his reply ' *To the Noble*
Captain, *who was in a D—-d Confounded Pet, because the
Author of the* Satyr against Wit *was pleas'd to Pray for
his Friend.—*.' But from the tenor of the verses it
would seem that he knew little of Steele personally.
It is clear, however, that Steele was already of sufficient
importance to be enrolled among the champions whom
Will's dispatched against the ' Cheapside bard,' and
it may therefore be inferred that, in 1700, his reputation as a Coffee-house notability was fairly estab-

lished.[1] It must, also, be concluded from Blackmore's mode of address that he was already a Captain.

With this controversy another minor point of interest is connected. One of the writers against Blackmore was Colonel Christopher Codrington, afterwards the benefactor of All Souls' College, to which he left his library. He was a scholar and soldier, who, like Steele, had been at Christ Church, passing afterwards to a captaincy in the 1st Regiment of Foot Guards. He had fought in Flanders with distinction; and had acquired a reputation as a wit and verseman. Hence, in his poem on Oxford in 1706, Tickell couples him with Steele :—

> When Codrington and Steele their verse unrein,
> And form an easy, unaffected strain,
> A double wreath of laurel binds their brow,
> As they are poets and are warriors too.

But the most interesting thing about Codrington was that he came from Barbadoes, where he had estates. Steele, as we shall see, was also to have property in that island; and it is not impossible that his acquaintance with the West Indian heiress whom he afterwards married may have been in some way connected with Colonel Codrington.

We have no right, however, to piece the imperfections of his story with speculations of our own, and must moreover hasten to the *Christian Hero*, which appeared just six years after the publication of *The Procession*. It bears

---

[1] Congreve, writing to Joseph Keally in January 1700, says, 'Dick Steel is yours'; and the *Poetical Miscellanies* of 1714 contain some lines by Steele on *The Way of the World*, which probably belong to this period.

no author's name on the title-page ; but Steele's signa-
ture is appended to the dedication.   In the *Apology for
Himself and his Writings*, which he published many
years afterwards, he gives a frank account of the circumstances which led to this somewhat unexpected
production from the pen of a soldier.   'He first
became an Author,' he says, 'when an Ensign of the
Guards, a way of Life exposed to much Irregularity ;
and being thoroughly convinced of many things, of
which he often repented, and which he more often
repeated, he writ, for his own private Use, a little Book
called the *Christian Hero*, with a design principally to
fix upon his own Mind a strong Impression of Virtue
and Religion, in opposition to a stronger Propensity
towards unwarrantable Pleasures.'   This is the frank
and perfectly characteristic admission of a man conscious of the contradiction between his principles and
his practice.   But the ball of biography gathers as it
rolls ; and it is one of the misfortunes of candour to
be always suspected, by those who are not candid, of
withholding more than it concedes.   Accordingly, the
writer of the memoir of Steele in the *Biographia
Britannica*, taking this sentence as his authority,
expands it thus :—' He spared not to indulge his
genius in the wildest excesses, prostituting the exquisite
charms of his conversation-talents to give his pleasures a
daintier and more poignant relish,'—that is to say, he
transforms the author of the *Christian Hero* from an
erring and repentant man, conscious of his own stum-
blings and failings, into a venal and calculating de-
bauchee.   'This secret Admonition'—continues Steele,
referring to the fact that his little essay was not at

first intended for publication—'was too weak; he therefore Printed the Book with his Name, in hopes that a
standing Testimony against himself, and the Eyes of
the World (that is to say) of his Acquaintance upon
him in a new light, might curb his Desires, and make
him ashamed of understanding and seeming to feel
what was Virtuous, and living so quite contrary a Life.'

Such is the author's account of the origin of the
Christian Hero. It is true that when the foregoing
sentences were written Steele was upon his defence,
and was besides recalling the events of a much earlier
day. Yet there is no reason for supposing that his
memory was materially at fault, or that distance unduly
romanced his recollections. For the book itself, it is
an orderly little treatise of some eighty or ninety pages.
By those who have never read it, it is sometimes spoken
of as if it were a maudlin *Whole Duty of Man* or such a
Practice of Piety as might be expected to be compounded
by a penitent Rake in the intervals of headache. But
its sub-title, which describes it with exceptional precision, defines it as 'An Argument proving that No
Principles but those of Religion are sufficient to make
a Great Man.' In modern parlance this is little more
than the doctrine preached to-day from so many pulpits
—the doctrine that religion, to be real, must be something more than a theory,—that it must be part and
parcel of the daily life. According to his own summary,
Steele illustrates this by examples, 'by a view of some
Eminent Heathen, by a distant admiration of the Life
of our Blessed Saviour, and a near examination of that
of His Apostle St. *Paul.*' This is the matter of the
first three chapters; the fourth proceeds to show the

common motives of human action are 'best us'd and improv'd, when Joyn'd with Religion,' and ' that True greatness of mind is to be maintain'd only by Christian Principles.' Having done this, it winds up by an ingenious and not impolitic parallel between Lewis the Fourteenth and William the Third, which, as might be anticipated, is very much to the advantage of the latter. The style, though somewhat diffuse and negligent, is straightforward and manly. Ripened and developed by practice, it becomes the style of the *Spectator*, with one of the essays in which part of it was afterwards incorporated. So little is the book known that a specimen of it may fairly be reproduced here. It is from the chapter on St. Paul, and Steele's way of giving reality to his picture is thoroughly his own :—

There is nothing expresses a Man's particular Character more fully, than his Letters to his Intimate Friends, we have one of that Nature of this Great Apostle to *Philemon*; which in the Modern Language would perhaps run thus.

' SIR,—It is with the deepest satisfaction that I every day hear you Commended, for your Generous behaviour to all of that Faith, in the Articles of which I had the Honour and Happiness to Initiate you ; for which tho' I might presume to an Authority to oblige your compliance in a Request I am going to make to you, yet chuse I rather to apply myself to you as a Friend than an Apostle ; for with a Man of your Great Temper I know I need not a more powerful pretence than that of my Age and Imprisonment : Yet it is not my Petition for my self, but in behalf of the Bearer your Servant *Onesimus*, who has robb'd you, and ran away from you ; what he has defrauded you of, I will be answerable for ; this shall be a demand upon me ; not to say that you owe me your very self : I call'd him your

Servant, but he is now also to be regarded by you in a greater Relation, ev'n that of your Fellow-Christian; for I esteem him a Son of mine as much as your self; nay, methinks it is a certain peculiar endearment of him to me that I had the happyness of gaining him in my confinement: I beseech you to receive him, and think it an act of Providence, that he went away from you for a Season, to return more Improv'd to your Service for ever.'

This Letter is the sincere Image of a Worthy, Pious and Brave Man, and the ready Utterance of a generous Christian Temper; How handsomly does he assume tho' a Prisoner, how humbly condescend tho' an Apostle? Could any request have been made, or any Person oblig'd with a better Grace? The very Criminal Servant, is no less with him than his Son and his Brother; for Christianity has that in it, which makes Men Pity, not Scorn the Wicked, and by a beautiful kind of Ignorance of themselves think those Wretches their Equals; it aggravates all the Benefits and good Offices of Life, by making 'em seem Fraternal; and the Christian feels the wants of the Miserable so much his own, that it sweetens the Pain of the oblig'd, when he that gives does it with an Air that has neither Oppression or Superiority in it, but had rather have his Generosity appear an inlarg'd Self-Love than diffusive Bounty, and is always a Benefactor with the mein of a Receiver.[1]

This expedient of bringing the remote home to men's hearts and bosoms by means of a nakedly modern paraphrase was afterwards frequently employed by Steele. He makes use of it when dealing with an extract from *Paradise Lost* in *Tatler* No. 217, and in translating a letter of recommendation from Horace in *Spectator* No. 493. There are other passages in which he gives

---

[1] *Christian Hero*, 1701, second edition, pp. 72-5.

indication of his future work. His recognition of women—and the women of the eighteenth century owe as much to Steele as those of the nineteenth to Tennyson's *Princess*—as reasonable creatures and not as the mere puppets of a false admiration or a flighty pursuit, already finds its expression in a passage which precedes that quoted above:—It is 'from Want of Wit and Invention in our Modern Gallants,' he says, 'that the Beautiful Sex is so absurdly and vitiously entertain'd by 'em: For there is [that?] in their tender Frame, native Simplicity, groundless Fear and little unaccountable contradictions, upon which there might be built Expostulations to divert a good and Intelligent young Woman, as well as the fulsome raptures, guilty impressions, senseless deifications, and pretended Deaths that are every day offer'd her.'[1] There are other pages of the *Christian Hero*, which, read by later events, as much foreshadow the future Essayist as the whole book reveals the writer, who, through good and evil repute, remained always and of set purpose, a moralist and teacher of ethics. At the same time it is possible for even enthusiasm to find too much in Captain Steele's little manual. His later works have, by contrast, condemned it to almost complete neglect; and had they never existed, its chief, if not its sole, claim to remembrance would probably lie in the fact that it is a tract written by a military man.

In the author's own day its success was qualified. A second and enlarged edition did, indeed, succeed the first, with a rapidity so unusual that Charles Gildon, in his *Comparison between the Two Stages*, boldly asserted

[1] *Christian Hero*, 1701, second edition, p. 71.

it to be no more than the original issue masquerading under a new title-page. But examination of the two editions shows unmistakably that the alterations in the second were considerable. The sale, however, must have fallen ·off immediately, for the third edition did not appear until 1710, and in 1710 Steele was no longer an unknown writer, but the popular author of the *Tatler*, concerning whose earlier efforts the public might well be curious. During the appearance of the *Spectator* a sixth edition was reached, and thenceforward its progress declined again. In the Dyce Library at South Kensington there is a copy of the second edition, which contains the following dedicatory lines in the author's own handwriting :—

> To
>   My Lov'd Tutour Dr. Ellis—
>
> With secret impulse thus do Streams return
> To that Capacious Ocean whence they're born:
> Oh Would but Fortune come wth bounty fraught
> Proportion'd to ye mind wch thou hast taught !
> Till then let these unpolish'd leaves impart
> The Humble Offering of a Gratefull Heart.
>   RICH^D STEELE.

Captain Steele thought so well of the first couplet that he subsequently made use of it for a more academic production.

CHAPTER II.

DRAMATIST AND GAZETTEER.

IF the welcome given by the general public to the *Christian Hero* was somewhat undecided, there is no doubt whatever about the way in which it was received by those for whom it had been especially intended. Its author—as he himself tells us in his *Apology* of later years—'from being thought no undelightful Companion . . . was soon reckoned a disagreeable Fellow.' As was inevitable, comparisons were frankly made between his precepts and his practice; and his critics did not scruple to class him with those '*Qui Curios simulant, et Bacchanalia vivunt.*' 'Every Body he knew,' he says, 'measured the least Levity in his Words and Actions, with the Character of a Christian Heroe.' From his adding that 'one or two of his Acquaintance thought fit to misuse him, and try their Valour upon him,' it would seem that his personal courage was also called in question, and that he was invited to defend his doctrines with his sword. It may be, indeed, that his sole duel, the precise date of which is nowhere recorded, belongs to this period. The particulars, based upon the authority of Dr. Thomas Amory, are thus given by Nichols.[1] Steele, being

---

[1] Nichols, *Tatler*, 1797, i. p. 216, and *ibid.*, 1806, i. p. 267.

consulted by a junior comrade as to a challenge he was about to send, prevented its being sent. His motives were misinterpreted by the companions of the young soldier, who was induced by them to challenge Steele himself. Faithful to his principles, Steele, who was then recovering from a fever, vainly endeavoured by raillery and every indirect expedient to avert a meeting. Ultimately he accepted the challenge, counting upon his superior skill to disarm his opponent without injuring him; and even when upon the ground, he took advantage of the accidental breaking of his shoe-buckle to urge a pacific settlement, but without success. For some time he parried his adversary's thrusts; but at last, to his own great distress, in a well-meant attempt to disable him, he ran him through the body, wounding him dangerously, but not fatally, although his life was at one period despaired of. While his condition was still critical, Steele's conduct was freely canvassed, being warmly defended by Lord Cutts and others. As regards himself, the main result of the occurrence was to intensify that horror of so-called satisfaction, to which, in his subsequent writings, he so often refers.

The exact date of this story, vaguely reported by its first narrators, cannot be given; and it may have preceded the publication of the *Christian Hero*, and not have followed it. But another circumstance, although it has the look of a *non-sequitur*, did unquestionably succeed Steele's lay-sermon, and that is the production of his first acted play. Finding himself, he says in the *Apology*, 'slighted, instead of being encouraged, for his Declarations as to Religion . . . it was now incumbent upon him to enliven his Character, for which Reason he writ the Comedy called *The Funeral*, in which (tho' full of Incidents that move Laughter) Virtue and Vice appear just as they ought to do.' The full title of the play referred to is *The Funeral; or, Grief à la Mode*. From the fact that the first edition bears the date of 1702, Genest and others seem to have concluded that it was first played in that year. But the advertisements in the *Post Boy* for December, 1701, show clearly that the 4to is only dated 1702 by anticipation; and that the piece, which is described on the 20th of December as being 'acted at the Theatre Royal in Drury-Lane,' the music of the songs having been announced a day or two before, must have been brought out in November or December, 1701.

The stress laid by Steele upon the part which virtue and vice play in his piece indicates a certain difference in his aims from those of his predecessors. The *Funeral*, indeed, appeared at a time when an appreciable reaction in stage morality was in progress. In some of the higher literary qualities, the comedy which had preceded the production of Congreve's *Way of the World* in 1700 has never since been equalled. But Wycherley's robustness and Vanbrugh's gay frivolity, the brisk and bustling vivacity of Farquhar, the dazzling brilliancy even of Congreve himself, had rendered little service to the purification of manners. Marriage as the sacrament of adultery, infidelity and libertinism as the indispensable equipment of the fine gentleman, pruriency and unchastity as the prevailing characteristics of the fine lady, ridicule of all that is honest and of good report as a general proposition,—these were the chief things

which the later drama of the Stuarts had offered for
the imitation of its audiences. Side by side, however,
with the uncontrolled lawlessness of the anti-Puritan
spirit, a spirit of righteous repugnance was also beginning to assert itself. As early as 1695, Sir Richard
Blackmore, in the Preface to *Prince Arthur*, had made
a manly but ineffectual protest against the impurity of
the Theatres. He desired, he said, in words far more
eloquent than any in his impregnable Epic,—words
which Steele afterwards quoted admiringly in the
Spectator—'to make one *Effort* towards the rescuing
the *Muses* out of the hands of these *Ravishers*, to
restore them to their sweet and chast Mansions, and to
engage them in an Employment suitable to their
Dignity.'[1] But his appeal was too inconspicuous, and
his performance too languid and drowsy, to do more
than cover his good intention with ridicule. A few
years later the cause was taken up by a much abler
man, who added to honesty of conviction controversial
powers of the highest order. In his *Short View of the
Immorality, and Profanity of the English Stage* Jeremy
Collier framed an indictment against the existing
drama which his arguments made unanswerable and
his energy resistless. The Wits might have pricked a
meaner man to death with epigram; but the terrible
Nonjuror in the armour of his fearless indignation
was invulnerable. He remained master of the field.

---

[1] Blackmore must sometimes have said fine things, or they were
turned into fine things by those who heard them. Steele in No. 11
of the *Theatre* quotes one of his sentiments, which certainly deserves preservation :—' He who rejoices at the superior merit of
another man, knows a greater thing of himself than he possibly
can know of another man.'

Dryden, soon to die, declined the combat; Congreve answered feebly; Vanbrugh (whose *Relapse* was specially dissected), Settle, and Dennis, all replied in vain. Gradually a new spirit of decency began to manifest itself, at least ostensibly, in the works of contemporary playwrights, and by 1702, Charles Gildon could write in his *Comparison between the Two Stages*, that 'Our Audiences are really mended in their tast of Plays, and notwithstanding all the Raillery we have put upon Mr. *Collyer*, it must be confest that he has done the Stage good Service in correcting some of their Errors.' That he should correct them all was not to be expected; still less can it be said that the drama became pure by reason of his impeachment of it; but it may fairly be affirmed that licence received a definite check, and that the proclamation of a moral purpose became henceforth the conventional ensign of the popular dramatist.

Steele's *Funeral* came upon the wave of this new order of things, and we have seen that the moral purpose of making 'Virtue and Vice appear just as they ought to do' was not absent from his programme. Moreover, his play has a great deal of fresh vivacity, and not a little originality of conception. An old nobleman, Lord Brumpton, believed to be dead, although he is only in a fit, is persuaded by his servant Trusty— one of the earliest examples of the trusty servant on the English stage—to continue to feign death in order to observe the effect of his loss upon the members of his household, in particular upon his young wife, who is by no means unwilling to become a young widow. The idea is not without some obvious improbabilities; and as Gildon did not fail to point out in his excellent contemporary criticism, much of the subordinate intrigue between Lord Brumpton's wards and their soldier-admirers is out of keeping in the house where the head of the family is lying dead, while the escape of one of the heroines to her lover in the very coffin itself, although justified by stage precedent, certainly implies a liberal allowance of *bonne volonté* on the part of the spectator. Indeed Steele's negligence in this respect can only be explained by the supposition that, knowing himself Lord Brumpton was not dead, he forgot to remember that several of his *dramatis personæ* were not equally well informed. But if the plot be open to question on this score, the characters are less assailable. Those belonging to the legal and funereal class, at whom the main assault of the satire is directed, are certainly exceedingly diverting. Mr. Sable, the undertaker, drilling his mutes, and expostulating, more in sorrow than in anger, with the unfortunate man, who, engaged at first upon the strength of his wobegone countenance, has provokingly grown haler and gladder with each week's access of unhoped-for prosperity,[1]—Mr. Puzzle, the lawyer and 'last great prophet of tautology,' instructing his clerk in the *longæ ambages* of testamentary phraseology, and the barbarous Law-Latin, the *Barnos, Outhousas, et Stabulas*, which Fielding ridiculed long after in the *Champion*,—fairly foreshadow the best cha-

---

[1] William Peer, the actor, on whose death Steele wrote an obituary *Guardian*, was a living exemplification of this. His chief impersonation was the lean apothecary in *Caius Marius*—Otway's version of *Romeo and Juliet*. But having the good fortune to be made property-man at Drury Lane, he speedily grew so corpulent as to be wholly disqualified for the part.

racter sketches in the *Spectator* and *Tatler*. The scene of the ragged recruits, too, one of whom has made his way from Cornwall by being whipped from constable to constable, and another who, in justification of his tattered condition, explains that, in his last regiment, 'the Collonel had one Skirt before, the Agent one behind, and every Captain of the Regiment a Button'—must have been hugely relished by the 'gentlemen of the Army,' who packed the house on the first night, and gallantly applauded their comrade's maiden effort. But Steele's most notable achievement in the *Funeral* is to be found in the freshness with which he has managed to invest his younger female characters. Lady Brumpton's woman Tattleaid administering mock consolation to her mistress with her mouth full of pins is a humorous picture which might be matched from earlier writers; but the dialogue between Lady Harriot and Lady Sharlot, with a little modernisation, would easily fit into a chapter by Trollope :—

Lady Harriot. Nay, good Sage Sister, you may as well talk to [*Looking at herself as she speaks*] me, as sit Staring at a Book which I know you can't attend——Good Dr. *Lucas* may have writ there what he pleases, but there's no putting *Francis* Lord *Hardy*, now Earl of *Brumpton*, out of your Head, or making him absent from your Eyes, do but look at me now, and Deny it if you can——

L. Sh. You are the Maddest Girle——   [*Smiling.*

L. H. Look'e you, I knew you could not say it and forbear Laughing—[*Looking over* Sharlot] Oh I see his Name as plain as you do—F..r..a..n *Fran..c..i..s, cis Francis* 'Tis in Every line of the Book.

L. Sh. [*Rising*] 'Tis in Vain I see to mind any thing in such Impertinent Company—but Granting 'twere as you say, as to my Lord *Hardy*——'Tis more excuseable to admire another than One's self——

L. H. No I think not—Yes I Grant you than really to be vain at One's person, But I don't admire myself—Pish! I don't believe my Eyes have that Softness—[*Looking in the Glass*] They A'n't so peircing : No 'tis only a Stuff the Men will be talking—Some People are such admirers of Teeth—What signifies Teeth? [*showing her Teeth*] A very Blackamore has as White Teeth as I—No Sister, I Don't admire my self, but I've a Spirit of Contradiction in me : I don't know I'm in Love with my self, only to Rival the Men——

L. Sh. Ay, but Mr. *Campley* will gain Ground ev'n of that Rival of his, your Dear self——[1]

L. Ha. Oh! what have I done to you, that you should name that Insolent intruder—A Confident Opinionative Fop—No indeed, If I am, as a Poetical Lover of mine Sigh'd and Sung, of both Sexes,

The Publick Envy, and the Publick Care,

I shan't be so easily Catch'd—I thank him——I want but to be sure, I shou'd Heartily Torment Him, by Banishing him, and then consider whether he should Depart this Life, or not.

L. Sh. Indeed Sister to be serious with you, this Vanity in your Humour does not at all become you!

L. Ha. Vanity! all the Matter is we Gay People are more Sincere than you wise Folks : All your Life's an Art —Speak your soul—Look you there——[*halling her to the Glass*] Are not you Struck with a Secret Pleasure, when you view that Bloom in your Looks, that Harmony in your Shape, that Promptitude of your Mein!

L. Sh. Well Simpleton, if I am, at First so Silly, as to

---

[1] Lady Sharlot's reply, imperfectly printed in the 1st edition, has been corrected from the later issues.

be a little taken with my self, I know it a Fault, and take Pains to Correct it.

L. Ha. Psaw! Psaw! talk this Musty Tale to Old Mrs. *Fardingale*, 'tis too soon for me to think at that Rate——

L. Sh. They that think it too soon to Understand themselves, will very soon find it too Late—But tell me honestly don't you like *Campley*?

L. Ha. The Fellow is not to be Abhorr'd, if the Forward thing did not think of Getting me so easily——Oh—I hate a Heart I can't break when I please——What makes the Value of Dear China, but that 'tis so Brittle——were it not for that, you might as well have Stone-Mugs in your Closet.

The *Funeral* was excellently cast. Lady Brumpton was one of the last characters of Mrs. Verbruggen, that charming actress of whom Cibber has given such an admirable vignette, while Lady Sharlot was played by Mrs. Oldfield, then in the first bloom of her youth and beauty. Cibber himself, who four years before had found a career with his own part of Sir Novelty Fashion, was Lady Sharlot's lover, Lord Hardy; and Wilks was Lady Harriot's. One of the minor characters, Mrs. Fardingale, was acted by the diminutive Henry Norris, the 'little Dickey' whose nickname, years afterwards, was to give rise to a curious misconception as regards Steele himself. There is no doubt that the play was a success, and that it would have been so without the countenance of the Duke of Devonshire, who witnessed its rehearsal, or the friendly military *claque*. Gildon, who examines it minutely, begins by a half-apology for criticising what so many good judges have approved, and he winds up with a high compliment to the character of the author, who, he says, is 'indued with singular Honesty, a noble

Disposition, and a conformity of good Manners; and as he is a Soldier, these Qualities are more conspicuous in him, and more to be esteemed.' He also commends the loyalty of his expressions,—a characteristic which, taken in connection with that timely reference to his Majesty in the *Christian Hero*, no doubt played its part in those 'Particulars enlarged upon to his Advantage,' which obtained for him the notice of William the Third, in whose 'last Table-Book,'—the *Apology* tells us,—the name of the author of the *Funeral* was noted for promotion.

But a mole-hill in the park at Hampton Court put an end to these expectations, as it did to so many others. On the 8th of March, 1702, King William died at Kensington; and two years elapsed before Steele again tempted fate as a dramatist. Strangely enough, his next play, *The Lying Lover; or, the Ladies' Friendship*, was in its profession much more what might have been expected from the author of the *Christian Hero* than was the *Funeral*. The *Funeral*, though unobjectionable enough in the days of Farquhar and Vanbrugh, was still far from deserving the reproachful title of 'homily in dialogue,' hastily given by Hazlitt to all Steele's comedies, and, it may be added, applied with greater reason to the first essays of sentimental comedy in France, the *drames sérieux* of La Chaussée. Nevertheless its tone was infinitely more 'cleanly and beneficial' than the Restoration Comedy which Collier had assailed. Steele's second play, however, according to his own account in the *Apology*, was a deliberate attempt to put the precepts of Collier, whose work he greatly approved, into practice, and 'to write a Comedy in the Severity he required.' He took for basis the *Menteur* of Corneille, which Corneille in his turn had adapted from the Spanish of Ruiz de Alarcon. In many of the passages, the Old and Young Bookwit of the *Lying Lover*, who correspond to the Geronte and Dorante of the elder play, closely follow their originals; but Steele's chief moral interpolation was a prison-scene, in which young Bookwit, who is supposed to have killed a man in his cups, is shown overwhelmed with remorse. This deviation from the recognised practice of contemporary comedy, heightened by the fact that the added passages were written in blank verse, while the rest of the play was in prose, accounts in some measure for the comparative failure of the piece. When it was produced in December, 1703, it was performed but six times, or in its author's summary words, 'damned for its Piety.'

There were, however, other reasons for its misfortune, and among the rest, inferiority to its predecessor. The character of the hero seems better suited to the Spanish or French stage than the English; and Steele did not improve Corneille by the needless extension of certain of the speeches. Yet the *Lying Lover* is not without its happy pages. Some of young Bookwit's mendacious romancing is highly successful; and there is a group of gaol-birds in Act iv. who suggest certain chapters of Fielding's *Amelia*. One of these, Mr. Charcoal, the chemist, who is described as never cheating a fool, but 'still imposing on your most sprightly Wits and Genius—Fellows of Fire, and Metal, whose quick Fancies, and eager Wishes, form'd Reasons for their undoing'—almost seems to glance indirectly at certain chemical misadventures of Steele's own, to which we shall presently refer.[1] There is also a clever scene in Act iii., not borrowed from Corneille, where the two heroines, both anxious to do execution upon the hero, endeavour, by perfidiously patching each other, to mitigate the effect of their respective charms; while the second Act contains a pleasant vignette of that popular eighteenth-century resort, well known, no doubt, to Captain Steele of Lucas's,—the new Exchange :—

Young Bookwit. No Faith, the New Exchange has taken up all my Curiosity.

Old Bookwit. Oh ! but, Son, you must not go to Places to stare at Women. Did you buy any thing ?

Y. Book. Some Bawbles.—But my Choice was so distracted among the pretty Merchants and their Dealers, I knew not where to run first.—One little lisping Rogue, Ribbandths, Gloveths, Tippeths.—Sir, cries another, will you buy a fine Sword-knot ; then a third, pretty Voice and Curtsie,—Does not your Lady want Hoods, Scarfs, fine green silk Stockins.[2]—I went by as if I had been in a Seraglio, a living Gallery of Beauties—staring from side to side, I bowing, they laughing—so made my Escape, and brought

---

[1] Compare also the following :—' *Char.* Yet let me tell you, Sir, because by secret Sympathy I'm yours—I must acquaint you, if you can obtain the favour of an opportunity and a crucible—I can show projection—directly *Sol*, Sir, *Sol*, Sir, more bright than that high luminary the Latines call'd so—Wealth shall be yours—We'll turn each Bar about us into golden Ingots—*Sir, can you lend me half a Crown ?* '

[2] Green silk stockings were made fashionable by Elizabeth, Countess of Chesterfield, touching whose *bas verds* Grammont tells a curious story. In Pepys' *Diary* that worthy gentleman is recorded to have bought a pair of these brilliant hose for his valentine.

your Son and Heir safe to you, through all these Darts and Glances.—To which indeed my Breast is not impregnable.[1]

The *Funeral* had been dedicated to the Countess of Albemarle; and its preface had contained a handsome compliment to John, Earl Somers. The *Lying Lover* was inscribed to the Duke of Ormond, in whose grandfather, the first duke, Steele gratefully recognised the patron of his childhood. When the preface which follows the dedication was written, the fate of the play must already have been decided; and Steele probably glances at contemporary criticism when he admits that the prison scene, notwithstanding its moral aspect, is perhaps 'an Injury to the Rules of Comedy.' 'But,'— he continues,—and the words deserve quotation for the reference they contain, 'Her Most Excellent Majesty has taken the Stage into Her Consideration; and we may hope, by Her gracious Influence on the Muses, Wit will recover from its Apostacy; and that by being encourag'd in the Interests of Virtue, 'twill strip Vice of the gay Habit in which it has too long appear'd, and cloath it in its native Dress of Shame, Contempt, and Dishonour.' The allusion here is obviously to Queen Anne's proclamation of the 17th of January, which had appeared only a few days before the *Lying Lover* issued from the press. Reverting to the orders already given to the Master of the Revels and the Comedians that 'Nothing be Acted in either of the Theatres [i.e. Drury Lane and Lincoln's Inn Fields] contrary to Religion or Good Manners,' it went on to forbid the wearing of Vizard masks by women (a practice which had given rise to great irregularities), and the presence of

[1] *The Lying Lover*, 1704, Act ii. p. 26.

strangers behind the scenes or upon the stage. Other proclamations followed this timely one ; but from the notices in the newspapers for several years later, it seems that going behind the scenes had become too inveterate a custom to be summarily discontinued.

By the earlier biographers the failure of the *Lying Lover* to keep the stage has generally been held to account for Steele's long intermission of his dramatic efforts. Whatever may be the explanation of this misconception, it is clear that it is a misconception, based upon the belief that the *Lying Lover* was the third of Steele's acted plays. In reality it was the second, being succeeded by another, which, until lately, has usually been placed before it. This was the *Tender Husband; or, The Accomplished Fools*, produced at Drury Lane in April, 1705, with scarcely more success than its forerunner. Why it met with no better reception is difficult to understand. Wilks, Mrs. Oldfield, Estcourt, Bullock, Penkethman,—most of the best comedians on the boards of that day were engaged in it; and apart from the equivocal character of some of the intrigue, which nevertheless can scarcely have caused any scruple of conscience to an eighteenth-century audience, it is brightly and effectively written. Moreover, several of the subordinate personages, if they do not actually stand *in loco parentis* to certain well-known dramatic figures of later date, are distinctly among their ancestors. There is a country gentleman, clearly of the race of Squire Western and the Tory Foxhunter, while his booby son, who is heir to fifteen hundred a year, who has been kept in ignorance that he has attained his majority, and who ' boggles a little at Marrying his Own Cousin,' is more than a mere indication of the future Tony Lumpkin.[1] But the closest anticipation of a later personage is that of the romance-reading Biddy Tipkin, whose head is stuffed with *Pharamond* and the *Grand Cyrus*, who sighs to be called ' Parthenissa,' objects ' to go out at a Door to be Married ' instead of out of a window, and hungers for the indispensable accompaniments of a courtship,—' Disguise, Serenade and Adventure,'—like the veriest Lydia Languish. ' Had *Oroondates* been as pressing as *Clerimont* '—she tells her impatient suitor—' *Cassandra* had been but a Pocket-Book,'—a fact which is undeniable, and is also in Molière. ' *La belle chose que ce seroit*,' says Mademoiselle Magdelon of the *Précieuses ridicules*, ' *si d'abord Cyrus épousoit Mandane, èt qu'Aronce de plain-pied fût marié à Clélie* ! ' Dennis, indeed, years afterwards, taunted Steele with taking Biddy Tipkin direct from this source. He would have shown more sagacity if he had pointed out another and more unmistakable debt to Molière. The episode of Parthenissa's lover, who disguises himself as a portrait painter, is plainly adapted, and in some places translated, from the *Sicilien ; ou, l'Amour Peintre*, of

[1] It is possible to make too much of minor resemblances. But Goldsmith clearly knew his Steele. The portrait of Mrs. Tipkin, deceased, with ' an Orange in her Hand, and a Nosegay in her Bosom, but a Look so pure and fresh-colour'd, you'd have taken her for one of the Seasons,' suggests the travelling limner's pictures of the seven Miss Flamboroughs in the *Vicar of Wakefield* ; while Beau Tibbs's hatred of your ' immense loads of meat,'—' extreme disgusting to those who are in the least acquainted with high life,' almost reads like a recollection of the Frenchified Mrs. Clerimont's condemnation of ' that vast load of Meat ' which is to form the wedding feast in Act v. of the *Tender Husband*.

the same author, a piece which must be held to have been unusually suggestive, since it is also supposed to have afforded hints both to Sheridan and Beaumarchais.

Addison, having by this time returned from Italy, and written the *Campaign*, contributed a rather colourless prologue to his friend's play; and there were also, Steele tells us in a later *Spectator*, 'many applauded Stroaks' in the piece itself from the same already eminent hand. Except upon the principle of assigning to Addison generally all the good things which it contains,—a plan which has been adopted by some of his admirers,—it is of course impossible to estimate the exact measure of this indefinite assistance. With the recollection of Addison's 'Will Wimble' fresh in one's mind, one might indeed be disposed to suspect that Captain Clerimont's definition of the vocation of a younger brother as consisting in 'Calling over this Gentleman's Dogs in the Country, Drinking his Stale-Beer in the Neighbourhood, or Marrying a Fortune,' must have proceeded from Addison's pen. Unfortunately Will Wimble has a nearer prototype in 'Mr. Thomas Gules' of *Tatler*, No. 256, one of those vague joint productions which cannot with certainty be assigned to one or other of the two colleagues. But if speculation upon this question is fruitless, the dedication to Addison of the play itself affords pleasant illustration of Steele's chivalrous attachment to his old schoolfellow, with whom, at this date, he declares himself to be in 'daily and familiar Conversation.' 'I look' (he says) 'upon my Intimacy with You, as one of the most valuable Enjoyments of my Life.

At the same time I hope I make the Town no ill
Compliment for their kind Acceptance of this Comedy,
in acknowledging that it has so far rais'd my Opinion of
it, as to make me think it no improper Memorial of an
Inviolable Friendship. I should not offer it to you as
such,' he goes on, ' had I not been very careful to avoid
everything that might look Ill-natured, Immoral, or
prejudicial to what the Better Part of Mankind hold
Sacred and Honourable.'

These last words were no doubt perfectly sincere,
although the modern reader who turns to the play
itself, and opens upon the dubious *rôle* of the elder
Clerimont's mistress, Mrs. Fainlove, may be forgiven a
certain amount of astonishment. But a very slight acquaintance with the stage-literature of the Augustan
age, and especially with the stage-literature of the
Augustan age while it still bore about it the half-
cleansed stains and smirches of Restoration drama, will
not fail to convince him that the practice indicated by
Steele's precepts still fell far short of the practice which
would be expected to follow such precepts now. Its
chief merit, in fact, consisted rather in refraining from
rewarding and glorifying vice, than in positively incul-
cating and rewarding virtue. Regarded in this light,
and making fair allowance for contemporary laxity of
expression, Steele's three comedies may be justly described as moral in their intention. That this intention
is more apparent in one case than another, is due to
the conditions under which they were produced. In
the *Funeral* the author of the *Christian Hero* went as
far as he dared in the way of stage reformation. That
is to say, he had to bear in mind both the imputation of

sanctimoniousness which the book had brought upon him, and the probable opposition of the Wits at Will's, upon whom, as he admits in the *Apology*, Collier 'had been too severe.' Direct moral sentiment plays but a small part in the first piece although it is undoubtedly there. In the *Lying Lover* the case is different. Steele had the *Funeral* behind him; and the Queen, at no time a lover of Theatres, was known to be opposed to the license of the stage. Writing a play—as was then possible—'in the severity Collier required,' he not only interpolated a long serious passage in Corneille's plot; but he bracketed it off, by writing it, after the mistaken fashion of the day, in blank verse. As a result, the piece was, as he puts it, ' damned for its Piety,' although the errors of its construction have quite as much to do with its failure. In the *Tender Husband* he seems to have contented himself with the more modest aim of being harmless, instead of didactic,—in other words, he tried to be simply amusing. Nevertheless, the *Tender Husband*, which certainly is amusing, was effectively acted, and, as the author says in the above quotation from his dedication, was ' kindly accepted by the Town,' seems to have lived exactly as long as its predecessor,—the space of about seven nights. The case for the useful as against the agreeable, when Steele, according to tradition, intermitted his labours as a playwright, was therefore fairly equal.

What is the explanation of this intermission, since, the sequence of the plays being rectified, it cannot be laid to the failure of the *Lying Lover*? The answer is simple. There was no real intermission. Though Steele did not actually produce any other play until the *Conscious Lovers* came out in 1722, there is absolutely nothing to show that, had the ways been open, and his other vocations and avocations permitted, he would not have speedily followed up the *Tender Husband* by another comedy. If Mr. Forster, who quotes the *Muses Mercury* of 1707, but who nevertheless accepts the tradition that the failure of the *Lying Lover* closed Steele's dramatic career for the present, had only looked a little deeper into that engaging miscellany, he would have seen that in its very first number, after reference to a forthcoming play by Farquhar, announcement is made of the fact that 'had not the Death of a Dear Friend hinder'd Capt *Steel* from finishing a Comedy of his, it wou'd also have been Acted this Season [1706–7].' As Steele was a contributor to the *Mercury*,—there are some slight verses by him in the January and February numbers, and that for September contains his *Prologue to the University of Oxford*,—it is most likely that this information was supplied by himself. In the September number there is also another 'paragraph.' 'As for *Comedies*'—says the chronicle of the stage—'there's no great Expectation of anything of that kind, since Mr. *Farquehar's* Death. The two Gentlemen, who would probably always succeed in the *Comick* Vein, Mr. *Congreve* and Capt. *Steel*, having Affairs of much greater Importance to take up their Time and Thoughts.' What occupied Congreve, who had, moreover, expressed his determination when the *Way of the World* failed, to write no more, need not concern us; but in the interval between January and September, Steele had been appointed Gazetteer. Hè had, therefore, quite enough to distract his attention from the chances of dramatic writing. Before he had ceased to be Gazetteer, he had succeeded with the *Tatler*; and to the *Tatler* followed the *Spectator*, the *Guardian*, the *Englishman*, and the cares of patriotic pamphleteering. Yet he seems never to have wholly relinquished his desire to write another comedy, for, as will be shown in a later chapter, he was engaged upon one in 1713, and it must have been frequently on his lips, since in the year following Swift twits him with his oft-deferred intention :—

> And, when thou'st bid adieu to cares,
> And settled Europe's grand affairs,
> 'Twill then, perhaps, be worth thy while
> For Drury-Lane to shape thy style :
> ' To make a pair of jolly fellows,
> The son and father, join to tell us,
> How sons may safely disobey,
> And fathers never should say nay ;
> By which wise conduct they grow friends
> At last—and so the story ends ! ' [1]

With this plot, says Swift, Steele had ' long threatened the town '—a sentence which is in itself almost enough to prove that he never willingly refrained from writing plays, although nearly seventeen years elapsed before the appearance of his next dramatic effort, the *Conscious Lovers*.

But it is a far cry from the *Tender Husband* of 1705 to the *Conscious Lovers* of 1722 ; and to 1705 we must return. Of Steele's doings at this period we know little or nothing, although we may safely assume that, in

---

[1] *First Ode of Horace, Book ii., addressed to Richard Steele,* 1714.

spite of the after-sneers of Dennis and others, some
part of his time, when he was not planning plays, was
absorbed by his military duties.   There is evidence in
the Marlborough correspondence that he was at Land-
guard Fort with his regiment in June and December
1703, and in August 1705, when he writes to Lord
Cutts 'from my lodgings at Mr. Keen's an apothecary's
in Bennet street, near S^{nt}. James's,' it is apparently
upon a question of advancement.   It is also probable
that the gap of our ignorance at this time will not be
improperly filled by the chronicle of that fruitless search
for the philosopher's stone with which Steele was twitted
in later life both by his friends and enemies.   Nay, if
the utterances of Mr. Charcoal in the *Lying Lover* are
accepted as relevant, we must conclude that he himself
was not unwilling to make capital of his ill success.

As far as his friends are concerned little has been
recorded respecting this incident.   In a prologue attributed to Addison, and spoken in Steele's presence in
1715, there is a couplet telling that

> Early in youth, his enemies have shewn,
> How narrowly he miss'd the Chemic Stone ;

and in a note to this Nichols says—'It is well known
that Steele once entertained hopes of being successful
in the pursuit of the Philosopher's Stone ; the laboratory
was at Poplar, and is now converted into a garden-
house.'   In the account which Mrs. Manley gives of
'Monsieur *le Ingrate*'—as she styles Steele—she is much
more explicit, and professes to have been one of the
chief personages in the drama—in fact, its *Dea ex
machina*.   According to her, Steele, not long after

Lord Cutts obtained him a commission, fell into the hands of an illiterate empiric, who, of course, was on the high road to the *magnum arcanum*, and only retarded in his progress by the lack of pence which vexes alchemists as much as other public men. Steele, says Mrs. Manley, was a ' Bubble to his Mind,' and he flung himself into the enterprise with all the hopefulness of his sanguine temperament. A house was taken (query, at Poplar), furnaces were built, and the young soldier's money, then his credit, quickly vanished in the quack's melting-pot. At this juncture his colleague introduced him to Mr. Manley, whose attitude in the transaction is exceedingly ambiguous. He thus became acquainted with Mrs. Manley, who grew interested in him. So it came to pass that when Steele, at the end of his resources, was about to sell his commission, she intervened, and managed to convince him that he was being grossly deceived. His commission was saved; but he was for some time hopelessly embarrassed, and had to go into hiding. ' Fortune'—Mrs. Manley continues— ' did more for him in his Adversity than would have lain in her Way in Prosperity; she threw him to seek for Refuge in a House, where was a Lady of vast Possessions; he marry'd her, she settled all upon him, and dy'd soon after.'

This story must be taken for what it is worth; and it is not easy to decide how much is truth and how much malicious exaggeration. When, years afterwards, the authoress of the *New Atalantis* dedicated her play of *Lucius* to Steele, she had made her peace with him, and could write as follows :—' I shall say no more, trusting to the Gallantry of Your Temper for further Proofs of

E

Friendship; and allowing You, like a true Woman, all the good Qualities in the World now I am Pleas'd with You, as well as I gave You all the ill One's when I was Angry with You.' We have thus—if need were—her own testimony to the animus of her earlier statements. But the fact remains that Steele's friends admitted the chemical hallucinations of his youth, while he himself, in a letter to his 'fair enemy,' of the 6th of Sept. 1709, frankly acknowledges her kindness in warning him when he 'was going on to his ruin '—an admission which does much to establish the substantial truth of her narrative.

Moreover, another part of that narrative has lately been corroborated by an unexpected discovery. Mrs. Manley's words as to the 'Lady of vast Possessions' coincide practically with the received but somewhat vague account of Steele's first wife, who had died, leaving him an estate in Barbadoes, which he himself tells us in one of his letters was let for 850*l.* per annum. Further tradition related that the lady derived her wealth from her brother, a West Indian planter, who had been taken prisoner by the French in returning to England, and had died in France. But when this first marriage took place, and what was the lady's name, were points which have hitherto baffled his biographers. The matter has now been set at rest by Mr. George A. Aitken,[1] whose researches among the records at Somerset House have disclosed a valuable series of minute facts upon the subject. He shows that a Major Robert Ford of Barbadoes made his will in December, 1704, leaving the bulk of his property to his sister, Mrs. Margaret Stretch, a widow. Major Ford was dead in 1705;

[1] *v. Athenæum*, May 1, 1886.

because Mrs. Stretch administered his estate in March of that year; and she herself was dead in January, 1707, when Steele, who had married her in the interim, administered her estate. Whether the first Mrs. Steele will ever become a personality in Steele's biography remains to be seen; but—thanks to Mr. Aitken—at least we now know her name and the period of her death, which must have taken place not later than December, 1706, as the warrant of administration sets forth that she had been dead fully fourteen days on January 4, 1707. It may further be added that she was evidently the 'Dear Friend' whose loss prevented Captain Steele from finishing the comedy referred to by the *Muses Mercury*.

Between December, 1706, and Steele's appointment as Gazetteer in the following May, it will be convenient to interpose some account of his connection with the Kit-Cat Club. Of this famous assembly he must have been one of the earlier members. The *Funeral* and the *Tender Husband*[1] were both published by Jacob Tonson, the bookseller, and Jacob Tonson, it is admitted, was the founder of the Club.

> For thou, whose fertile Genius does abound
> With noble Projects, didst this Order found—

sings Blackmore, also a member, apostrophising a mythical BOCAJ, who, upon inquiry, turns out to be nothing but 'Jacob' reversed.

One Night in Seven, at this convenient Seat,
Indulgent BOCAJ did the Muses treat,
Their Drink was gen'rous Wine, and *Kit-Cat's* Pyes their
  Meat—

---

[1] The *Lying Lover* was published by Bernard Lintott.

he says again, lapsing not only into 'a needless Alex-
andrine,' but committing one of those reprehensible
triplets which Swift afterwards satirised in the *City
Shower*.   Kit, or Christopher Catt, sometimes regarded
as a fictitious personage, was a Quaker and 'pudding
pye man' in Shire Lane by Temple Bar, at whose shop
Tonson's flock first assembled.   His portrait by, or
rather attributed to Kneller, was exhibited, not many
years ago, at South Kensington.   From Shire Lane he
moved to the Strand, ultimately occupying the Fountain Tavern.   In summer the Kit-Cats migrated to the
Upper Flask at Hampstead, an inn on the edge of the
heath, still existing as a private house, and betraying
its eighteenth-century origin by its entrance hall and
low-ceiled rooms.   In its gardens stood, up to 1876, a
mulberry tree, more famous than Hogarth's at Chiswick,
under which, in the all-golden afternoon, Steele must
often have lingered with Addison, or chatted with
Vanbrugh and Garth and Congreve.

'All the first Members for their Place were fit,
    Tho' not of Title, Men of Sense and Wit,'—

says the Kit-Cat Laureate.   But title, as the Whig
leaders grew more and more to lean upon letters, seems
gradually to have intruded into the ranks, and names
like Halifax and Somerset, Wharton and Somers, were
numbered among its notabilities.   One of the rules
obliged each member to name a lady as his 'toast';
and the couplet or quatrain he composed in her honour
was engraved on the club glasses.   Several of these,
written by Halifax, in 1703, for the famous 'little

Whig,' Lady Sunderland, for Madame Spanheim, the beautiful daughter of the Prussian Ambassador, for Lady Mary Churchill and others are to be found in his works; and verses by Addison are also extant. In the Marlborough correspondence are the following lines by Steele, which belong to a somewhat later date. Writing to Leonard Welsted in 1716, he says, 'I have writ three Couplets for the Toasts: they are to be printed under their names for the Kitt Catt Club. These are the verses:—

> " Bright dames when 1st We meet unheeded passe
> We read frail charms on Monuments of Glasse
> In Joylesse Streams the Purple Chrystall flows
> Till each is nam'd for whome each bosome glows
> Then Friendship Love and Wine unite their fires
> Then all their Homage pay where each admires." '

The couplets have no particular merit; and seem hardly intended to be used separately. But they show the vitality of Tonson's symposium. If to quote them is to anticipate, there is, before the date of this chapter, one occurrence connected with the Club proceedings, at which it is just possible that Steele assisted. Our account of it is derived from Lady Stuart's pleasant anecdotes of Lady Mary Wortley Montagu. One day, she tells us, at a meeting of the Kit-Cats to choose toasts for the year, the whim seized Lady Mary's father, Lord Kingston, to nominate his daughter, then said to be eight years old. He did so upon the ground 'that she was far prettier than any lady upon their list. The other members demurred, because the rules of the club forbade them to elect a beauty whom they had never seen. "Then you shall see her," cried he; and in the gaiety of the moment sent orders home to have her finely dressed and brought to him at the tavern, where she was received with acclamations, her claim unanimously allowed, her health drunk by every one present, and her name engraved, in due form, upon a drinking glass. The company consisting of some of the most eminent men in England, she went from the lap of one poet, or patriot, or statesman, to the arms of another, was feasted with sweetmeats, overwhelmed with caresses, and, what perhaps already pleased her better than either, heard her wit and beauty loudly extolled on every side. Pleasure, she said, was too poor a word to express her sensations; they amounted to ecstasy. Never again, through her whole future life, did she pass so happy a day.'[1]

Steele's connection with the Kit-Cat Club, however, is a fact rather instinctively perceptible to the picturesque biographer than actually inscribed with legibility upon the records of his life. But in August, 1706, he was appointed Gentleman Waiter to Prince George of Denmark, with a salary of 100*l.* per annum;[2] and in the following May, by his own showing, he received a Government post to which incidental reference has already been made. 'His next Appearance as a Writer'—says he, speaking of himself years after in the *Apology*—'was in the Quality of the lowest Minister of State, to wit; in the Office of Gazetteer: Where he worked faithfully according to Order, without ever erring against the

[1] *Letters and Works of Lady Mary Wortley Montagu*, 1861, i. 53.

[2] Boyer's *Annals*, 1706.

Rule observed by all Ministries, to keep that Paper very innocent and very insipid.'[1] 'It is believed'—he adds—'it was to the Reproaches he heard every Gazette Day against the Writer of it, that the Defendant [i.e. Steele] owes the Fortitude of being remarkably negligent of what People say, which he does not deserve.' There is a letter among the MSS. at Blenheim, which, in a measure, confirmed these words—at all events as far as the reproaches are concerned. As it has only been imperfectly printed in the Report of the Historical Manuscripts Commission; and as, moreover, it exhibits Steele at work in his new office, we reproduce it *verbatim et litcratim*:—

'May 10th, 1707.

'MY LORD I presume to Acquaint Your Lordship that Mr Burchet inform'd me He had Orders from the Prince to attend your Lordship with a Complaint against the Article from Ostend in the last Gazette, where 'tis said a Fleet arriv'd to the Great Satisfaction and Advantage of the People there.

'This Article, it seems, is interpreted as an insinuation y^t they had not a Convoy in due time, and that their having a safe One at last look'd like a matter of Extraordinary Good Fortune. All that I can say for my self is that I was directed to take notice of that Circumstance by Mr Addison at Your Lordship's Order and us'd Mr Stepny's very Words tho' I made no such Apology when I was urg'd to know whence I had my Order or Advice, only In Generall acknowledg'd it a Great Misfortune to offend His Royall Highness but

---

[1] Compare Pope's *Dunciad*, i. 215:—
'No Gazetteer more innocent than I.'

said that as to the words themselves I thought I should rather have gain'd approbation than displeasure.

'There is a dissatisfaction also about ye Late Sea-fight; Mr Burchett indeed told me I had better stay till a further account but such as there was I might have at the Office ; but it being Mr Hopkins's and Mr Addison's Opinion that I had before stay'd too long, and that 'twould look as if the Government had a mind to Stifle the Account, I went to the Admiralty and made a Relation from their Letters.

'Your Lordship will please to pardon my taking this liberty of acquainting you with the matter before the Gentleman comes to You from His Royall High-nesse thô I beleive the offence is taken much lower. I shall look at such Impotent cavills with a great deal of Indifference while I beleive you think I have done my Duty, and promise my self your Lordships protection in matters where an ill intention is forc'd upon expressions from an ill inclination in the Reader to

'My Lord,
 'Y^r Lordship's Most Devoted
   'Most obedient and
    'Most Humble Servant
     'RICH^D STEELE.'
'My Lord the Secretary.'

The 'Mr. Burchet' above mentioned was Josias Burchet, Secretary to the Admiralty ; and 'Mr. Stepny' was George Stepney, Halifax's friend, the poet and Envoy to the States-General. The Prince was Prince George of Denmark, whom Queen Anne had created Lord High Admiral in 1702 ; and 'My Lord the Secretary,' to whom the letter is addressed, was Marlborough's son-in-law, Lord Sunderland, who, in the preceding December, had succeeded Sir George Hedges as Secretary of State, finding Addison and the Mr. Hopkins of whom Steele speaks, already installed as Under Secretaries. It is sometimes supposed that Steele was indebted to Addison for his appointment as Gazetteer. But his patron on this occasion—as will appear in a future chapter—was Arthur Maynwaring, another member of the Kit-Cat Club, who obtained it for him, not from Lord Sunderland, but from Lord Sunderland's fellow-Secretary of State, Robert Harley, afterwards Earl of Oxford. The salary had previously been 60*l.*, but Harley increased it to 300*l.* subject to an annual tax of 45*l.* The office of the two Secretaries of State was in the old Cockpit, which formerly stood on the site of the present Privy Council Office.

CHAPTER III.

LOVER AND LETTER-WRITER.

AT the close of 1706, for we are now able to fix the date approximately, there came to the funeral of Steele's first wife a mourner who was destined to play a considerable part in his subsequent career. From her presence upon this occasion, it may be inferred that the deceased lady was her friend, and Steele may therefore have made her acquaintance previous to this period. On the other hand, he may have seen her for the first time at the close of 1706. In either case, the relation so established appears to have improved with opportunity, and to have ultimately ripened into an attachment. Whether there was more of expediency than passion about his first marriage is difficult to say, and it is never without certain disadvantages to purity of motive that a gentleman in difficulties woos and wins an heiress and a widow. But it is clear from the promptitude and vigour of his suit to his second wife that Steele had not upon the preceding occasion exhausted his supply of those methods and arguments which serve to abridge the formalities of courtship. In August, 1707, he is definitely in the field with a proposal, and thenceforth matters progress so rapidly that he is married in the following September.

Miss Mary Scurlock—for such was the maiden name of the second Mrs. Steele—was at this time about eight or nine and twenty. She was the daughter of Jonathan Scurlock, deceased, of Llangunnor in Carmarthen; and is said to have been possessed of considerable personal charms. She had also valid expectations, for her mother's estate produced an income of about 400*l*. per annum. Nothing very definite can be affirmed respecting her character, as but few specimens of her correspondence have been preserved, and it would be unjust to take those as strictly representative. From her husband's letters to her she appears to have been somewhat capricious and *exigeante*, and to have combined the apparently irreconcilable qualities of economy and extravagance. But we do not know to what extent she may have been tried by the vagaries of her impulsive better-half; and without implying any special derelictions upon his part, it is manifest that his sanguine temperament and facile geniality were not calculated to foster a faultless domestic life. Nevertheless, there is little doubt that she was sincerely attached to him; and there can be no doubt whatever that he was devoted to her. This may be read plainly in every one of the four hundred and odd thoroughly characteristic epistles which she ('thrifty and prudent of everything that told against him'—says Mr. Forster a little uncharitably) so carefully preserved; and most of which were given to the world in 1787, without suppression of a single line, by John Nichols, the antiquary. The originals, on all sorts of paper, in all sorts of hands, are still to be seen in the British Museum Library, to which he afterwards presented them. It has sometimes been forgotten, in speaking of this famous correspondence, that it was never intended for publication. There was nothing here of that finessing in view of a wider audience which one finds in the otherwise admirable letters of Walpole and Pope. On the contrary, it was the express wish of the writer that his effusions—and they are literally. effusions—should be shown 'to no one living.' 'Let us be contented,' he says, 'with one another's thoughts upon our Words and Actions, without the intervention of other people, who cannot Judge of so delicate a circumstance as the commerce between Man and Wife.'[1] It has been forgotten, also, that they were entirely intimate and personal communications, which cannot be rightly tried by any test applicable to more guarded utterances. 'As Keys do open Chests, so Letters open Breasts,' says the old motto of the *Epistolæ Ho-Elianæ*, and if the adage be true of any written words, it is certainly true of these. They come to us exactly as they slipped from the rapid and impetuous pen of Steele ; and they have all the marks of the moment, seldom more than a moment, when they were penned. They were thrown off at all times, in all places, and they record truthfully all his fugitive hopes, regrets, yearnings, feelings and failings. They treat of all themes, from Prince George's death and the most pious aspirations to the despatch of a bottle of tent, or the safe-conduct of a parcel of walnuts. It would occupy too large a part of this strictly limited memoir to examine

[1] Letter dated September 9, 1707.

them at any length. But those which were composed between the appointment of their writer as Gazetteer and the establishment of the *Tatler* in April, 1709, cover the period of Steele's brief courtship, and the first year of his marriage. A man's letters at such a time may be supposed to exhibit the best side of his character, and these are fair samples of the collection as a whole. We, therefore, propose to devote this chapter to giving some account of this particular group, premising that our transcripts are made, not from the reprints by Nichols, but from the letters themselves in the British Museum.

The first missive to the beautiful Mrs. Scurlock—for, according to the fashion of those days, 'Miss,' when not a term of opprobrium, was confined to very young girls[1]—is dated the 9th of August, 1707. That is to say, Nichols assigns this date to it; because, for some reason not now wholly intelligible, the dates in many cases have been changed or cut away. It is a *billet-doux*, despatched to the lady through the orthodox channel of a *fille-de-chambre*, and asks for an interview. We must assume that it met with no response, since two days later the impatient suitor makes a declaration in form :—

'MADAM,—I writ to you on Saturday by Mrs. Warren, and give you this trouble to urge the same request I made then, which was that I may be admitted

---

[1] There is a good contemporary illustration of this in Cibber's *Lady's Last Stake*, 1707, among whose *dramatis personæ* are a 'Mrs. Conquest' and a 'Miss Notable.' The former is a young unmarried woman, the latter a girl.

to wait upon You. I should be very far from desiring
this if it were a Transgression of the most severe rules
to allow it; I know you are very much above the little
Arts which are frequent in your sex of giving unnecessary torment to their Admirers; therefore hope you'le
do so much Justice to the Generous passion I have for
You, as to let me have an opportunity of acquainting
y^u upon what motives I pretend to your Good opinion.
I shall not trouble you with my Sentiments till I know
how they will be receiv'd, and as I know no reason why
difference of Sex should make our Language to each
other differ from the ordinary rules of right reason, I'
shall affect plainesse and sincerity in my discourse to
you, as much as other Lovers do perplexity and rap-
ture. Instead of saying I shall die for you, I professe
I should be glad to Lead my life with you; you Are as
Beautifull as Witty as prudent, and as good humour'd
as any woman breathing, but I must confesse to you I
regard all those excellencies as you will please to direct
'em for my Happinesse or Misery. With Me, Madam,
the only lasting motive to Love is the hope of It's becoming Mutuall; I begg of you to let Mrs. Warren
send me word when I may attend you. I promise you
I'le talk of nothing but indifferent things, tho' at the
same time I know not how I shall approach you in the
tender moment of first seeing you after this declaration which has been made by, Madam,

> ' Y^r most Obedient &
> 'Most Faithfull H^{mble} Ser^{vt}
> ' Rich^D Steele.'

This appeal, the manly frankness of which has been

praised by Coleridge and others, is entirely consistent with those views as to the 'reasonable service' of women already expressed by the writer in the *Christian Hero*. Apparently Steele himself was not ill-satisfied with his performance, for it figured two years later in *Tatler*, No. 35, as the production of an imaginary Cynthio, and was prefaced by the words, 'He will undoubtedly succeed; for he accosts her in a Strain of Familiarity, without breaking through the Deference that is due to a Woman whom a Man would chuse for his Life. I have hardly ever heard rough Truth spoken with a better Grace than in this his Letter.'

But whatever fate attended the fictitious Cynthio, the real Richard appears to have received due notice through Mrs. Warren that he might wait upon her mistress. He accordingly does so, only to find that the coquettish Mrs. Scurlock, by an artifice common enough in courtship, has, as he puts it, 'commanded him to expect the happinesse of seeing her at another time of more Leisure.' Thereupon, 'under her own Roof,' he pens her a flaming letter in which the emotion of the minute is stronger than the calmer reflection which had dictated its predecessor. 'All great passion makes us dumb'—he says—and then he proceeds to tell her 'The Vainest Woman upon Earth never saw in Her Glasse half the attractions which I veiw in you, your Air, y^r Shape, your Every glance Motion and Gesture have such peculiar Graces that you possesse my whole Soul, and I know no life but in the hopes of your approbation; I know not what to say but that I Love y^u with the Sincerest passion that ever enter'd the Heart of Man. I will make it the businesse of my

Life to find out means of Convincing You that I prefer y^u to All that's pleasing upon earth.'

The promised interview must have followed hard upon this, for if Nichols's dates be correct, a few hours later it had already taken place. Henceforth the letters come thick and fast, alternately warm and impulsive, or sensible and grave and pious, as the pen was held by the Steele whose heart or whose head was in the ascendant. Meanwhile Mrs. Scurlock, who must have been staying with friends in London, announces her engagement to her mother, who is detained in Carmarthen by ill-health. After reference to a certain 'wretched impudence' (by which we must understand an unsuccessful suitor), whom the imperious beauty has treated as he deserves, she goes on to speak of her latest admirer. 'I Cant'—she says—'recomend ye person to y^u as having a great Estate, Title &c., wch are generally A parants Chief Care, but he has a Competency in worldly goods to make easie, wth a mind so richly adorn'd as to Exceed an Equivalent to ye greatest Estate in ye World in my opinion, in short his person is w^t I like, his temper is w^t I'm sure will make you as well as myself perfectly happy, if ye respect of a Lover wth ye tender fondness of a dutyfull Son can make y^u so, & for his understanding & Morals I refer y^u to his Christian Hero wch I remember y^u seem'd to approve, by this I believe y^u know his name, but least memory maint befriend me, tis ye survivour of ye person to whose funerale I went to in my illness.'

From the passages which follow this, the lady seems to be as anxious as Steele for speedy marriage. In begging for her mother's consent, she calls him 'her first &

only inclination,' adding the not unusual postscript that she ' shall never meet wth a prospect of happiness if y^s shou'd vanish.' She lays stress, also, upon the tattle and gossip which accompany a long engagement, and finally, with a touch of that forethought, which gained her afterwards her pet name of ' Prue,' points out as the ' main matter of all ' that his business must suffer seriously by his frequent visits to her.

The mother's reply was favourable, though she appears to have asked for further particulars, which Steele supplied in a long and interesting letter of the 3rd of September, 1707. In the interim from Lord Sunderland's Office at Whitehall, and from Steele's lodgings in Smith Street, Westminster, the assault goes on unremittingly. It is doubtful whether a maiden fortress was ever so bombarded by ' paper bullets of the brain.' He writes to his lady love in the anticipation of meeting; he writes to her in the pleasure of retrospect; he is rhetorical, lyrical, pietistic, and, though he does not deal much in the ' babyisms and dear diminutives ' of modern courtship, occasionally sufficiently extravagant and sentimental. She must give him ' either a Fan, a Mask or a Glove she has wore [sic] or he cannot Live,' otherwise she must expect him to kiss her hand, or when he next sits by her, to steal her handkerchief. She is ' too Great a Bounty to be receiv'd at once,' therefore he must be prepared by degrees, ' least the mighty Gift distract him with Joy.' His soul is stolen from itself, he says elsewhere, all its attention is broken. His books are blanks, and his friends intruders. He is left alone for a moment, he tells her in one little notelet, and he steals it to remind his ' Charmer and

F

Inspirer' that he is hers devotedly. ' Oh hasten Ye Minutes! bring on the happy Morning wherein to be ever her's will make me look down on thrones! Dear Molly I am tenderly, passionately faithfully thine.' And so on, *da capo*.

It seems almost cruel to read these unfeigned utterances, in cold blood. But Steele's *caveat* to his correspondent referred to the inquisitive of his own day rather than the inquisitive of ours. As we have seen, one of the letters subsequently appeared in the *Tatler*, and six more, communicated by an imaginary ' Andromache,' as examples of *billets-doux* written to her forty years before, were printed in *Spectator* No. 142. The originals at the British Museum still exhibit the variations which prepared them for Mr. Nutt's press in the Savoy. Over the following is scrawled :—' He was when He writ the following letter as agreeable and pleasant a man as any in England ' :—

'Aug' 30, 1707

'MADAM,—I begg pardon that my paper is not Guilt but I am forc'd to write from a Coffee-house where I am attending about businesse. There is a dirty Croud of Busie faces all around me talking politicks and managing Stocks while all my Ambition, all my wealth is Love! Love, which animates my Heart, sweetens my Humour, enlarges my Soul, and affects every Action of my Life. ' Tis to my Lovely Charmer I owe that many Noble Ideas are continually affix'd to my words and Actions ; tis the naturall effect of that Generous passion to create some similitude in the Admirer of the object admir'd. Thus my Dear am I every day to Improve from so sweet a Companion. Look up, My Fair One to that Heav'n which made thee such, and Join with me to Implore Its influence on our Tender Innocent hours and beseech the Author of Love, to blesse the Rights He has ordain'd, and mingle with our happinesse a just sense of our Transient Condition, and a resignation to His Will which only can regulate our minds to a steddy endeavour to please each other. I am for ever Y^r Faithful Ser^{nt}

'R : STEELE.'

Here is another over which is—'The Two next [1] were written after the day for our marriage was fixed':—

'Sepbr 1st 1707
'S^{nt} James's Coffee-house

'MADAM,—It is the hardest thing in the World to be in Love and yet attend businesse. As for me, all that speake to me find me out, and I must Lock my self up, or other people will do it for me.

'A Gentleman ask'd me this morning what news from Lisbon, and I answer'd She's Exquisitly handsome. Another desir'd to know when I had been last at Hampton Court, I reply'd twill be on Tuesday come se'nnight. Prethee Allow me at least to kisse your hand before that day, that my mind may be in some Composure. Oh Love

'A thousand Torments dwell about thee
Yet who would Live to Live without thee?

Methinks I could write a Volume to you but all the Language on earth would fail in saying how much, and with what disinterested passion I am Ever Y^{rs}

'RICH^D STEELE.'

[1] Only one of these two is reprinted here.

It is curious to note on the faded MS. Steele's hasty corrections. He first turns 'guilt' into 'guilded,' in Letter No. 1, then strikes out that and writes 'finer' over it. In Letter 2, among other changes, 'Hampton Court,' which might have betrayed the writer, is changed to 'Windsor,' and the quotation is omitted altogether. But it would have been more curious still if 'Andromache' had printed the eminently characteristic epistle which, in the original correspondence, succeeds a few hours later to No. 1 :—

'Saturday-night [Aug. 30, 1707]

'DEAR, LOVELY MRS. SCURLOCK,—I have been in very Good company where your Health under the Character of the Woman I lov'd best has been often drank. So that I may say I am Dead Drunk for your sake, which is more y^n I dye for you.

'Y^{rs} R : STEELE.'

Some of Steele's biographers have taken this letter too seriously. It is a manifest exaggeration ; and it is probable that the writer was at the moment much more 'fou o' love divine' than of any less celestial vintage. The man who *inter pocula* can write a fairly legible hand, and remember to be witty, is not very far gone. But the note is interesting because it shows that if 'good company' was Steele's rock ahead, he was honest enough not to conceal it during his courtship; and, as he married the lady, it may fairly be inferred that she regarded it as a venial error.

In the second of these three epistles, it will be observed, Steele speaks of a certain 'Tuesday come se'nnight.' This it is supposed was the wedding day, and reckoned from the Sunday on which the letter was dated would be the 9th of September, 1707. There is some reason for suspecting that Mrs. Steele's prudery kept the matter private for some weeks, pending her mother's expected arrival in London from Wales. But the whole affair is exceedingly obscure, and the alteration of the dates of the letters makes it obscurer still. It is not, however, until the 7th of October that Steele openly directs his communications 'to Mrs. Steele.' Previous to this, although he signs himself in one instance 'your most obliged Husband,' they are superscribed to 'Mrs. Scurlock' or to 'Mrs. Warren,' her maid.

The newly-married couple, shortly afterwards, took a house in Bury Street, further identified in those days of unnumbered dwellings as the 'Last House but two on the left hand' or, more exactly still, as the '3rd door right hand turning out of German Street' (Jermyn Street). Here the Gazetteer and gentleman-in-waiting would be in convenient proximity to the Palace and the Cockpit, to say nothing of the Mall and the coffee-houses. Here, too, Mrs. Steele could readily slip on her mob ; and, with the faithful Warren, trip to morning prayers at the neighbouring church of St. James's. The Bury Street house existed early in the century; but it has long since disappeared. Steele and his 'adorable Molly' must have gone into it some time in November, 1707; and from a passage in one of his letters it seems that he had previously been living with Addison. 'Mr. Addison does not remove till tomorrow,' he says ; 'therefore I cannot think of moving my Goods out of His Lodgings,'—a sentence which throws a light upon those close relations with the

Under Secretary which were revealed in the already-quoted letter to Lord Sunderland. He began his housekeeping upon the liberal scale of a man, who, in addition to a pretty wife, has plantations in the West Indies, hopes of an estate in Wales, and innumerable Castles in Spain. There are signs of numerous domestics; and like everyone else of importance he set up his coach. Besides this he took a little cottage at Hampton Wick, which from its proximity to the Palace there, he christened unambitiously by the name of 'The Hovel.' Finally, he seems to have committed the indiscretion of inviting his mother-in-law to become part of his establishment. All this is to be gathered from his letters, which pass almost as freely as before, and, as frankly reveal their writer's idiosyncrasy. The Barbadoes property does not seem to be quite responding to the expectations formed of it, and it is greatly upon his mind, involving much running hither and thither and much transacting of belated business at taverns and the like. Then he has his first fit of the gout; and makes pleasant fun of his crutches and his infirmity, which obliges him to sit still while his little wife dances. Nor are there wanting traces of those misunderstandings of early married life, which are almost inevitable where the husband and wife are no longer very young, and have each formed habits of their own. Steele's vagrant easy good-fellowship, and his interest in all sorts and conditions of men, must have tried his new companion, who was sedentary in her tastes, and perhaps, as the French say, a little *froide et pincée* besides. Then, early in the correspondence, comes another shadow. In one letter Steele, begging pardon for ' every Act of Rebellion,' refers to his having been impatient ' of her kind concern [in] interesting herself with so much affection in all which relates to him ; ' and she, confessing that it is but ' *an addition to our uneasiness* to be at variance ·with each other,' asks his forgiveness if she has offended him, not without a touch of lingering soreness :—' God forgive you for adding to the sorrow of an heavy heart, that is above all sorrow but for your sake.' The words ' an addition to our uneasiness,' coupled with a passage in one of Steele's letters to his mother-in-law which speaks ' of the Generall complaints under which every body at present is sighing, whose concerns are wholly in Land,' make it clear that the money difficulties which accompanied Steele during the greater part of his career had already begun to disquiet him. But the best idea of his life at this time will be obtained by transcribing some more of his letters, in all cases following the original manuscripts. Here is one that was written on the 8th of December, 1707 :—

' DEAR RULER,—I cant Wait upon you to-day to Hampton Court. I have the West Indian businesse on my hands, and find very much to be done before Thursday's post. I shall dine at Our Table at Court, where the Bearer knows how to come to me with any Orders for

'Your Obedient Husband & Most Humble Ser^{nt}

' RICH^D STEELE.

' My duty to my Mother.'

' My mother ' was of course Mrs. Scurlock, who, by

this time, was in residence at Bury Street. The next
two letters, the first of which is dated ' Devill Tavern,
Temple Barr,' are apologies because he cannot return
home to dinner; in a third a friend has stopped him
on the road, and he writes that he is drinking his wife's
health, and will ' come within a Pint of Wine.' Then
he is busy a few weeks later about Barbadoes :—

' Tennis Court Coffee-House
' May 5, 1708

' DEAR WIFE,—I hope I have done this day what
will be pleasing to you; In the mean time shall lye
this night at a Barbers, one Legg, over against the
Devill Tavern at Charing Crosse. I shall be able to con-
front the fools who wish me Uneasy and shall have the
Satisfaction to see thee Chearfull and at Ease.

' If the Printer's boy be at Home send Him hither;
and let Mrs. Todd send by the Boy my Night-Gown,[1]
Slippers & clean Linnen. You shall Hear from me
early in the morning.'

Unless the news from Ostend or Paris were unusually heavy, it is difficult to understand what could
make it necessary for ' Mr. Gazetteer,' who resided in
Bury Street, St. James's, to which place this missive is
addressed, to relinquish his *domus et placens uxor* for
' one Legg's ' at Charing Cross, which was but a stone's
throw away. Perhaps, at his own home, there were
importunate inquirers out of whose way it was desir-

---

[1] That is, his Morning, or Dressing-Gown. ' I am in my night-
gown every morning between six and seven,' says Swift in the
Journal to Stella.

able to keep. In a few days, however, Richard is himself again, and at eleven o'clock, on the 19th of May, 1708, writes from Lord Sunderland's Office as follows :—

'DEAR PRUE [It is the second time he uses this name],—I desire of you to gett the Coach and y^r self ready as soon as you can conveniently and call for me here from whence we will go and spend some time together in the fresh Air in free Conference. Let my best Periwigg be put in the Coach-Box, and my new Shoes, for 'tis a Comfort to [be] well dress'd in agreeable Company. You Are Vitall Life to Y^r Oblig'd Affectionate Husband & Humble Ser^{nt}

'RICH^D STEELE.'

Steele was particular about what Gay calls the 'curling honours of the head,' and according to old Richard Nutt, one of the first printers of the *Tatler*, never rode out on airing but in a fine black full-bottomed periwig, the price of which in those days would be nearly fifty pounds. This, or some earlier example, is doubtless the object of his solicitude, and on this particular day in May, we may imagine him driving slowly round and round the Ring in the Park in free, and, for the moment, cloudless conference with the lady whom he calls his ' Ruler,' and behaving, no doubt, as became ' as agreeable and pleasant a man as any in England.' But alas! a day or two after there must have been bad news from Barbadoes, or Steele had met another friend on his way home, for there has evidently been a second quarrel. On the 1st of June he tells her that he shall ' be at the office exactly at seven, in hopes of seeing the beautifullest object that can present itself to his eyes—her fair self,' and then, four days later, comes this :—

' DEAR PRUE,—What you would have me do I know not. All that my fortune will compasse you shall always enjoy and have no body near you that You do not like except I am my self disapproved by you for being devotedly

' Y^r Obedient Husband :

' RICH^D STEELE.

' I shan't come home till night.'

On the 7th of June matters are no better :—

' DEAR PRUE,—I enclose to you a Guinnea for y^r Pockett. I dine with Ld Hallifax.

' I wish I knew how to Court you into Good Humour, for Two or Three Quarrells more will dispatch me quite. If you have *any* Love for me believe I am *always* pursuing our Mutuall Good. Pray consider that all My little fortune is to [be] Settled this month and that I have inadvertently made me self Liable to Impatient People who take all advantages. If you have [not] patience I shall transact my businesse rashly and Lose a very great sum to Quicken the time of y^r being ridd of all people you don't like.

' Y^{rs} Ever   RICH^D STEELE.'

In August Mrs. Steele seems to have moved to her country house at Hampton Wick, into possession of which Nichols supposes Steele to have entered some time between the 11th of June and the 11th of August. The situation seems still to have been considerably strained from Steele's next letter:—

'Aug^{st} 12th, 1708.

'MADAM,—I have your letter wherein you let me know that the little dispute we have had is far from being a Trouble to you, neverthelesse I assure you, any disturbance between us is the greatest affliction to me imaginable. You talk of the Judgement of the World I shall never Govern my Actions by y^t, but by the rules of morality and Right reason. I Love you better than the light of my Eyes, or the life blood in my Heart but when I have lett you know that you are also to understand that neither my sight shall be so far inchanted, or my affection so much master of me as to make me forgett our common Interest. To attend my businesse as I ought and improve my fortune it is necessary that my time and my Will should be under no direction but my own. Pray give my most Humble Service to Mrs Binns. I Write all this rather to explain my own thoughts to you than answer your letter distinctly. I enclose it to you that upon second thoughts you may see the disrespectfull manner in which you treat

'Y^r Affectionate Faithfull Husband:

'R : STEELE.'

In a letter which follows a few days later he tells her that he dined yesterday with Lord Halifax 'where the Beauties in the Garden (presumably Mrs. Steele and her friend Mrs. Binns) were drank to.' He has done a deal of business of which he will give an account when they meet. Then follow two letters which throw a light upon what has preceded :—

'Aug. 18, 1708

'DEAR PRUE,—I have your letter, and all the Great severity you complain of is that you have a Husband Who loves you better than His life who has a great deal of troublesome businesse out of the [fatigue?] of which He removes the dearest thing alive.

'Y^{rs} Faithfully in Spite of y^r self,

'RICH^D STEELE.'

'August 20th, 1708

'DEAR PRUE,—Yours by penny post[1] came to my hands but Just now. You extremely mistake me in beleiving me capable of any Cruelty or Unkindnesse to you. I scorn that any man living should have more honour and regard to His Wife than my self. You speak with Heat to me but I will not answer you in that stile but make it my utmost aim to make you easy and happy to which you [sic] nothing but doing me the Justice to believe me with all the attention Imaginable

'y^r Faithfull Husband

'RICH^D STEELE.

'I have paid Mr. Addison His whole thousand pound and have settled every man's payment except one which I hope to perfect tomorrow. Desmaiseaux is gone to the Bath for His Health.

[1] There had been a penny post since 1683. It was abolished in 1711. There was even a halfpenny post for the London district when Steele wrote the above letter. (Ashton's *Social Life in the Reign of Queen Anne.*)

' I enclose a Guinnea and an half & will send more
to-morrow or monday if I don't come my self. I am
Mrs. Binn's servant.'

It is clear from the former of these two letters that
Mrs. Steele had been persuaded to go to Hampton
Court mainly to get her out of the way during her
husband's difficulties; it is also clear that Addison had
been obliged to help his friend by the loan of a considerable sum, which, if words mean anything, had
recently been paid by funds from Barbadoes or elsewhere. After this the sky seems to brighten, and the
correspondence shows that for the time, at least, Mrs.
Steele's equanimity is restored, or in process of restoration. Here is one of the indications :—

' Aug⁺⁺ 28th, 1708

' DEAR PRUE,—The Afternoon Coach shall bring you
ten pounds. Your letter shows you are passionately in
Love with me. But We must take our portion of life
as it runs without repining and I consider that Good
nature added to that Beautifull form God has giv'n you
would make an happinesse too great for Humane life.
  ' Yʳ Most Oblig'd Husband
   ' & Most Humble Serᵛ
     ' RICHᴰ STEELE.'

· Here is another :—

' Aug⁺ᵗ 30th, 1708

' DEAR PRUE,—I sent ten pounds by the Afternoon
Coach of Saturday and hope you receiv'd it safe. The
manner in which you write to me might perhaps to
another look like neglect and want of Love, but I will

not understand it so but take it to be only the uneasi-
nesse of a doting fondnesse which cannot bear my
Absence without disdain.

'I hope We shall never be so long asunder more,
for it is not in your powér to make me otherwise than
Yʳ Affectionate Faithfull & Tender Husband

'RICHᴰ STEELE.'

A fortnight later the situation still seems doubtful :—

'Septʳ 13th 1708

'DEAR PRUE,—I write to you in Obedience to what
you Ordered me, but there are not words to Expresse
the Tendernesse I have for you. Love is too harsh a
Word for it, but if you knew how my Heart akes when
you Speake an Unkind word to me, and springs with
Joy when you smile upon me, I am sure you would
place your Glory rather in preserving my happinesse
like a good Wife, than tormenting me like a Peevish
Beauty. Good Prue write me word you shall be over-
joyed at my return to you, and Pity the Awkard
figure I make when I pretend to resist you by Complying always with the reasonable demands of yʳ
Enamour'd Husband

'RICHᴰ STEELE.'

'I am Mrs. Binn's servant.'

This careful reference to Mrs. Steele's companion
Mrs. Binns, which recurs in many of the letters, looks
as if Steele was more than usually anxious to conciliate
this lady and secure her good offices. It may be,
indeed, that the wholesome dread of confidantes which

he afterwards expressed through Sir Roger de Coverley
dates from this time. A few more examples and we
shall have done with our specimens of Steele as a letter
writer :—

'Sep^{br} 19th 1708 five in the Evening

' DEAR PRUE,—I send you seven pen'orth of Wall
nutts at five a penny. Which is the greatest proof I
can give you at present of my being with my whole
Heart Y^{rs}

' RICH^{D} STEELE.'

Then follow two PSS. But apparently the walnuts
were too great a temptation to be resisted, for when
the letter was folded and addressed he wrote outside in
the corner :—' There are but 29 Walnutts.'

'Sep^{br} 20th 1708

' DEAR PRUE,—If a Servant I sent last night gott to
Hampton-Court you receiv'd 29 Walnutts and a letter
from me. I enclose the Gazette and am with all my
Soul y^{r} Passionate Lover & Faithfull Husband

' RICH^{D} STEELE.

' Since I writ the Above I have found half an
hundred more of Walnutts which I send herewith.
' My Service to Binns.'

'Sep^{br} 21st 1708

' DEAR DEAR PRUE,—Your pretty letter, with so much
good nature and Kindnesse wch I receiv'd yesterday is
a perfect pleasure to Me. I am at present very much
out of Humour upon other account Tryon having putt
off the payment of my 800*l.* which I ought to have

received yesterday till further time. But I hope when Mr. Clay comes to town to-morrow He will see me Justified.

'I am, With the Tenderest Affection, Ever y^{rs}
'Rich^D Steele.'

'Sep^{br} 27th 1708 Monday—se'en at night

'DEAR PRUE,—You see you are obey'd in every thing and that I write over night for the day following; I shall now in earnest by Mr. Clay's good conduct manage my businesse with that method as shall make me easy. The news I am told, you had, last night, of the taking of Lille does not prove true but I hope we shall have it soon.[1] I shall send by to-morrow's Coach. I am, Dear Prue a little in Drink but at all times

'Y^r Faithfull Husband
'Rich^D Steele.'

'Sep^{br} 28th 1708
'Secretary's office between six and seven at night
[Torn away]

'I thought it better to enclose this thus than to direct so small a sum to you. I have but half as much left in my Pockett but shall be much richer on Thursday Morning. My Dear Wife it is not to be imagin'd by you the tender Akings my Heart is frequently touch'd with when I think of you. Mr. Clay has shown Himself a man of Addresse in Settling my Affairs in Spite of the Tricks and Artifices of those I have [to] deal with.

[1] The city of Lille finally surrendered to Prince Eugène on the 22nd of October, 1708. Boufflers then retired into the citadel, and was besieged by the Allies for seven weeks more.

'I recommend Thee, my Heart's Desire, to the Good God who made thee that Amiable Creature thou Art to keep thee safe and happy. My Service to Your Companion Binns. I am

'Y^r Devoted Affectionate

'Husband & Humble Ser^{vt}

'RICH^D STEELE.'

Later in the evening, or, to be exact, at the 'Half hour after ten,' with a candour equal to that of the day before he writes again as follows:—'It being three hours since I writ to you I send this to assure you I am now going very soberly to bed, and that you shall be last thing in my thoughts to-night as well as the first to-morrow morning.—I am with the Utmost Fondnesse Y^r Faithfull Husband RICH^D STEELE.'

The selection from Steele's letters at this period, of which the foregoing are examples, might be indefinitely extended, with but little gain in variety of interest. Tender aspirations; apologies for unkept engagements; schemes for infallible advancement; hopes of unravelling obscure pecuniary entanglements;—these continue as heretofore to make up the staple of his communications to the capricious beauty, who still remains at Hampton, while her husband is bustling among bailiffs, lawyers, and gentlemen-in-waiting. Now he is at Sandy-End with Addison, lying there the night, and going on in his (Addison's) coach-and-four to visit a friend; now, with the aid of Stephen Clay, the young barrister of whose death he afterwards wrote so feelingly in the *Spectator*, No. 133, he is endeavouring to bring the shadowy and intractable

G

Tryon to book;[1] now he is scribbling a notelet to Prue which Jervas the painter will throw over her garden wall on his way to Hampton Court, and now despatching to that lady a quarter of a pound of the best Bohea, which, in this particular year of grace, costs just 5*s*. Then the Lord Chamberlain is expected in town immediately, from whom he hopes for an order for a very handsome apartment, into which (when he gets it) he will remove forthwith; and then, a day or two later, he is putting in with all the force he can command for the place vacated by the death of Mr. Harrison, 'a gentleman usher of the Privy Chamber' (200*l*. a year salary, and 100*l*. perquisites). Later again he writes from beside the dead body of his master, Prince George of Denmark, who departed this life, after making no great figure in it, on the 28th of October, 1708. By this he loses his salary as gentleman usher, but regains it in another way, as Queen Anne gave all her husband's attendants annuities which, in Steele's case, equalled his salary. Meanwhile Mrs. Steele returns to London and goes into lodgings in Kensington Square. Why she did not return to Bury Street is explained by the fact that there are difficulties with the landlady, by whom an officer has been put into the house. This corner turned, a new hope arises out of the appointment of Addison in December as Secretary to the Lord-Lieutenant of Ireland, which creates a vacancy at the Cockpit for an Under Secretary of State. Steele at once makes application for the post,

---

[1] 'Rowland Tryon, *Merchant*,' appears among the subscribers to the 1710-11 edition of the *Tatler*. But the indefatigable Nichols gives no definite information respecting him.

as eagerly as ever. The result may be told from the recently published *Wentworth Papers*. 'Mr. Addisson' —says gossiping and incoherent Peter Wentworth— 'is certain of going over secretary to Lord Wharton, and Mr. Steele put in for his place, but Lord Sunderland has put him off with a promise to get him the next place he shall ask that may be keep with his Gazette. I hear it is one of the Scotch members that is to come into Mr. Addisson place, but I don't know his name yet.' This is confirmed by another of Steele's letters in which it is stated that the fortunate candidate was a North Briton (Mr. R. Pringle). And so time wears on until we come to the first serious enterprise of Steele's life, the establishment of the *Tatler* and the eighteenth-century essay,—a subject to which the ensuing chapter will be devoted.

But before beginning, it may be well for a moment to consider Steele's personality as revealed by the correspondence which has here been quoted and referred to. From the scant and often doubtful biographical particulars scattered through the first two chapters no very definite picture of the man was to be constructed. But in his letters to his wife his character, and especially his character in undress, is disclosed with considerable distinctness. He is loyal, he is affectionate, he is amiable, he is thoroughly generous and good-hearted, but he is hopelessly sanguine, restless, and impulsive. It is to these defects that most of his inconsistencies are to be traced, without accusing him either of careless profusion or exceptional conviviality. Because, in one or two of his letters to his wife, both before and after marriage, reference is made to his

having taken wine freely, there is no reason for concluding that he drank more than any of his contemporaries, whose letters to their wives (if equally
candid) we have not had the privilege of perusing.
Because there are evidences that he had little or no
money, it is equally unnecessary to conclude that he
was without it because he had spent it recklessly or
foolishly.   On the contrary, the whole of his communications go rather to show that he counted upon money
that never came to him.   Upon paper his means, as
stated in his own promising programme, were ample
enough.   His West Indian property was worth 850*l.*
per annum; he had 300*l.* from the *Gazette*, 100*l.* as
gentleman-in-waiting, and the income of his wife's
mother was 400*l.*   But, as a matter of fact, the figures
were much less than this.   The Barbadoes estate was
encumbered with an annual debt of 180*l.*; the salary
from the *Gazette* was saddled with 45*l.* taxes, and whatever Mrs. Scurlock could leave the newly married
couple at her death, she seems, from one of Steele's
letters to her, to have allowed them no more than 160*l.*
per annum during her lifetime.   This, moreover, is
ominously described as 'liable to certain debts.'   It is
also probable that the value of the Barbadoes estate was
considerably exaggerated; and it is besides admitted
that times were exceptionally hard for the holders of
such property.   It is equally plain that Steele had
great difficulty in getting his money.   Indeed it is
even doubtful whether, owing to the protracted nego-
ciations so often mentioned, he received any money at
all from this source during the first year of his married
life.   If this be the case, his income during that time

would only be about 500*l*., a sum obviously inadequate
to maintain an establishment in Bury Street, a country
box at Hampton Wick, and an equipage to match,
however much these splendours might have been
justified by his estimated means. Add to this that as
a quondam Captain of Fusileers [1] and man about town,
he no doubt started with debts of his own; and it
requires no further argument to prove that, without
extravagance of any kind, he had at the outset all the
elements of embarrassment,—an embarrassment from
which he never after seems to have succeeded in wholly
freeing himself.

These were conditions, which were certainly unfavourable to happiness; and it can scarcely be supposed
that Steele's wedded life was of that idyllic serenity,
which the charm of his individuality and the warmth
of his attachment would seem to promise. In the
absence of any utterances from Mrs. Steele herself, it
would be unwise to infer too much respecting her from
her husband's letters. But it is impossible not to read
those letters without receiving a certain vague impression which is not entirely to her advantage. As an
unmarried woman she had been a beauty and a ' scornful lady,' to use the seventeenth-century synonym for
a coquette,—and she apparently continued to retain as a
wife a good deal of that affected disdain and tenacity of
worship which had characterised her as a spinster. She
seems also to have been given to vapours, and variable

---

[1] From the absence of any reference to his military pay in his
account of his means, as given to his mother-in-law, it must be inferred that previous to the 3rd of Sept. 1707, the date of his letter to
her, he had sold his commission. . . .

beyond the licence of her sex; and from her injunction to her husband, when choosing a house, to get one near a church, was probably something of a *dévote*. The general effect produced upon one is that, notwithstanding intervals of genuine tenderness and even indulgent toleration, she was on the whole 'gey ill to live with,' and that when things went wrong, she was by no means sparing of complaints and recriminations which Steele's self-reproachful and promptly repentant nature must have found especially hard to bear. Yet he seems to have loved her dearly. Although, as we have seen, his language once or twice strikes a more dignified note than usual, he is undeviating in his cordiality of tone. To the last she is his 'Absolute Governesse,' his 'capricious Beauty,' his 'dear dear Prue.' When years afterwards he writes of her in the dedication to the *Ladies Library*, it is with the same steadfast loyalty, and the brief note which records her death speaks of her as his 'dear and honoured Wife.'

It must, however, be admitted that, on her side, there was some ground for disillusion. To have married a gentleman with a court appointment and 'a Competency in worldly goods,' who was irregular in his habits, and always at his wits' end for a guinea, was scarcely a satisfactory change from the flattered existence of a prospective Fortune, or the indolent *sommeils du matin* (dear to Millamant) of irresponsible maidenhood.[1] And the escape from impecuniosity is less

---

[1] This privilege she does not seem to have wholly abandoned after marriage. 'I wish sleeping so long this morning, after I came out to Work may not do you harm,' her husband writes; and again, 'Rising a little in a morning . . . would not be amisse.'

easy for the woman than for the man. Steele, with
his elastic vitality and his keen interest in human
nature, could easily fling to the Cretan winds both
Barbadoes and the bailiffs over a bottle with an op-
portune 'school-fellow from India.' But it must have
been far otherwise for 'dearest Prue,' nursing the
wreck of her expectations in tearful *tête-à-tête* with
the sympathetic Mrs. Binns, or waiting nervously, in
an atmosphere of Hungary Water, for the long-ex-
pected tidings that her husband's vaguely-defined
'affairs' were at last successfully composed. If she
was peevish and irritable, her peevishness and irrita-
bility were not without a certain justification.

From the date of his appointment as Gazetteer in
May, 1707, Steele seems to have done little in the way
of literature. As already stated, in September of the
same year, he published a *Prologue to the University of
Oxford*, the first couplet of which—

> ' As wand'ring Streams by secret Force return
>   To that capacious Ocean whence they're born '—

is an economical *réchauffé* of part of his address to
Dr. Ellis in the Dyce Library copy of the *Christian Hero*.
In the concluding lines he apostrophises the academic
dons as follows—

> 'Ye calm Spectators of a guilty Age,
>   Pity the Follies of the World and Stage,
>   Free from what either act, or represent,
>   Weigh both the Character and the Intent.
>   And know, Men as they are our Authors drew,
>   But what they should be, we must learn from you ;'

a commendation, which, it may be observed, would

scarcely be borne out by some of the contemporary entries in Mr. C. E. Doble's excellent edition of Hearne. But if Steele escaped literary criticism by non-production, he seems to have been still unable to secure unmixed approbation for his official announcements. 'The paragraph you mention'—he writes to an Irish friend in October, 1708—'was very much censured in the town; but I acted so as to answer it where I am accountable. As to the rest, I take my employment in its very nature to be what is the object of censure, since so many interests are concerned in the matters I am to relate twice a week: but I am armed cap-a-pee with old sentences; among which I prefer that of Horace with L.300 *per annum* salary—

> *Populus me sibilat at mihi plaudo*
> *Ipse domi simul ac nummos contemplor,'* etc.

'My way of life,' he adds, 'should make me capable of entertaining with much politics; but I am not a bit wiser than you knew me.[1]' It would have been happier for Richard Steele, and for literature generally, if he had maintained this assumed incapacity in matters political. Yet his labours on the *Gazette* can scarcely be regretted, since they certainly played their part in the initiation of the *Tatler*.

[1] *Literary Relics*, etc., by George-Monck Berkeley, 1789, pp. 397-9, where this letter is more fully printed than by Nichols.

CHAPTER IV.

'MR. BICKERSTAFF'S LUCUBRATIONS.'

So much engrossed by the Barbadoes business are
Steele's letters for 1708 that they scarcely contain any
reference to his daily associates, with the exception of
Addison. But during this year he must have seen
much of Swift. In November, 1707, not long after
Steele's marriage, Swift had come to England; and he
remained in this country until June, 1709. His object
was to obtain for the Irish clergy the same remission
of First Fruits and Twentieths payable to the Crown
which had been conceded to their English brethren;
and he had counted upon the aid of Sunderland and
Somers. Upon this occasion, however, his efforts were
unsuccessful. But in the weary waiting-time which
ensued, he had frequent communications with Steele
and Addison, the latter of whom he already knew and
respected. 'The triumvirate of Addison, Steele and
me'—he writes to Ambrose Philips—'come together
as seldom as the sun, moon and earth; but I often
see each of them.' His note-book contains frequent
entries of dinners with one or other at the St. James's
Coffee-house, at the Fountain of the Kit-Cats, at the
old George in Pall Mall. Congreve, no doubt, was

sometimes of that illustrious company, and Swift's friend, Colonel Hunter, and Anthony Henley, the Hampshire 'Squire who is supposed to have contributed to the *Tatler*. There would be meetings also at Lord Halifax's house in New Palace Yard, or at his country seat by the Thames. Nor was the intercourse of the trio wholly of the table and the tavern. At his lodgings in the Haymarket Swift would be within easy distance of both Bury Street and Steele's office.[1] He must have made the acquaintance of ' dearest Prue,' by whom, he wrote afterwards, Steele was henpecked ; and there is evidence that even in bureaucratic Whitehall itself, he sometimes guided the pen of the too garrulous Gazetteer. When all the world was hungering for the long-deferred surrender of Lille, whereof mention was made in the foregoing chapter, it was Swift, apparently, who prevented the premature announcement of an engagement. ' We are now every day expecting news from abroad of the greatest importance,' he tells Archbishop King in August. ' In the last *Gazette* it was certainly affirmed that there would be a battle ; but the copy coming to the office to be corrected, I prevailed with them to let me soften the phrase a little, so as to leave some room for possibilities.' The *Gazette* still exists ; but to be written by a Steele and corrected by a Swift is not now among its privileges.

Pruning luxuriances in the Gazetteer's foreign news was not, however, the only literary influence which the dominating spirit of Swift exercised upon his docile associate, One of the first books to which the forth-

[1] In March, 1709, writing to Colonel Hunter at Paris, he asks him to address his letters ' at Mr. Steele's office, at the Cockpit.'

coming *Tatler* drew attention was the *Project for the Advancement of Religion and the Reformation of Manners*, which, under the mask of a 'Person of Quality,' Swift wrote in 1708. It does not seem to have been quite decided by the Dean's biographers whether he intended to be wholly didactic or partly ironic in this remarkable tract, which he dedicated to that Countess of Berkeley upon whom he had previously palmed off his *Meditation on a Broomstick*. But much in it, and especially certain passages with regard to the contemporary stage, must have been thoroughly to Steele's taste, while several of the social practices which fell under its condemnation, as gaming, intemperance, profanity, and the like, are exactly those which Steele in his subsequent character of Censor (and it is to be observed that Swift especially recommends the appointment of Censors) most persistently attacked. It was to be expected therefore that Steele, who knew the anonymous author, would commend his work. All Will's Coffee-house, he declares, have read it and approved it; and one of that company, by whom Mr. Forster thinks we are to understand Addison, observed of it that the author 'writes very like a Gentleman, and goes to Heav'n with a very good Mien.' More direct, however, than the effect which the *Project* exercised upon Steele's future enterprise was that of another of Swift's literary exercises for 1708—the famous predictions which he levelled against the almanack-makers. His chief victim upon this occasion, as is well known, was the cobbler and starmonger, John Partridge, the author of an annual *Merlinus Liberatus*, whose death he gravely predicted at a certain day and hour. By itself this was nothing; but when the time arrived, Swift gravely announced that his prophecy was accomplished. It was in vain for Partridge to assert his existence; his decease was related with the gravest circumstantiality; his elegy was written in spite of his protestations, and the mystification, into which the whole of Will's gradually entered, was carried to such a point that the company of stationers applied for an injunction against the continued publication of Almanacs bearing the name of Partridge. The pseudonym of 'Isaac Bickerstaff,' which Swift had borrowed from a locksmith's door, and which was borne many years later by an actual playwright, became 'famous through all Parts of *Europe*;' and when, early in 1709, Steele was meditating the establishment of his new paper, he appropriated, probably with Swift's concurrence, the name which Swift had already made familiar. The *Tatler*, No. 1 of which appeared on the 12th of April, 1709, was announced as 'by Isaac Bickerstaff, Esq.'

It is one of the snares of literary inquiry that far too much importance is attached to remote causation. Those who have attempted to account for the sudden and apparently unpremeditated appearance of the *Tatler* have sometimes done so by tracing the germ of its inception to this or that of its periodical predecessors. But with a man like Steele to-day is far more suggestive than yesterday. If the *Tatler* appeared suddenly, it was probably because it was executed almost as soon as it was conceived, and its proximate cause is to be found in the surrounding conditions. Steele, we know, had been vainly seeking some lucrative employment to increase his income. He had failed to obtain the post of gentleman usher of the Privy Chamber: he had failed to obtain the succession to Addison's Under-Secretaryship of State. His thoughts would naturally revert to literature, and not unreasonably to some form of literature in which he could turn to account his exceptional advantages as Gazetteer. From these considerations the idea of a paper or Journal of News of a superior kind must almost necessarily follow. Then it is clear that Swift's *Project* had suggested to him, as indeed he later admits, a way ' of undervaluing the World with Good Breeding,' which was very different from that of the ordinary moral teacher, and could scarcely be over-estimated ' in observing upon the Manners of the Pleasurable as well as the Busie Part of Mankind.' Thus would grow up the scheme of that unique ' Letter of Intelligence,' which was to be the *Tatler*, ' consisting of such Parts as might gratify the Curiosity of Persons of all Conditions, and of each Sex.' Nothing further was needful but to give it an impetus at the outset by some device calculated to attract public attention. This was supplied by attributing the authorship to the all-popular Bickerstaff, who from being a name of Swift's became a personage of Steele's.

The *Tatler*, in all probability, had no more recondite origin than this. In the course of its career its scope widened, and modifications no doubt took place both in its matter and its manner. But the above circumstances are sufficient in themselves to account for the initial appearance on eighteenth-century breakfast tables of the homely double-columned folio sheet— ' Tobacco paper ' and ' Scurvy Letter,' an outraged

correspondent styled it—which was to be succeeded by
so many imitators. Perhaps the best way of giving
some idea of its general purport will be to describe
briefly the first four numbers, which were ' Printed for
the Author,' and issued *gratis*, announcement being
made that after a certain time the price would be a
penny. The motto of the first and many subsequent
numbers was the well-worn *Quicquid agunt Homines
nostri Farrago Libelli*. To Nos. 1, 2 and 3 was prefixed
an introduction, in which Mr. Bickerstaff, after proclaim-
ing that the end and purpose of his paper is to teach
people what to think, goes on as follows:—' I shall
from Time to Time Report and Consider all Matters of
what Kind soever that shall occur to Me, and publish
such my Advices and Reflections every *Tuesday, Thursday*, and *Saturday*, in the Week, for the Convenience
of the Post. It is also resolv'd by me to have something
which may be of Entertainment to the Fair Sex, in
Honour of whom I have taken the Title of this Paper.'
A few lines farther on he says that he shall arrange
his relations under these heads:—' All Accounts of
Gallantry, Pleasure, and *Entertainment*, shall be under
the Article of *White's Chocolate-House* ; *Poetry*, under
that of *Will's Coffee-house* ; *Learning*, under the Title of
Græcian ; *Foreign* and *Domestick News*, you will have
from *St. James's Coffee-house* ; and what else I shall on
any other Subject offer, shall be dated from my own
Apartment.' Finally, recurring to the proposed price, he
adds :—' I once more desire my Reader to consider, That
as I cannot keep an Ingenious Man to go daily to *Will's*,
under Two-pence each Day merely for his Charges ; to

White's, under Sixpence ; nor to the *Græcian*, without allowing him some Plain *Spanish*, to be as able as others at the Learned Table ; and that a good Observer cannot speak with even *Kidney* at *St. James's* without clean Linnen. I say, these Considerations will, I hope, make all persons willing to comply with my Humble Request (when my *Gratis* Stock is exhausted) of a Penny a Piece, especially since they are sure of some proper Amusement, and that it is impossible for me to want Means to entertain 'em, having besides the Helps of my own Parts, the Power of Divination [the opponent of Partridge was, it will be remembered, an astrologer], and that I can, by casting a Figure, tell you all that will happen before it comes to pass.' This last faculty, however, he designs to ' use very sparingly, and not speak of any Thing till it is pass'd, for fear of divulging Matters which may offend our Superiors.'

In accordance with this *avant propos*, *Tatler* No. 1 leads off, under the article of White's, with the account of the deplorable condition of a ' very pretty Gentleman ' who has lost his heart to a lady whom he saw out of a tavern window in Pall Mall while he was washing his teeth. Under Will's is an account of the acting at Drury Lane for Betterton's benefit of Congreve's *Love for Love*, in which Mrs. Barry, Mrs. Bracegirdle and Doggett, though not then attached to the house, took their parts. From the unusual success of this representation Mr. Bickerstaff augurs that ' Plays will revive, and take their usual Place in the Opinion of Persons of Wit and Merit, notwithstanding their late Apostacy in Favour of Dress and Sound '—an obvious

hit at the prevalent rage for opera.[1] His next sentence
gives a curious picture of the eighteenth-century playhouse audience, which, on this occasion, was unusually
splendid and distinguished. 'This Place is very much
alter'd since Mr. *Dryden* frequented it, where you us'd
to see *Songs*, *Epigrams*, and *Satyrs*, in the Hands of
every Man you met, you have now only a Pack of Cards ;
and instead of the Cavils about the Turn of the Expression, the Elegance of the Style, and the like, the
Learned now dispute only about the Truth of the Game.'
After the Poetical and Dramatic comes the Foreign and
Domestic News, part of which is attributed to Mr.
Humphrey Kidney, the then well-known waiter and
keeper of book-debts at St. James's Coffee-house, and
the communication from 'my own Apartment' deals with
the obtrusive and indecent vitality of Partridge the
astrologer, as evidenced by his *Almanack* for the year
1709. The number concludes with an advertisement of
Swift's latest pamphlet on the same subject, the well-
known *Vindication of Isaac Bickerstaff, Esq.*, with which,
for his own part at least, he practically concluded this
protracted jest.

The second number of Steele's paper is mainly
occupied by a poem from the pen of Swift's friend, 'little
Harrison,' based, according to Steele's introduction,
upon 'a real Accident which happen'd among my
Acquaintance.' This is a pleasant versification, under
the title of ' *The Medicin*,' of the old story from Burton's
Anatomy of the lady who is cured of loquacity by
holding water in her mouth, and still finds its place

---

[1] ' The taste for plays is expired '—he had written to Keally in
the previous October. 'We are all for operas,' etc. Swift's corr
spondence tells the same tale.

in humorous anthologies.[1]   Number 3 contains the
earliest of those fine and sympathetic theatrical papers
of which Steele afterwards produced so many examples.
It is an account of the acting of Mrs. Bicknell (always
a favourite of the author) in Wycherley's _Country Wife_;
and while doing justice to the literary merits of that celebrated comedy, manages to do justice also to its dubious
morality.   At the same time the _Tatler_ admits that he
does not go as far as some of his contemporaries in their
views of the stage.   'I cannot be of the same Opinion
with my Friends and Fellow-Labourers, the _Reformers of
Manners_, in their Severity towards Plays, but must allow,
that a good Play, acted before a well-bred Audience,
must raise very proper Incitements to good Behaviour,
and be the most quick and prevailing Method of giving
young People a turn of Sense and Breeding.'   Then,
after a grave and kindly rebuke of a certain 'Young
Nobleman' who had discomposed the audience by coming
to the theatre flustered with wine, he proceeds to make
merry over the last new poem at the coffee-houses,
Blackmore's mechanical _Instructions to Vanderbank_ [a
tapestry designer], which recommends the execution
of all Marlborough's campaigns in arras.   This happy
idea Mr. Bickerstaff thinks might be advantageously
extended.   'As, suppose an Ingenious Gentleman

---

[1] The news in this number from 'my own Apartment' contains
a sarcastic paragraph which is worth quoting.   Since Lewis XIV.
has reached the age of sixty-three, 'there has not dy'd'—says Mr.
Bickerstaff—'one Man of the _French_ Nation, who was Younger
than his Majesty, except a very few, who were taken near the Village
of _Hockstet_ in _Germany_ [Blenheim]; and some more, who were
straitned for Lodging at a Place call'd _Ramelies_, and died on the
Road to _Ghent_ and _Bruges_.'

should write a Poem of Advice to a Callico-Printer :
Do you think that there is a Girl in *England*, that
would wear any Thing but *The Taking of Lisle* ; or, *The
Battle of Oudenarde*? They would certainly be all the
Fashion, 'till the Heroes abroad had cut out some more
Patterns. I should fancy small Skirmishes might do
for Under Petticoats, provided they had a Siege for
the Upper. If our Adviser was well imitated, many
industrious People might be put to Work. Little Mr.
Dactile, now in the Room [i.e. at Will's] who formerly
writ a Song and a Half, is a Week gone in a very
pretty Work, upon this Hint: He is writing an Epigram to a Young Virgin who knits very well; 'tis a
Thousand Pities he is a *Jacobite* : But his Epigram is
by way of Advice to this Damsel to knit all the Actions
of the *Pretender* and the Duke of *Burgundy* last Campaign in the Clock of a Stocking.'

The last of the *gratis* numbers, No. 4, after brief
preliminary, opens with a pair of feminine portraits,
after Steele and Pope's friend Jervas. Whether they
were intended for real beauties, the annotators say not.
But they are in Steele's best manner :—' All Hearts '—
he writes from White's—' at present pant for two Ladies
only, who have for some Time engross'd the Dominion
of the Town. They are indeed both exceeding Charming,
but differ very much in their Excellencies. The Beauty
of *Clarissa* is Soft, that of *Chloe* Piercing. When you
look at *Clarissa*, you see the most exact Harmony of
Feature, Complexion, and Shape; you find in *Chloe*
nothing extraordinary in any one of those Particulars,
but the Whole Woman irresistible. *Clarissa* looks Languishing; *Chloe* Killing. *Clarissa* never fails of gaining

Admiration; *Chloe*, of moving Desire. The Gazers at *Clarissa* are at first unconcern'd, as if they were observing a finé Picture. They who behold *Chloe*, at the first Glance, discover Transport, as if they met their dearest Friend. These different Perfections are suitably represented by the last Great Painter *Italy* has sent us, Mr. *Jervase*. *Clarissa* is, by that Skilful Hand, plac'd in a Manner that looks artless, and innocent of the Torment she gives; *Chloe* drawn with a Liveliness that shows she is Conscious, but not Affected, of her Perfections. *Clarissa* is a Shepherdess; *Chloe*, a Country Girl. I must own, the Design of *Chloe's* picture shows, to me, great Mastery in the Painter, for nothing could be better imagin'd than the Dress he has given her, of a Straw-Hat and Ribbon, to represent that Sort of Beauty which enters the Heart with a certain Familiarity, and cheats it into a Belief, that it has receiv'd a Lover as well as an Object of Love. The Force of their different Beauties is seen also in the Effects it makes upon their Lovers. The Admirers of *Chloe* are eternally Gay and well-pleas'd: Those of *Clarissa* Melancholy and Thoughtful. And as this Passion always changes the natural Man into a quite Different Creature from what he was before, the Love of *Chloe* makes Coxcombs; that of *Clarissa*, Madmen.[1] There were of

---

[1] Can Steele have here been thinking of Waller's charming lines
' To Amoret ? '—

'AMORET! as sweet and good
As the most delicious food,
Which, but tasted, does impart
Life and gladness to the heart.

SACHARISSA'S beauty's wine
Which to madness doth incline :
Such a liquor, as no brain
That is mortal can sustain.'

each Kind just now here.   Here is One that Whistles,
Laughs, Sings, and Cuts Capers, for Love of *Chloe*.
Another has just now writ Three Lines to *Clarissa*,
then taken a Turn in the Garden, then came back
again, then tore his Fragment, then call'd for some
Chocolate, then went away without it.

'*Chloe* has so many Admirers in the Room at present'
[i.e. at White's] 'that there is too much Noise to proceed
in my Narration : So that the Progress of the Loves of
Clarissa and *Chloe*, together with the Bottles that are
drank each Night for the One, and the many Sighs
which are utter'd, and Songs written, on the Other,
must be our Subject on future Occasion.'

The Theatrical News of the same Number, after a
whimsical outburst *à propos* of the Owen M'Swiney's
new Opera of *Pyrrhus and Demetrius*, concludes with
the following passage, which is quite in the spirit of
Fielding's *Pasquin* and Hogarth's *Strolling Actresses* :—
'Advices from the upper End of *Piccadilly* say, that *May-
Fair* is utterly abolish'd ; and we hear, Mr. *Pinkethman*
has remov'd his Ingenious Company of Strollers to *Greenwich* : But other Letters from *Deptford* say, the Company is only Making thither, and not yet settled ; but
that several Heathen Gods and Goddesses, which are
to descend in Machines, landed at the *Kings-Head-
Stairs* last Saturday.   *Venus* and *Cupid* went on Foot
from thence to *Greenwich* ; *Mars* got drunk in the Town,
and broke his Landlord's Head ; for which he sat in
the Stocks the whole Evening ; but Mr. *Pinkethman*
giving Security that he should do nothing this ensuing
Summer, he was set at Liberty.'   Diana—the record
goes on to tell—owing to a misadventure quite out of

keeping with her celestial character, 'was committed by Justice *Wrathful.*' 'But,' it is added, 'there goes down another *Diana* and a *Patient Grissel* next Tide from Billingsgate.' The number concludes with the following Advertisement :—' Upon the Humble Petition of the Running Stationers, &c. this Paper may be had of them, for the future, at the Price of one Penny.' At this price it continued to be sold,—the only subsequent difference being that, after No. 26, there was a special issue with a blank leaf 'to write Business on' for the benefit of country subscribers. This cost a halfpenny more.

Steele, as will be evident from the above summary of the opening numbers, struck at the outset most of the notes which later distinguished the periodical. The reference to cards in theatres, and the rebuke to the young nobleman flustered with wine, have each their amplification in subsequent papers devoted to drunkenness and gambling. Many excellent theatrical and literary utterances succeeded to the criticism of the *Country Wife* and the *Instructions to Vanderbank,* while the contrasted portraits of Chloe and Clarissa and the sketch of the distraught lover of No. 1 are no more than ordinary examples of those efforts for the entertainment of the 'Fair Sex,' which excited the robust cynicism of Swift. The tale or incident is, indeed, not yet represented.; but it is close at hand in the little tragedy of Valentine and Unnion at the siege of Namur, which figures in No. 5, and nothing afterwards attempted in the burlesque way is much happier than the paragraph devoted to the *splendeurs et misères* of Mr. Penkethman's company of strolling comedians.

Upon the political department there is less need to lay stress. Although Steele seems to have attached great, and perhaps unreasonable, importance to this, it was not, by its nature, destined to be an enduring feature; and as the plan of the paper developed, it finally faded away altogether. At first with some anonymous aid, such as that afforded by Harrison's poem in No. 2, Steele seems to have provided the whole of the copy himself. Swift's well-known *Description of the Morning*, indeed, is included in No. 9, but it is introduced rather as a quotation than as the contribution of its author, who at this time was visiting his mother at Leicester on his way back to Ireland; and there is nothing that with any certainty can be attributed to him before No. 32, which, under the name of Madonella, coarsely ridicules poor Mary Astell and her 'Protestant Nunnery.' The first letter of John Hughes, another occasional contributor, does not appear until No. 64, and beyond the humorous account of the Staff family in No. 11, which is assigned to a certain Captain Twisden, who was killed at the siege of Mons, there are no signs that Steele had any stated assistants, with but one exception; nor did any of the above-mentioned writers render, at any period, any material aid to his enterprise. But, as soon as the sixth number was issued, Addison, who had left London on his way to his Irish Secretaryship two days before the *Tatler* first came out, recognised his friend's pen by its reproduction of a remark of his own in reference to the propriety of Virgil's epithets. Shortly after he seems to have tendered his services, first in the way of hints and suggestions, then in the form of finished papers, which

towards the close of the series, when he had again returned to London permanently, became pretty numerous,
and fairly regular in their appearance.

There can be no need now to attempt to lessen the
value of Addison's contributions to the *Tatler*, or to
underrate their importance in perfecting the eighteenth-century Essay. Steele himself, with that royalty
of acknowledgment which characterised him, frankly
admits this. ' I have,' he says, in that oft-quoted
passage from the general Preface to volume iv. of the
collected edition of 1710-11, ' only one Gentleman,
who will be nameless, to thank for any frequent Assistance to me, which indeed it would have been barbarous in him to have denied to one with whom he has
lived in an Intimacy from Childhood, considering the
great Ease with which he is able to dispatch the most
entertaining Pieces of this Nature. This good Office
he performed with such Force of Genius, Humour, Wit,
and Learning, that I fared like a distressed Prince, who
calls in a powerful Neighbour to his Aid; I was undone
by my Auxiliary; when I had once called him in, I
could not subsist without Dependance on him.' ' That
paper [i.e. the *Tatler*] '—he says again, with perfect
sincerity and truth, when defending himself many
years after in the Preface to the second edition of the
Drummer—' was advanced indeed! for it was raised to
a greater thing than I intended it! For the elegance,
purity, and correctness, which appeared in his [Addi-
son's] Writings were not so much my purpose; as (in
any intelligible manner, as I could) to rally all those
Singularities of human life, through the different Pro-
fessions and Characters in it, which obstruct anything

that was truly good and great.' These words, despite some friendly enthusiasm, accurately define the nature of Addison's aid. He imported into the undertaking a higher standard, not of motive, but of execution, and a more finished literary style. He found in it, moreover, opportunities for the exercise of qualities of his own which his Italian Travels, and his 'Gazette in rhyme,' had not hitherto afforded him. In his friend's varied pages, his keen observation, his sub-humorous gravity and his fine irony, his discursive learning and his delicate lapidary art, were all invaluable; while his position as a contributor made it unnecessary for him to depart from those contemplative modes of composition which are generally essential to the making of masterpieces. And many of his papers in the *Tatler* are little masterpieces, not afterwards excelled by any of the maturer efforts of the *Spectator*. The delightful sketch of the fatuous poetaster, Ned Softly, fooled to the top of his bent by his compliant listener; the Labruyère-like full-length of that 'Broker in Learning,' Tom Folio, great only in type and title-pages; the admirable *genre*-piece of the 'Political Upholsterer' and his shabby consistory of quidnuncs, combing out their old campaign-wigs in the Mall, and discussing 'what the Swede intend, and what the French,'—these are productions which are in no wise inferior to the *Citizen's Journal* or *Sir Roger de Coverley at the Play*. Nor are there many, if any, essays in the later *Spectator* which can be said to compete successfully with the *Adventures of a Shilling* or the Rabelaisian fancy of *Frozen Voices*.

But the praise that cannot be withheld from the merit of Addison's performance must not mislead us into forgetting that he was, after all, only a contributor, and a contributor moreover whose aid was tendered when the periodical for which he worked was already well established. No doubt he assisted greatly in extending and maintaining it; but by the time he began to write continuously,—that is after No. 80,—it had already found its *raison d'être*. It was Steele who originated and designed it; it was Steele upon whom fell the burden and heat of the day; and upon Steele devolved the duty of providing an unfailing supply of material. Neither these conditions, nor Steele's own literary habits, were favourable to the best kind of work. We find, as we might expect to find, frequent traces of haste and hurry; we find also, not, as in Addison's case, careful elaborations from some remote suggestion, but rapidly improvised utterances springing from the casual prompting of the moment—a face at a window, a word in a club, a cry from a crowd. Addison seems to have transported his idea from the coffee-house to his quiet Whitehall office; Steele to have found his in the street and scribbled it down in the coffee-house. What Steele with his 'veined humanity' and ready sympathy derived from 'conversation,'—to use the eighteenth-century term for intercourse with the world, he flung upon his paper then and there without much labour of selection; what Addison perceived in his environment when, to use Steele's expression, he began 'to look about and like his company,' he carried carefully home to carve into some gem of graceful raillery or refined expression. Each writer has, naturally, the defects of his qualities. If Addison delights us by his finish, he repels us by his restraint and absence of fervour; if Steele is careless, he is always frank and genial. Addison's papers are faultless in their art, and in this way achieve an excellence which was beyond the reach of Steele's quicker and more impulsive nature. But for words which the heart finds when the head is seeking; for phrases glowing with the white heat of a generous emotion; for sentences which throb and tingle with manly pity or courageous indignation, we must turn to the essays of Steele.

In the dedication of the first volume of the *Tatler*, Steele described its general purpose as ' to expose the false Arts of Life, to pull off the Disguises of Cunning, Vanity, and Affectation, and to recommend· a general Simplicity in our Dress, our Discourse, and our Behaviour.' The *Tatler* had existed for some time when this definition of its mission was penned; and it must be regarded rather as a description of what it had become, than a forecast of its intention. Still, whether Steele had borrowed his idea from Swift's *Project* or not, the reformation of manners had always been his aim. As in his comedies he had endeavoured—according to his lights—to reconcile morality and the stage, so in the pages of the *Tatler*, he strove to reconcile morality and the world. In a series of papers beginning with No. 26 he continued the campaign against duelling, which he had already begun in the *Lying Lover*; and his assaults upon the prevalent vice of gaming, with its train of swindlers and sharpers, seem to have been effectual at all events in arousing the greatest alarm and irritation among the cogging community. There is a familiar story of two well-dressed gamblers who, entering a coffee-house, while

smarting under some of Steele's paragraphs, swore
loudly and lustily that they would cut the Captain's
throat to teach him better manners. 'In this country,'
said my lord Forbes, then a guidon in the Horse
Guards, 'you will find it easier to cut a purse,'—and
the bullies were unceremoniously hustled out at doors,
'with every mark of disgrace.' Lord Forbes was not
the only man who supported Steele in his 'Endeavour
to banish Fraud and Couzenage from the Presence and
Conversation of Gentlemen.' In the last *Tatler*, Mr.
Bickerstaff makes his public acknowledgments to two
other military men, Brigadier Andrew Bisset and
Major-General Davenport of the Horse Guards, both of
whom had expressed their willingness to protect him
from any danger to which he might be exposed in his
righteous crusade. Steele himself regarded his attempts
in this way with pardonable satisfaction. Long after, in
the *Apology*, he referred to them complacently; and in
the Preface to the fourth volume of the collected *Tatler*,
they form the subject of its peroration. 'As for this
Point'—he says—'never Hero in Romance was carry'd
away with a more furious Ambition to conquer Giants
and Tyrants, than I have been in extirpating Gamesters
and Duellists. And indeed, like one of those Knights
too, tho' I was calm before, I am apt to fly out again,
when the Thing that first disturbed me is presented to
my Imagination. I shall leave off when I am well,
and fight with Windmills no more: Only shall be so
Arrogant as to say of my self, that, in Spite of all the
Force of Fashion and Prejudice, in the Face of all the
World, I alone bewailed the Condition of an *English*
Gentleman, whose Fortune and Life are at this Day

precarious ; while His Estate is liable to the Demands of Gamesters, through a false Sense of Justice ; and to the Demands of Duellists through a false Sense of honour. As to the First of these Orders of Men, I have not one Word more to say of them : As to the latter I shall conclude all I have more to offer against them (with Respect to their being prompted by the Fear of Shame), by applying to the Duellist what I think Dr. *South* says somewhere of the Lyar, *He is a Coward to Man, and a Bravo to God.'*

But gaming and duelling were not the only windmills against which Queen Anne's Quixote turned his lance. Profanity, profligacy, the neglect of the marriage tie, are all successively the subject of his censure. The moral essay pure and simple, however, belongs less to the discursive *Tatler* than to the more leisurely *Spectator*, and it is far easier to select examples from the latter than the former. Nevertheless the *Tatler*, upon such themes as Praise, Flattery, Pride, Deference to Public Opinion and the like, contains some notable papers from Mr. Bickerstaff's pen. The popular subject of Good Breeding is one to which he frequently recurs ; and in No. 69 there is a passage on True Distinction which seems to anticipate a teaching since made familiar by the author of the *Book of Snobs*. In Steele's day, when—as he says elsewhere—'the gilt chariot, the diamond ring, the gold snuff-box, and brocade sword-knot' were the essential parts of a fine gentleman, and when, also, the distinctions of rank were more rigidly defined than at present, such an utterance as the following must have had all the boldness of novelty :—

'It is to me a very great Meanness, and something much below a Philosopher, which is what I mean by a Gentleman, to rank a Man among the Vulgar for the Condition of Life he is in, and not according to his Behaviour, his Thoughts and Sentiments, in that Condition. For if a Man be loaded with Riches and Honours, and in that State of Life has Thoughts and Inclinations below the meanest Artificer ; is not such an Artificer, who within his Power is good to his Friends, moderate in his Demands for his Labour, and chearful in his Occupation, very much superior to him who lives for no other End but to serve himself, and assumes a Preference in all his Words and Actions to those, who act their Part with much more Grace than himself ? *Epictetus* has made use of the Similitude of a Stage-Play to human Life with much Spirit. It is not, says he, to be consider'd among the Actors, who is Prince, or who is Beggar, but who acts Prince or Beggar best.[1] The Circumstance of Life should not be that which gives us Place, but our Behaviour in that Circumstance is what should be our solid Distinction. Thus, a wise Man should think no Man above him or below him, any further than it regards the outward Order and Discipline of the World : For if we take too great an Idea of the Eminence of our Superiors, or Subordination of our Inferiors, it will have an ill Effect upon our Behaviour to both. But he who thinks no Man above him but for his Virtue, none below him but for his Vice, can never be obsequious or assuming in a wrong Place, but will frequently emulate Men in Rank below him, and pity those above him.'

Good breeding, with its designed reticences, and its endless catalogue of minor observances, was not the only novelty which Steele presented to his readers. When he says, in *Tatler* No. 271, that 'it has been

---

[1] *Encheiridion*, Sect. xvii.

a most exquisite Pleasure to me to frame Characters of Domestick Life,' he is making a statement which had far more significance to them than to us over whose heads the ends of the English Novel have passed. In Steele's day of promenades and outdoor life, of meetings and greetings, of clubs and assemblies, the fireside with its simple duties and unobtrusive cares, had been wholly neglected by the historian. It was Steele who first, before Fielding and Richardson, before Goldsmith and Sterne, crossed the threshold of the home, and lifted the veil upon the idyll of the hearth. His pictures, as Mr. Bickerstaff, of his sister Jenny and her husband Tranquillus; his admirable advice to her upon the occasion of their first matrimonial quarrel; his delightful account of the three lads, his nephews, and their respective bearings in the presence of a 'beautiful Woman of Honour,' are charming in themselves and still fresh and wholesome in their teaching. But his highest mark in this way is reached in three papers numbered 95, and 114, and 181. The last contains the well-known passage respecting his father's death, which has already been reproduced in Chapter I. The first is the description of a visit which he pays to an old friend and his wife; the second records her death. The visit is a finished piece of literary *genre*-painting. Arriving at the house, he is led in by a pretty girl 'that we all thought must have forgot me.'

'Her knowing me again was a mighty Subject with us, and took up our Discourse at the first Entrance. After which they began to rally me upon a Thousand little Stories they heard in the Country about my Marriage to one of my Neighbour's Daughters : Upon which the Gentleman my Friend said, Nay, if Mr. *Bickerstaff* marries a Child of any of his old Companions, I hope mine shall have the Preference ; there's Mrs. *Mary* is now Sixteen, and would make him as fine a Widow as the best of them : But I know him too well ; he is so enamoured of the very Memory of those who flourished in our Youth, that he will not so much as look upon the modern Beauties. I remember, old Gentleman, how often you went Home in a Day to refresh your Countenance and Dress, when *Teraminta* reigned in your Heart. As we came up in the Coach, I repeated to my Wife some of your Verses on her. With such Reflexions on little Passages which happen'd long ago, we pass'd our Time during a chearful and elegant Meal.'

After dinner, the lady leaves the room, and the husband falls easily to praises of her, softened all the more by the unmistakable evidences of her failing health. That fading in her countenance, he says, is caused by her watching with him in his fever. The anticipation of losing her haunts him continually ; and the pleasure he used to take in telling his boy stories of the war, and asking the girl questions about her doll, is turned into inward reflection and melancholy.

'He would have gone on in this tender Way, when the good Lady entered, and with an inexpressible Sweetness in her Countenance told us, she had been searching her Closet for something very good to treat such an old Friend as I was. Her Husband's Eyes sparkled with Pleasure at the Chearfulness of her Countenance ; and I saw all his Fears vanish in an Instant. The Lady observing something in our Looks which showed we had been more serious than ordinary, and seeing her Husband receive her with great Concern

under a forced Chearfulness, immediately guessed at what
we had been talking of ; and applying herself to me, said,
with a Smile, Mr. *Bickerstaff*, don't believe a Word of what
he tells you, I shall still live to have you for my Second,
as I have often promised you, unless he takes more Care of
himself than he has done since his coming to Town. You
must know, he tells me, That he finds *London* is a much
more healthy Place than the Country ; for he sees several
of his old Acquaintance and School-fellows are here young
Fellows with fair full-bottomed Periwigs. I could scarce
keep him this Morning from going out open-Breasted. My
Friend, who is always extreamly delighted with her agreeable Humour, made her sit down with us. She did it with
that Easiness which is peculiar to Women of Sense ; and
to keep up the good Humour she had brought in with her,
turn'd her Raillery upon me. Mr. *Bickerstaff*, you remember you followed me one Night from the Playhouse ;
supposing you should carry me thither to-morrow Night,
and lead me into the Front-Box. This put us into a long
Field of Discourse about the Beauties, who were Mothers
to the present, and shined in the Boxes Twenty Years ago.
I told her, I was glad she had transfer'd so many of her
Charms, and I did not question but her eldest Daughter
was within half a Year of being a Toast. We were pleasing our selves with this fantastical Preferment of the young
Lady, when on a sudden we were alarm'd with the Noise of
a Drum, and immediately entered my little Godson to give
me a Point of War. His Mother, between Laughing and
Chiding, would have put him out of the Room ; but I
would not part with him so. I found, upon Conversation
with him, tho' he was a little noisy in his mirth, that the
Child had excellent Parts, and was a great Master of all
the Learning on t'other Side Ten Years old. I perceived
him a very great Historian in *Æsop's* Fables ; but he
frankly declared to me his Mind, That he did not delight in

that Learning, because he did not believe they were true ; for which Reason, I found, he had very much turned his Studies, for about a Twelvemonth past, into the Lives of Adventures of Don *Bellianis* of *Greece*, *Guy* of *Warwick,* the *Seven Champions*, and other Historians of that Age. I could not but observe the Satisfaction the Father took in the Forwardness of his Son ; and that these Diversions might turn to some Profit, I found the Boy had made Remarks, which might be of Service to him during the Course of his whole Life. He would tell you the Mismanagements of *John Hickathrift*, find Fault with the passionate Temper in *Bevis* of *Southampton*, and loved St *George* for being the Champion of *England* ; and by this Means, had his Thoughts insensibly moulded into the Notions of Discretion, Virtue, and Honour. I was extolling his Accomplishments, when the Mother told me, That the little Girl who led me in this Morning, was in her Way a better Scholar than he. *Betty* (says she) deals chiefly in Fairies and Sprights ; and sometimes in a Winter-Night, will terrify the Maids with her Accounts, till they are afraid to go up to Bed.'

A month after, in *Tatler* No. 114, comes a pathetic account of her death, and the grief of her heartbroken husband and children—an account so vivid in its realism that it is hardly possible not to believe it based upon an actual occurrence. Steele—the story goes— overpowered by his emotion, was unable to complete the paper, and a frigid academic close was supplied by Addison. But there is nothing in Addison like Steele's share in these two essays, and even the malice of Addison's editor, Dr. Hurd, who invariably attributes all the weak points of his work to his colleague, is obliged to admit tacitly that, in this especial instance, the position is reversed. There are other examples of Steele's descriptive power in the *Tatler*, but in these he attains the measure of his strength.

At this hour of the day it is probable that neither the moral essay of the Augustans, nor the picture of home life under Anne, would greatly attract the *blasé* nineteenth-century reader. An army of imitators, lumbering in the heavy footsteps of Johnson, made the one unendurable; while a long array of illustrious novelists have carried domestic portraiture to a perfection never dreamed of in Steele's amiable philosophy. But the social sketches of the *Tatler* must always retain a certain interest. The whole of the time is mirrored in its pages. We see the theatre, with Betterton and Bracegirdle on the stage, or that 'romp' Mrs. Bicknell dancing; we see the side-box bowing 'from its inmost rows' at the advent of the radiant 'Cynthia of the minute'; we hear the shrill cries of the orange wenches, or admire at the pert footmen keeping guard over their mistresses' bouquets. We see the church with its high pews, and its hour-glass by the pulpit; we hear, above the rustle of the fans, and the coughing of the openbreasted beaux, the sonorous periods of Burnet or Atterbury; we scent the fragrance of Bergamot and Lavender and Hungary-water. We follow the gilded chariots moving slowly round the Ring in Hyde Park, where the lackeys fight and play chuck-farthing at the gates; we take the air in the Mall with the Bucks and Pretty Fellows; we trudge after the fine lady, bound, in her glass chair, upon her interminable 'how-dees.' We smile at the showy young Templars lounging at Squire's or Serle's in their brocaded 'night-gowns' and strawberry sashes; we listen to the politicians at White's or the Cocoa-Tree; we company with the cits at Batson's, and the Jews and stock-brokers at Jonathan's. We cheapen our Pekoe or Bohea at Motteux's China Warehouse; we fill our boxes with musty or 'right Spanish' at Charles Lillie's in Beaufort Buildings; we choose a dragon cane or a jambee at Mather's toy shop in Fleet Street. We ask at Lintott's or Tonson's for 'Swift in Verse and Prose'; we call for the latest *Tatler* at Morphew's by Stationers' Hall. It is not true that Queen Anne is dead: we are living in her very reign: and the Victorian era with its steam and its socialism, its electric light and its local option, has floated away from us like a dream.

The *Tatler*—the magician of this miracle—expired prematurely in January, 1711, when it had reached its 271st number. The ostensible or colourable reason for this unexpected termination was that the public had penetrated the editor's disguise, and that the object of the work was wholly lost by his (Steele's) 'being so long understood as the Author. I never designed in it to give any Man any secret Wound by my Concealment, but spoke in the Character of an old Man, a Philosopher, an Humorist, an Astrologer, and a Censor, to allure my Reader with the Variety of my Subjects, and insinuate, if I could, the Weight of Reason with the Agreeableness of Wit. The general purpose of the Whole,' he goes on, ' has been to recommend Truth, Innocence, Honour, and Virtue, as the chief Ornaments of Life ; but I considered, that Severity of Manners was absolutely necessary to him who would censure others; and for that Reason, and that only,

chose to talk in a Mask. I shall not carry my
Humility so far as to call myself a vicious Man; but
at the same Time must confess, my Life is at best but
pardonable. And with no greater Character than this,
a man would make an indifferent Progress in attacking
prevailing and fashionable Vices, which Mr. *Bickerstaff*
has done with a Freedom of Spirit that would have lost
both its Beauty and Efficacy, had it been pretended to
by Mr. *Steele.*'

This, if it signifies anything, must be taken to
imply that some of Steele's contemporaries, as in the
case of the *Christian Hero*, had been too narrowly
contrasting 'the least Levity in his Words and Actions'
with the unimpeachable precepts of the Shire Lane
Philosopher. But other reasons have been suggested
for the premature cessation of Mr. Bickerstaff's *Lucubrations*, and for these we must turn to the obscure and contradictory records of Augustan politics.
Through the influence of Maynwaring, Steele, it will
be remembered, had obtained his appointment as
Gazetteer from Harley, then one of the two Secretaries
of State, the other being Marlborough's son-in-law,
Lord Sunderland. Early in 1708, after the Gregg
episode, Harley had been removed from the Ministry.
But before the *Tatler* was well into its fourth volume,
the whirligig of time, and his own dark and tortuous
diplomacy, had brought Harley back to power. The
Sacheverell trial of 1710 gave an extraordinary impetus to the Tory cause, and precipitated the down-
fall of the Whigs, already broken by doubts and
divisions. First Lord Sunderland, from whose office
at Whitehall so many of Steele's letters are super-

scribed, received his dismissal, and was succeeded by a red-hot Tory, Lord Dartmouth. A greater catastrophe ensued; 'Sid Hamet's Rod' was broken; and the disgrace of the Lord Treasurer Godolphin prepared the impending fall of Marlborough.

At first sight it seems strange that these wholly supernal mutations should have any connection with the fortunes of that 'lowest Minister of State,' the Gazetteer. But in January, 1710, probably in pursuance of the promise made to him by Lord Sunderland when he was refused the reversion of Addison's Under-Secretaryship, Steele was appointed a Commissioner of Stamps, a vacancy having been created by the nomination of one John Molesworth as Envoy to the Court of Tuscany. His new office added 300*l.* a year to his income. Not very long after this,—in fact in the very July of Sunderland's dismissal,—there appeared in the *Tatler* three papers, which rightly or wrongly, for even now the matter does not seem quite certain, were supposed to be levelled at Harley. It is pretty clear that Steele himself was not the writer of these—indeed he twice expressly denied the authorship of one of them.[1] But his position with respect to the periodical clearly imposed upon him the responsibility for their appearance; and when, in the following month the Tories, with Harley at their head, came into power, he was not unnaturally the object of their suspicion and resentment. Late in September, Swift,

[1] In the Preface to vol. iv. of the *Tatler*, 1711, and *Guardian* No. 53. This was a fictitious letter from Downes the Prompter in No. 193 comparing the affairs of the stage and state. It seems to have been the main cause of offence; but the offence now is not very perceptible. No. 191 satirises Harley as *Polypragmon*.

with whom the Whigs had been vainly coquetting, came
again to England ; and one of the earliest records he
has to make in his famous journal to Mrs. Johnson and
Mrs. Dingley is that Steele, to whose office 'at the
Cockpit near *Whitehall*,' his (Swift's) letters are to be
directed, 'expects every day to be turned out of his
employment,' i.e. as Gazetteer. '*Steele*,' he says again
next day, 'will certainly lose his *Gazetteer's* place, all
the world detesting his engaging in parties.' A month
later the foreboding has come true ; Steele is turned out,
and Swift has cast in his lot with the party in power.
The diary of the 22nd of October contains a long passage
respecting his no doubt well-meaning efforts in behalf
of his friend, whose remaining appointment of Commissioner of Stamps was thought to be also in jeopardy.
'I was this morning,' says he, 'with Mr. *Lewis*, the
under-secretary to Lord *Dartmouth*, two hours talking
politicks, and contriving to keep *Steele* in his office of
stampt paper : he has lost his place of *Gazetteer*, three
hundred pounds a year, for writing a *Tatler*, some
months ago, against Mr. *Harley*, who gave it him at
first, and raised the salary from sixty to three hundred
Pounds. This was devilish ungrateful ; and *Lewis* was
telling me the particulars : but I had a hint given
me, that I might save him in the other employment ;
and leave was given me to clear matters with *Steele*.'
Accordingly, he says, he went the same evening 'to sit
with Mr. *Addison*, and offer the matter at distance to
him, as the discreeter person ; but found *Party* had so
possessed him, that he talked as if he suspected me,
and would not fall in with any thing I said. So I stopt
short in my overture, and we parted very dryly ; and

I shall say nothing to *Steele*, and let them do as they will; but if things stand as they are, he will certainly lose it unless I save him; and therefore I will not speak to him that I may not report to his disadvantage.' 'Is not this vexatious?'—he goes on—'and is there so much in the proverb of proffered service? When shall I grow wise? I endeavour to act in the most exact points of honour and conscience, and my nearest friends will not understand it so.' Later—on the 15th of December—comes another entry. '*Lewis* told me a pure thing. I had been hankering with Mr. *Harley* to save *Steele* his other employment, and have a little mercy on him, and I had been saying the same thing to *Lewis*, who is Mr. *Harley's* chief favourite. *Lewis* tells Mr. *Harley* how kindly I should take it, if he would be reconciled to *Steele*, &c. Mr. *Harley*, on my account, falls in with it, and appoints *Steele* a time to let him attend him, which *Steele* accepts with great submission, but never comes, nor sends any excuse. Whether it was blundering, sullenness, or rancor of party, I cannot tell; but I shall trouble myself no more about him. I believe *Addison* hindered him out of meer spight, being grated to the soul to think he should ever want my help to save his friend,' etc.

Such is Swift's version of the matter as, in 1710, he jotted it down from day to day for the benefit of two young women at Dublin. When, three years afterwards, political differences had widened the breach between himself and Steele, he gave, in the pamphlet called the *Importance of the Guardian Considered*, a more unfriendly account of some of the circumstances. It is not necessary to quote it at length. Soon after the Sacheverell trial, he says, Steele 'would needs corrupt his Paper with Politicks' and libel Harley, 'who had made him Gazetteer.' The result was that, when the new Ministry came in, to avoid being discarded, he had to resign. It is further stated that when Steele, according to form, had first tendered his thanks to Harley for his appointment, Harley had given the whole credit to Arthur Maynwaring, who had recommended him. Then, Swift goes on to say, Steele had complained to a gentleman of Harley's treatment, alleging 'that he never had done Mr. Harley any Injury, nor received any Obligation from him.' The gentleman (query, was the gentleman Swift himself) thereupon advanced the *Tatler* articles, of which Steele at once declared he was only the publisher, 'for they had been sent him by other Hands.' This the gentleman thought 'a very monstrous kind of Excuse,' whereupon Steele rejoined:—'Well, I have Libelled him, and he has turned me out, and so we are equal. But neither would this be granted: And he was asked whether the place of Gazetteer were not an Obligation? No, said he, not from Mr. *Harley*; for when I went to thank him, he forbad me, and said, I must only thank Mr. *Mainwaring*.'

It would be unwise to attach too much importance to this statement, penned in all the bitterness of party feeling, and aggravated by personal irritation. But even from this it is possible to deduce certain conclusions by no means so unfavourable to Steele as his antagonist would have us to believe. If, as Swift says, Steele did not regard himself as indebted to Harley, it is difficult to fix upon him the charge of ingratitude,

especially as tradition has, rightly or wrongly, associated
his real benefactor Maynwaring with the offending
utterances in the *Tatler*.[1]   His error, if error it were,
lay in the negligence or want of judgment, which
permitted the employment of a non-political paper for
political purposes.   But considering how he was surrounded by the opponents of Harley,—by Addison, by
Henley, by Halifax, by Sunderland, to the last of whom,
as we have said, he probably owed his Commissionership of Stamps, it is easy to understand what pressure
would be put upon him to harass a common enemy.
As regards the backwardness to fall in with Swift's
schemes which Swift in his journal professes to regard
as so disheartening, it seems even more capable of
solution.   Steele and Addison had not gone over, as
Swift had, to the Tories, nor in the turn things had
taken, were they inclined, after the fashion of some of
their more time-serving colleagues, to cling to him like
drowning men ;[2] and although neither of them thought
it necessary to come to open rupture with Swift the
friend, it is most probable that both of them resented
the patronising assistance, which at this moment may
fairly be supposed to have been more than usually
arrogant and exultant, of Swift the politician.   With
respect, also, to that famous visit to Harley which
Steele never paid, it would seem that if he failed upon
this occasion, he had at some later time an interview

---

[1] Mr. Forster says (*Essays*, 1858, 116): 'The fictitious letter of
prompter Downes was certainly by Maynwaring.' But we have found
nothing to warrant so express a statement.

[2] 'The *Whigs* were ravished to see me, and would lay hold on
me as a twig while they are drowning.' (*Journal to Stella*, Sept. 9,
1710.)

with the new Lord Treasurer, which, whether Swift
knew of it or not, was wholly satisfactory in its results.
For this he himself is the authority. 'When I had
the Honour of a short Conversation with you, you were
pleased not only to signifie to me, That I should remain
in this Office, but to add, that if I would name to you
one of more Value, which would be more commodious
to me, you would favour me in it.' [1]

The proof that he remained in his Commissionership is furnished by a letter of the 4th June, 1713, containing the above extract, the object of which letter is
the resignation of this very post. It appears therefore
that Harley, who took from him the Gazetteer's place
he had given him, refrained from taking from him the
Commissionership he had not given him. That he
did so without some tacit understanding is improbable.
But whether it was definite or indefinite,—whether it
amounted to an armistice, or an armed neutrality, as
Mr. Forster suggests, are things we may never know.
What is clear is, the *Tatler* came to an end, and came
to an end so suddenly that—according to Swift—even
Addison, whom he met on the very day of its decease,
knew nothing of the matter—a rather incomprehensible
statement, which is nevertheless confirmed by Steele
himself.[2] It is clear also that politics had something
to do with its cessation, for Steele, in his valedictory
address, says that he has been blamed for touching
' upon Matters which concern both the Church and
State;' while the new paper which speedily followed
the *Tatler* announced in its first number that its author

[1] *Apology for Himself and his Writings*, 1714, p. 86.
[2] *Vide* Preface to the Second Edition of the *Drummer*, 1722.

had 'resolved to observe an exact Neutrality between the Whigs and Tories,' unless, he adds discreetly, 'I shall be forc'd to declare myself by the Hostilities of either side.[1] And whatever may have been the proximate cause of the discontinuance of Mr. Bickerstaff's utterances, weariness of the work, and poverty of invention, could scarcely be the reason, since the *Spectator* was begun in the short space of two months afterwards, and continued for nearly two years with unabated vigour.

Something of the popularity which the *Tatler* had attained at the time of its completion may be gathered from a little tract addressed by John Gay in May, 1711, 'to a Friend in the Country.' It is entitled *The Present State of Wit*, and gives a curious contemporary account of Periodical Literature, and especially of Steele's paper. It confirms the supposed connection of politics with its conclusion by enumerating among the causes currently assigned for that event, this—'That he [Steele] laid it down as a sort of submission to, and composition with, the Government, for some past offences,' and it goes on to say that 'However that were, his disappearance seemed to be bewailed as some general calamity. Every one wanted so agreeable an amusement,

[1] It has also been considered, and often repeated, by the present writer among the rest, that the loss of the Gazette sealed the sources of Steele's foreign intelligence, and thus entailed a change of plan. But a re-examination of the paper shows that the news-element had practically disappeared from the *Tatler* long before Steele ceased to be Gazetteer. The last accounts from St. James's Coffee-house are, it is true, dated the 15th of September, 1710, only a short time before he lost his appointment in October. But there had been nothing else since the previous May, and beyond this one has again to travel back a long way for Mr. Kidney's communications.

and the Coffee-houses began to be sensible that the *Esquire's Lucubrations* alone had brought them more customers, than all their other News Papers put together.'

Gay then proceeds to give his 'own Thoughts of this Gentleman's Writings' in a sequence of passages which deserve to be quoted entire :—

'I shall,—he says—in the first place, observe, that there is a noble difference between him and all the rest of our Polite and Gallant Authors. The latter have endeavoured to please the Age by falling in with them, and encouraging them in their fashionable vices and false notions of things. It would have been a jest, some time since, for a man to have asserted that anything witty could be said in praise of a married state, or that Devotion and Virtue were any way necessary to the character of a Fine Gentleman. BICKER-STAFF ventured to tell the Town that they were a parcel of fops, fools, and coquettes ; but in such a manner as even pleased them, and made them more than half inclined to believe that he spoke truth.

'Instead of complying with the false sentiments or vicious tastes of the Age—either in morality, criticism or good-breeding—he has boldly assured them, that they were altogether in the wrong ; and commanded them, with an authority which perfectly well became him, to surrender themselves to his arguments for Virtue and Good Sense.

'It is incredible to conceive the effect his writings have had upon the Town ; how many thousand follies they have either quite banished or given a very great check to ! how much countenance, they have added to Virtue and Religion ! how many people they have rendered happy, by showing them it was their own fault if they were not so ! and, lastly, how entirely they have convinced our young fops and young fellows of the value and advantages of Learning !

'He has indeed rescued it out of the hands of pedants, and fools, and discovered the true method of making it amiable and lovely to all mankind. In the dress he gives it, it is a most welcome guest at tea-tables and assemblies, and is relished and caressed by the merchants on the Change. Accordingly there is not a Lady at Court, nor a Banker in Lombard Street, who is not verily persuaded that Captain STEELE is the greatest Scholar and best Casuist of any man in England.

'Lastly, his writings have set all our Wits and Men of Letters on a new way of Thinking, of which they had little or no notion before : and, although we cannot say that any of them have come up to the beauties of the original, I think we may venture to affirm, that every one of them writes and thinks much more justly than they did some time since.'

Nothing that can be said to-day can much improve upon this contemporary view of the effect produced by Steele's labours, coming as it does from the pen of an observing literary man, and, though he disclaims politics, a Tory.[1] In this valuable pamphlet Gay gives some other interesting particulars respecting the *Tatler's* imitators—too large a field for these brief pages—and the inauguration of the *Spectator* by the two friends, whose literary conjunction he compares to that of Somers and Halifax 'in a late reign.' 'Meantime,' he adds, among his concluding words, 'all our unbiassed well-wishers to Learning are in hopes that the known

---

[1] Swift thought the *State of Wit* emanated from the rival party. 'The author'—he says—'seems to be a Whig. . . . But above all things he praises the *Tatlers* and *Spectators*; and I believe *Steele* and *Addison* were privy to the printing of it.' (*Journal to Stella*, May 14, 1711.)

Temper and prudence of one of these Gentlemen [Addison] will hinder the other [Steele] from ever lashing out into Party, and rendering that Wit, which is at present a common good, odious and ungrateful to the better part of the Nation,'—by which, it is to be feared, this impartial chronicler intended to signify the Tory Party. So difficult was impartiality under Anna Augusta!

When the final number of the *Tatler* was issued, three volumes of the reprinted papers, under title of ' *The Lucubrations of Isaac Bickerstaff, Esq.*,' had already made their appearance. A fourth speedily followed, the preface to which contained that famous compliment to Addison, already quoted. The first volume was dedicated to Arthur Maynwaring; the second to Edward Wortley Montagu, Lady Mary's husband; the third to Lord Cowper; and the fourth, which is headed ' *From the Hovel at* Hampton-wick,' April 7, 1711, to Charles, Lord Halifax. There is pleasant reference in the opening lines of this last to the former intercourse of the statesman and the writer. ' I could not '—says Steele— ' but indulge a certain Vanity in dating from this little Covert, where I have frequently had the Honour of your Lordship's Company, and received from you very many Obligations. The elegant Solitude of this Place, and the greatest Pleasures of it I owe to its being so near those Beautiful Mannors wherein you sometimes reside.' Halifax was Ranger of Bushey Park, and Mr. Bickerstaff must often have been his guest in the sombre red-brick Lodge which he left to Newton's niece, the fair and fortunate Catherine Barton.

CHAPTER V.

'THE SPECTATOR.'

THAT wonderful and unique record, the *Journal to Stella*, contains, besides the quotations in the last chapter, other references to Steele for the period between Swift's coming to London in September, 1710, and the appearance of the *Spectator* in the following March. As might be anticipated, they are less numerous than those relating to Addison, with whom Swift dines frequently at Lord Mountjoy's and elsewhere. He dines also with Addison and Steele together at Westminster and Kensington, and he sups with Steele at Addison's. 'This evening'—he writes on the 19th of November—'I christened our coffee-man *Elliot*'s child, where the rogue had a most noble supper, and *Steele* and I sat among some scurvy company over a bowl of punch.' But notwithstanding the apparent cordiality implied by this entry, an earlier one of some weeks before shows that the rejection of his good offices was still rankling in his mind. 'We have scurvy *Tatlers* of late : so pray do not suspect me. I have one or two hints I design to send him, and never any more : he does not deserve it. He is governed by his wife most abominably, as bad as [Marlborough ?]. I never saw her since I came, nor has he ever made me an invitation ;

either he dares not, or is such a thoughtless *Tisdall* fellow[1] that he never minds it. So what care I for his wit? for he is the worst company in the world till he has a bottle of wine in his head.' Later, when the last *Tatler* came out, he says he was to have drunk punch at Dartineuf's with Addison 'and little Harrison, a young poet whose fortune I am making. *Steele* was to have been there, but came not, nor never did twice, since I knew him, to any appointment.' Further on there are evidences of an interruption in his older and firmer friendship with Addison. Already in November he had admitted that they saw each other less frequently than formerly, although they were ' still at bottom as good friends as ever,' if ' differing a little about party.' ' I believe our friendship will go off, by this damned business of party,' he says, a month later. ' He [Addison] cannot bear seeing me fall in so with this ministry; but I love him still as well as ever, though we seldom meet.' He dines with him nevertheless at his lodgings; but it is no longer the same. They are ' grown common acquaintance ; yet what have I not done for his friend *Steele*?' And then he goes on to recall bitterly Steele's failure to keep his appointment with Harley. There is a half-remorseful, half-wounded note in these utterances which is creditable to Swift's fidelity to his old allies. But that there should be no estrangement was past hoping for. Steele and Addison probably knew, or, if they did not know, must have guessed, what Swift refrained from confiding to Stella,

---

[1] There are two Tisdalls in the Swift records. One, Dr. William Tisdall of Belfast, had been a suitor to Stella; the other was a citizen of Dublin. The former is probably here intended.

—namely this, that he had been for some time past employing his terrible plain English and his ironic common sense in the *Examiner*, on behalf of the Tories, with an effect against which Maynwaring, Henley, Kennet, and the writers of the rival *Medley* strove in vain. Moreover, they could scarcely have regarded with much favour the inconsiderate promptitude that led him (albeit no doubt fully entitled to make use of the style and fashion of 'Bickerstaff') to set up the above-named 'little Harrison' in a continuation of Steele's concluded *Tatler*. To hope that, in the circumstances, anything like effusive goodwill should survive between them was surely to expect too much of ordinary human nature. If Swift, on what was for the time the winning side, found it possible to separate friendship from faction, it was not so easy for those who were in the opposition.

But we are straying from Steele and his domestic history. During the progress of the *Tatler* his letters are few in number, and of no especial interest. On the 26th of March, 1709, just before Mr. Bickerstaff put forth his first Lucubration, his eldest daughter, Eliza-beth, was born. She was christened on the 6th of April, Addison and Wortley Montagu being her godfathers. A year later—on the 25th of May, 1710—came a second child, Richard, who was christened on the 24th of June, one of his sponsors being Lord Halifax. The Barbadoes business still drags on its obscure phases without at any point becoming particularly intelligible. On the 5th of May, 1709, when there are four letters in one day, references to an 'insufferable brute,' and going 'to see a convenient place,' seem to suggest a crisis of difficulties with Mrs. Vandeput, the landlady of the

K ·

Bury Street house, especially as Mrs. Steele is addressed shortly afterwards as ' At Mr. Sewell's, in King Street, near Whitehall Coffee-house.' But Bury Street can scarcely have been given up at this time, for Steele, a year later, still writes from it. In other letters we get hints of him as he hurries to and fro—finishing the next *Gazette* at the Cockpit, scribbling off a *Tatler* at Nutt's, the printer in the Savoy, or making up his accounts at Tonson's. 'Here is next door a fellow '—he says in one of them—'that makes old wigs new,' and ' Dear Prue ' is enjoined to send by bearer both of those in the bed-chamber. Then there is the inevitable ' tiff,' which seems on this occasion to have been exception-ally severe, for the letter closes without the usual affectionate subscription :—

'November 20, 1709

'DEAR WIFE,—I have been in great pain of body and mind since I came out. You are extremely cruel to a generous nature, which has a Tenderness for you that renders your least *dis-humour* insupportably afflict-ing. After short starts of passion not to be inclined to reconciliation, is what is against all rules of Chris-tianity and justice. When I come home I beg to be kindly received, or this will have as ill an effect upon my fortune as on my mind and body.

'RICH. STEELE.'

In the letter that follows—though with a long in-terval between—is a charming touch. His wife has been sick,—it tells us, and after his writing he has come up to see her (she was apparently staying with Mrs. Binns) ' and found she was herself gone a-visiting.'

Thereupon her ' affectionate, tender, observant, and indulgent husband' writes her a little notelet to say that
he wishes he had known she had been so well, as ' it
would have given what he was writing a more lively
turn.' Towards the end of August, 1710, he seems to
have been in serious pecuniary difficulties, perhaps even
under temporary restraint. This, however, would be
little more than a shrewd conjecture on the part of
Nichols were it not that it receives support from a
passage in Swift's *Journal*. ' Yes '—he says—' *Steele*
was a little while in prison, or at least in a spunging-
house, some time before I came, but not since.' Swift
came to London on the 7th of September, 1710, and
may therefore refer to this occasion.

With another of the letters in this group Swift is
more directly concerned. It has already been incidentally referred to in Chapter I., but deserves a word more
in this, its proper place. In May, 1709, Mrs. Manley
published the first volume of those ' Secret Memoirs of
her contemporaries, now generally known as the *New
Atalantis*. Although containing an uncomplimentary
portrait of Steele as ' Monsieur *le Inqrate*,' it had been
several times advertised in the *Tatler*, when, in a letter
signed ' Tobiah Greenhat,' referring to Mary Astell under
the name of ' Madonella,' applied to her by Swift, mention
was made of the book in terms which, if unsavoury, were
scarcely undeserved. Mrs. Manley at once addressed an
expostulation to Steele, who replied as follows :—

' September 6, 1709

' MADAM,—I have received a letter from you, wherein you tax me, as if I were *Bickerstaff*, with falling upon

you as author of *Atalantis*, and the person who honoured me with a character in that celebrated piece. [What has happened formerly between us can be of no use to either to repeat.] I solemnly assure you, you wrong me in this, as much as you know you do in all else you have been pleased to say of me. [I had not money when you did me the favour to ask the loan of a trifling sum of me.] I had the greatest sense imaginable of the kind notice you gave me when I was going on to my ruin; and am so far from retaining an inclination to revenge the humanity with which you have treated me, that I give myself a satisfaction in that you have cancelled with injuries a friendship, which I should never have been able to return.

'This will convince you how little I am an Ingrate; for I believe you will allow, no one that is so mean as to be forgetful of kindnesses [1] ever fails in returning injuries. As for the verses you quote of mine,[2] they are still my opinion; and your sex, as well as your quality of a gentlewoman (a justice you would not do my birth and education), shall always preserve you against the pen of your provoked most humble servant,

'Rich. Steele.'

Notwithstanding this disclaimer, further adverse references appear to have found their way into the *Tatler*, and to the third part of her *chronique scanda-*

---

[1] Mrs. Manley discreetly changes this word to 'services.'
[2] The verses, as quoted by Mrs. Manley, are—

> 'Against a woman's wit 'tis full as low,
> Your malice as your bravery to shew.'

leuse[1] Mrs. Manley prefixed a furious Dedication to Mr. Bickerstaff, in the body of which, with certain judicious suppressions indicated above by square brackets, she printed the foregoing letter. It is interesting in more respects than one. In the first place, while protesting generally against the injustice of Mrs. Manley's picture, it confirms her statement that she had rendered service to Steele at a critical moment of his career. In the second place, it shows that if Steele had sometimes to bear the praises of papers which he had not written, he had also occasionally to endure the blame of others of which he was equally guiltless. His position as nominal author of the *Tatler* made this unavoidable. But Swift,—and the choice of fathering the initial paragraph of offence seems to lie between him and Addison, for Steele distinctly disowns it,—should have remembered this, when, a year after Steele's death, he wrcte of his 'flourishing by imputed wit,' and might have admitted that such a procedure had its disadvantages as well as its merits. The piquant part of the story is that Swift's *volte-face* in politics brought him almost immediately into close relations with the amiable 'Rivella,' who succeeded him,—*haud passibus æquis*,—in the *Examiner*, worked as one of his 'under spur-leathers,' and must ultimately have enjoyed no inconsiderable share of his favour, since, in that famous list of friends which he drew up in his later days, she

[1] *Memoirs of Europe, towards the Close of the Eighth Century . . . . done into English by the Translator of the New Atalantis,* 1710. Steele is also attacked in the body of the book as *Stelico,* and (*inter alia*) it is stated that it is not politic to reward him too much, lest he should 'indulge too far his native Genius to Laziness, and being govern'd by his Wife' (p. 237).

is classed among the grateful ones,—a distinction that his darkened and distorted memories could not accord to Steele.

But from the contests of party, and the breaches begotten of faction, it is pleasant to turn to the new paper which, three months after the termination of the *Tatler*, entered upon a career of even greater success. On the 1st of March, 1711, appeared Number 1 of the *Spectator*. It was a folio sheet, a little smaller than its predecessor, and like that predecessor in its last days, confined to a single essay. The first of these was by Addison, and sketched lightly, with the subtle touches characteristic of its writer, the taciturn and contemplative 'Looker-on,' a sheetful of whose thoughts was to appear every morning—Sundays excepted. For, unlike the *Tatler* in this respect, the *Spectator* came out daily. In the second paper, couched in Steele's happiest style, followed a description of a club where, as the introductory essay had announced, all ' Matters of Importance' connected with the new venture were ' laid and concerted.' It contained the first rapid sketch of that famous Knight of Worcestershire, whose name was destined to become so well known in English letters. Besides Sir Roger de Coverley, there were vignette portraits of a Templar, a Clergyman, a Merchant, a Soldier, and a Fine Gentleman. Then a third paper by Addison, the subject of which was a Vision of Public Credit, succeeded, and the *Spectator* was fairly launched. How it first came to be planned and written are points which it is not likely will ever now be explained, perhaps because there is no particular explanation to give. Tickell, who held a strong brief for Addison,

says that ' the Plan of the *Spectator*, as far as regards
the feigned Person of the Author, and of the several
characters that compose his Club, was projected in
concert with SIR RICHARD STEELE,' and he makes this
his excuse for including Steele's *Spectator* No. 2 among
Addison's works, because, without it, many passages
would be obscure. ' As for the distinct Papers '—
he says—' they were never or seldom shewn to each
other, by their respective Authors ; who fully answered
the Promise they had made, and far outwent the
Expectation they had raised, of pursuing their Labour
in the same Spirit and Strength with which it was
begun.' The inference from this is that there was
no very elaborate programme. Probably it was orally
arranged that Addison should justify the title, and
depict the assumed Author, and that Steele should
devise a Club composed of sufficiently varied personages to act as his assistants. To push conjecture
further, it may also be assumed that the Soldier, the
Merchant and the Clergyman were to be the chief care
of Steele, while the Templar, the Fine Gentleman and
the Tory Squire were to fall to Addison.

If this were the intent at the outset, it was considerably modified during the progress of the paper. Of
the different representatives of society who made up
the Spectator Club, only one or two come really to the
front in the subsequent essays. The clergyman from
first to last never emerges from the background, nor has
the Templar any active identity. Sir Andrew Freeport,
the merchant, on more than one occasion delivers himself of some commendable utterances on commerce ;
but he is rather a voice than a character. Captain

Sentry, the soldier, is credited with an excellent discourse on courage and magnanimity, and a long letter relating to the management of his uncle's estate, both from the pen of Steele. The airy coxcombry of Will Honeycomb, the fine gentleman and *homme de ruelle*, who after a lifetime passed in the pursuit of beauties in brocade, declines in his failing maturity upon a country girl, who has captivated him in a grogram gown, receives rather ampler illustration. But the interest of the whole group seems to have been absorbed in the development of Sir Roger de Coverley, the Tory Country Gentleman, who speedily becomes not only the central figure in the Club, but the chief attraction of the paper. That this is not mainly owing to Addison it would be idle to assert. If one runs over one's recollections of the worthy Knight, it is generally Addison's pictures of him that one first recalls. Sir Roger being rowed to Spring Garden by the one-legged waterman who had fought at La Hogue; Sir Roger going to see the *Distrest Mother* with an escort for fear of the Mohocks; Sir Roger inspecting the transformation of his portrait into the sign of the 'Saracen's Head;' Sir Roger in church, at the assizes, at Westminster Abbey, with the gipsies, and lastly, in that admirable letter from Mr. Biscuit the butler which describes his death—all these bear the signet and sign-manual of Addison. But, since it is the life of Steele we are writing, and not that of his friend, it must be admitted that some of the contributions of Steele to this subject are only inferior when compared with the best of Addison's. There is excellent doctrine in the paper on Sir Roger's servants, and a charming love-scene in that depicting the huntsman's wooing. That, too, in which Sir Roger shows Mr. Spectator his family portraits is full of fine insight and discrimination. The Tilt-yard champion who carries away his adversary on the pummel of his saddle and sets him down before his Mistress's gallery 'with laudable Courtesy and pardonable Insolence;' the Maid of Honour, his wife, who afterwards had ten children, and, despite a Court education, excelled at a hasty-pudding and a white-pot; the prodigal who left the estate 'with ten thousand Pounds Debt upon it,' but was 'every way the finest Gentleman in the World,' and who is drawn with one hand on a desk, 'looking as it were another Way, like an easy Writer, or a Sonneteer;' the prudent Economist and Knight of the Shire who would have been killed in the Civil Wars had he not been 'sent out of the Field upon a private Message, the day before the Battel of *Worcester*:'—it is scarcely possible to suppose, that even under Addison's more restrained and accomplished handling, these could have been greatly bettered. But the best of Steele's contributions to the Coverley series is the description of Sir Roger's unhappy attachment to the perverse widow. The poor gentleman's rhapsody on the lady's beautiful hand; his account of his conquest when she appeared as a suitor at the assizes; and how, upon the negative encouragement that she had been heard to declare that he was 'the Tamest and most Human of all the Brutes in the Country,' he furbished up his equipage and set out to pay her a visit of ceremony, only to find that in the presence of those 'profound Casuists,' his mistress and her confidante, he was as mute as a stock-fish,—

are surely in the truest and kindliest spirit of humour.
'Chance,'—he says—'has since that time thrown me
very often in her way, and she as often has directed
a Discourse to me which I do not understand. This
Barbarity has kept me ever at a Distance from the
most beautiful Object my Eyes ever beheld. It is thus
also she deals with all Mankind, and you must make
Love to her, as you would conquer the Sphinx, by
posing her. But were she like other Women, and
that there were any talking to her, how constant must
the Pleasure of that Man be, who could converse with
a Creature— But, after all, you may be sure her Heart
is fixed on some one or other; and yet I have been
credibly informed; but who can believe half that is
said! After she had done speaking to me, she put
her Hand to her Bosom, and adjusted her Tucker.[1]
Then she cast her Eyes a little down, upon my be-
holding her too earnestly. They say she sings excellently, her Voice in her ordinary Speech has something
in it inexpressibly sweet. You must know I dined
with her at a publick Table the Day after I first saw
her, and she helped me to some Tansy in the Eye
of all the Gentlemen in the Country: She has certainly the finest Hand of any Woman in the World.'[2]

Much ink has been shed in the endeavour to identify
Sir Roger's obdurate idol with Mrs. Katharine Bovey or
Boevey, to whom a magnificent monument was erected

---

[1] The maintenance in its integrity of this '*decus et tutamen* of
the female neck' appears to have engaged much of the attention of
the Essayists of Anne's day. When later it began to be discarded,
Mr. Nestor Ironside of the *Guardian* expressed himself strongly
on the subject.

[2] *Spectator*, No. 113.

in Westminster Abbey by her bosom friend and execu-
trix Mrs. Mary Pope. It was to this lady that Steele
afterwards dedicated volume two of *The Ladies Library*,
and several pages are devoted to her laudation, under
the name of Porcia, in Mrs. Manley's *Atalantis*. She
was learned, she was beautiful, she was a widow, she
had (as stated) a confidante, and if these and other
minor parallelisms are to be held as conclusive, there
is nothing more to say. In the same fashion, Sir
Roger de Coverley has been connected with a certain
Sir John Pakington or Packington, a Tory knight
of Worcestershire; and Will Honeycomb's prototype has been sought in a Colonel Cleland. But
though there were several Clelands, and Steele undoubtedly knew one, Mr. Carruthers, who, in his life of
Pope, went rather minutely into the matter, seems
unable to decide that any of them bore any particular
resemblance to Steele's fine gentleman. Drake, again,
says that Sir Andrew Freeport was reported to be
copied from Mr. H. Martin, one of the authors of
The British Merchant; and the model for Captain
Sentry has been detected in Colonel Magnus Camperfeld or Kempenfelt, father of the Admiral, sung by
Cowper, who afterwards went down in the ' Royal
George.' There is a shade of plausibility in this last
comparison. Like Steele, Camperfeld had entered the
army as a volunteer ; like Steele, he had served in the
Coldstream Guards ; and it is not impossible that
they were brought into actual relations, as Camperfeld
was a lieutenant from 1692 to 1702, during part of
which time Steele was an ensign. But against all these
indications, conjectures and suppositions must be set

the facts, that Tickell, who should have known; regarded
the whole of the characters as feigned,[1] and that any
resemblance to real personages will have to be reconciled with the warning more than once repeated, of the
writers themselves. ' I know very well '—says Mr.
Spectator in No. 262, after describing the pains he
has taken to avoid such ' ill-natured Applications,'—
' the Value which every Man sets upon his Reputation,
and how painful it is to be exposed to the Mirth and
Derision of the Publick, and should therefore scorn
to divert my Reader, at the Expence of any private
Man.'

With the exception of Addison, none of Steele's
colleagues rendered any essential aid in evolving the
character of Sir Roger de Coverley. Eustace Budgell,
Addison's cousin, a writer who is now chiefly remembered by one of Pope's stinging couplets, made some
minor contributions, the best of which is a description
of the knight in the hunting field. Budgell's papers,
however, according to Johnson and tradition, were considerably edited by Addison. Another essay, which
exhibits Sir Roger in an equivocal character as taking
a woman of the town to a tavern, was for some time
attributed to Steele. But though it fell to him in his
capacity of editor to apologise for this jarring incident,
there is no reason for supposing him guilty of more
than accepting it for publication without sufficient consideration, or even examination, an accident which
seems to have happened to him on more than one
occasion. The sketch is not in his style, and was
attributed by the earlier editors to Tickell, to whom

---

[1] Preface to Addison's Works, 1721.

it is now usually assigned. Johnson, in his life of
Addison, connected this with Sir Roger's death by
assuming that Addison put an end to him to prevent
the recurrence of similar indiscretions. In this case
his resentment must have been somewhat tardily exhibited, for there is an interval of more than four
months between the paper referred to, and No. 517,
which describes the Knight's last hours and funeral.
The true reason was that by this time Steele was con-
templating the discontinuance of the *Spectator*; and
Addison, foreseeing, as Budgell tells us, that ' some
nimble gentleman would catch up his pen the moment
he quitted it,' determined, as Cervantes did with Don
Quixote, ' to kill Sir Roger that no body else might
murder him.' The words show how completely he had
appropriated the character for which he had done so
much. And there can be no doubt that to many in that
day even, Sir Roger de Coverley was the chief interest
in the *Spectator*, as in this he seems to be the sole
attraction; and that his decease found other contemporary mourners besides the great Bentley, who—says
Dr. Jebb—took it most seriously to heart.

Apart from the fortunate popularity attaching to
the central figure, and the advantages arising from a
narrower field of operation, it can scarcely be affirmed
that the *Spectator* greatly excelled the *Tatler*, especially when attention is confined to its more enduring
characteristics. If we withdraw the critical work of
Addison, part of which, according to Tickell, was not
prepared expressly for its pages, and to-day has lost
much of its value,—if we withdraw the moral essays
of Steele, now grown tedious by frequent imitation,

what remains is neither better nor worse than the staple material of the *Tatler*. In the social paper neither writer surpassed what he had done before. As already stated, Addison's best work in the *Spectator*, though perhaps more sustained, is not superior to his best work in its predecessor; while Steele in that predecessor is distinctly stronger. He never, even by the prose monody on Stephen Clay, rose to the level of the paper in the *Tatler* on the death of his father, nor did he afterwards repeat the admirable account of Mr. Bickerstaff's visit to his Friend. Nor are the well-known stories of *Inkle and Yarico* and *Brunetta and Phillis* really any happier than the more neglected episodes of *Valentine and Unnion* and *Clarinda and Chloe*, while for a *Stage Coach Journey* and a *Ramble from Richmond to London*, it would be easy to find fair equivalents in the earlier periodical. In some of the theatrical essays, it is true, the *Spectator* shows improvement—notably in the excellent criticism of the *Scornful Lady* and the touching paper on the death of Estcourt. But, upon the whole, the *Tatler* exhibits Steele at his highest, and certainly it contains the best of his efforts in a vein to which he never again returned. Indeed, if diversity of achievement is to be regarded as the test of merit, he should be chiefly studied in the earlier and fresher work, to which he was by far the larger contributor.

Addison, on the other hand, has the advantage in the *Spectator* as regards the number of his contributions. Out of a total of 555, his papers are 274 as opposed to 236 by Steele. This leaves but 45 for Budgell, John Hughes, and with the exception of Pope (whose *Messiah* appeared in *Spectator* 378) the other comparatively undistinguished assistants. Had these, as a matter of fact, added nothing to its pages, little would have been lost to the value of the *Spectator*, the honours of which belong exclusively to the two friends. Until December, 1712, it was continued daily with increased success, and a vitality that survived even the baleful Stamp Act, which Swift had foreseen a year earlier, and had vainly endeavoured to avert. While the *Flying Posts* and *Observators* of Grub Street sank under the fatal halfpenny tax, the little leaflet of Steele and Addison doubled its price, and still found readers enough, who, unlike the 'ingenious T. W.' mentioned in a former chapter, were willing to pay half as much again for the indispensable adjunct to the breakfast-table that was better than lace to their coffee. Towards the close of its career the reduced sale must have amounted to nearly ten thousand copies a week,[1] a number which —as Mr. Forster observes—to give a corresponding popularity in the present day, must be multiplied by six; and we have Steele's own authority for saying that no less than nine thousand of each of the four volumes already published when the last number came out had at that time been disposed of.[2] As in the concluding

---

[1] *Spectator*, No. 555. In *Spectator* No. 10 Addison says the sale at the outset was three thousand daily, and this probably increased as time went on.

[2] A half-share in these four volumes, and three more, was, on the 10th of November, 1712, 'granted bargained sold assigned transferred and set over' by Steele and Addison to Samuel Buckley, one of the two booksellers for whom the *Spectator* was printed. The sum paid by Buckley was 575*l*. Two years later he reassigned this share to Jacob Tonson, Jun., for 500*l*. (Bohn's Addison's *Works*, 1868, vi. 630-1.)

Tatler, Steele does not omit, when winding up the *Spectator*, to make admiring reference to his still-anonymous auxiliary :—' I am indeed much more proud of his long continued Friendship, than I should be of the Fame of being thought the Author of any Writings which he himself is capable of producing. I remember when I finished the *Tender Husband*, I told him there was nothing I so ardently wished, as that we might some time or other publish a Work written by us both, which should bear the name of *the Monument*, in Memory of our Friendship.'

Why the *Spectator* was thus brought to an end in the face of the ' Partiality of the Town ' is difficult to understand, and is nowhere very satisfactorily explained. Possibly its cessation had no more serious origin than a disagreement with the publisher or printer; possibly it may be attributed to the fact that, in the already high-running strife of Whig and Tory, Steele was again uneasily gravitating towards politics. This suggestion is the one that has found the most favour; and if report is to be believed, he had already betrayed symptoms of such a tendency in the *Spectator* itself. ' I believe he will very soon lose his employment,'—writes Swift to Stella in July, 1712,—' for he has been mighty impertinent of late in his *Spectators*; and I will never offer a word in his behalf.' What these impertinences were is now obscure; but outside the paper, Steele had, during its progress, given vent to his feelings, under the name of *Scoto-Britannicus*, in a fervent little tract entitled, *The Englishman's Thanks to the Duke of Marlborough*,[1] prompted by the

[1] Already, in 1710, he had greeted Marlborough's triumphs with

disgrace of that great Captain in December, 1711. This appeared in January; and with a fate that befell several of Steele's future political pamphlets, was speedily followed by an adverse outburst from Swift,—in this instance, the bitter *Fable of Midas*. Then again, the fourth volume of the *Spectator* was dedicated, in noble words, to the fallen hero, over whose infirmities and failing health Swift was rejoicing, in the hope that his death might leave the ministry more at ease; while the fifth was an offering to that very Thomas, Earl of Wharton, whom Swift had attacked so mercilessly in the seventeenth *Examiner*, and upon whose *Short Character* he had exhausted all the resources of his pitiless pen. That, pending a political antagonism so marked and earnest on either side, there could be much private sympathy between himself and his former allies scarcely requires demonstration.

Consequently, during the long period which, in the *Journal to Stella*, corresponds to the existence of the *Spectator*, there are, in addition to that given above, but few allusions to Addison and Steele, and those chiefly in the earlier part of it. 'I have not seen Mr.

an imitation of *Horace*, Bk. i. 6, the final lines of which pleasantly depict his labours in the *Tatler* :—

> 'In trifling cares my humble Muse
> A less ambitious track pursues.
> Instead of troops in battle mix'd
> And Gauls with British spears transfix'd,
> She paints the soft distress and mien
> Of Dames expiring with the spleen.
> From the gay noise, affected air,
> And little follies of the fair,
> A slender stock of fame I raise
> And draw from *others* faults *my* praise.'

Addison, these three weeks,' he says in the March in which the *Spectator* first appeared,—' all our friendship is over.' Of the paper he speaks kindly enough :— ' Tis written by Mr. *Steele*, who seems to have gathered new life, and have a new fund of wit. . . they have all of them had something pretty.' Two lines further, he says he has told Harley and St. John that he has been foolish enough to spend his credit with them in favour of Addison and Steele, but that he shall never do so more. ' The *Spectator* is written by *Steele*, with *Addison's* help,' he says later still,—' 'tis often very pretty ; '— he never sees either of them ; and his letters are directed to Erasmus Lewis, not to Addison, as they had been after Steele lost his Gazetteership. At last, in July, 1711, he dines with them at young Jacob Tonson's, and Addison talks as usual, as if they had seen one another yesterday, and Steele and he are very easy, ' although I writ him lately a biting letter, in answer to one of his, where he desired me to recommend a friend of his to lord treasurer '—a sentence which shows that if Steele would not accept favours for himself, he could ask them for other people. After this, with exception of one reference to Steele, to be mentioned presently, there is nothing material recorded of either for months to come. Meanwhile Swift's sleepless and imperious political activity continues, and the *Journal* gives constant indications of it. He goes on writing in the *Examiner* until June, 1711, when it is surrendered to Mrs. Manley—' to confound guessers.' But he is still busy on all sorts of pamphlets, squibs and tracts— sometimes dictated to Barber, his printer, afterwards the alderman and lord mayor, sometimes worked up from

hints and notes by his ' under spur-leathers,' as he calls
them, sometimes taking the form of paragraphs for
the Tory *Post Boy*, made ' as malicious as possible, and
very proper for *Abel Roper*, the printer of it.' ' Roper
is my humble slave,' he says,—a statement which shows
how absolute was his authority over his meaner colleagues of the ministerial press.

The one reference to Steele above alluded to occurs
in a letter to Stella dated the 1st of July, and is as
follows:—' *Steele* was arrested the other day for making
a lottery, directly against act of Parliament.[1] He
is now under prosecution ; but they think it will be
dropped out of pity.' Probably this was an exaggerated
report ; for there is no indication that circumstances
ever assumed so serious an aspect. Steele's projecting
spirit, it seems, had seduced him into a new and infallible scheme, of which he declares himself to be part
author, for the making of money. It is described, not
very lucidly, in a letter signed by himself, which, in
Spectator 413, follows one of Addison's papers on the
Pleasures of the Imagination. As far as it is intelligible,
it appears to have been a kind of adjunct to the State
Lottery. But four numbers later, came out an advertisement to the effect that the ' Multiplication Table,'
as it was called, was under an information from the
Attorney-General, and that it had been abandoned, all
sums which had been paid into the said Table being
returned. It is therefore most likely that Swift's
account, if not, in Nichols's words, ' invidiously stated,'
was the result of inaccurate gossip.

[1] *I.e.* The Act against illicit lotteries which became law on the
24th of June, 1712.

Steele's correspondence for the period contained in this chapter throws no particular light upon his domestic life. There are a few letters to his wife, not very different in tone or character from those which have already been quoted. There are obscure references to some missed preferment, the effect of which has been to make the retention of his Commissionership a certainty; and he seems about July, 1712, to have moved from Bury Street into a house on the east side of Bloomsbury Square, to which in August he invites his mother-in-law. From an allusion on this occasion to some little 'frowardnesses of Prue,' which, with his uneasy circumstances, have prevented such civilities hitherto, taken in connection with passages in a previous letter, it would appear that his wife and her mother were not always on the best of terms. Before going to Bloomsbury he had been in retirement at a little cottage on Haverstock Hill, of which Drake gives an engraving, and whence, on summer evenings, the Kit-Cats were wont to fetch him as they adjourned to the Upper Flask. It lay midway between Camden Town and Hampstead; and previous to Steele's time had served as a retreat for Sir Charles Sedley, who died there. It existed until 1867, when it was pulled down; but Steele's name is still preserved in the neighbourhood. Whether he resorted to it from financial trouble (as Nichols seems only too ready to conclude) or simply for seclusion must be matter of conjecture. In March, 1712, a second son Eugene had been born; a circumstance which, some months later in the year, prompted two or three interesting letters to his mother-in-law, the object of which is to induce her to make definite provision for her grandchildren. One of them, dated October, 1712, contains a noteworthy paragraph :— ' You are well acquainted that I have had no fortune with your daughter ; that I have struggled through great difficulties for our maintenance ; that we live now in the handsomest manner, supported only by my industry.' Whether this is to be taken as implying that Mrs. Scurlock had made them no allowance is doubtful ; but the concluding sentence shows distinctly that, for the moment at all events, there was remission of his money difficulties.

The most interesting of the letters, however, at this time, are some addressed to young Mr. Alexander Pope, now residing with his parents at Binfield, and not yet the author of the *Rape of the Lock*. In *Spectator* No. 253, Addison had noticed, and certainly not ' damned with faint praise,' Pope's *Essay upon Criticism*. Early in 1712, Pope wrote one of his alembicated epistles to thank Steele, who denied the authorship of the paper, but promised to make his correspondent acquainted with the writer. A few months later Pope seems to have submitted his *Messiah* to Steele, by whom, in a letter from his Haverstock Hill hermitage, it was examined and genially commended, subsequently making its appearance in the *Spectator* No. 378. A further letter from Pope, which was printed in No. 532, contains his prose version of the Emperor Hadrian's *Animula, vagula*, etc., the connection of which with the verses known as the *Dying Christian to his Soul* constitutes an episode in Pope's enigmatical correspondence of far too debatable a character to justify our entering upon it, even if it bore

materially upon Steele's biography.   But in one of
Steele's letters to Pope, dated November, 1712, he
hints at a new design he has in contemplation, in
which he is anxious for Pope's assistance.   This was
plainly the coming *Guardian*; and there can therefore
be no doubt that it must have been projected some
weeks before the *Spectator* came to an end.

CHAPTER VI.

PATRIOT AND POLITICIAN.

EARLY in 1713 we get a glimpse of Steele and his doings from the correspondence of a new and unprejudiced observer. In the month of January there came to London, on sick leave from Trinity College, Dublin, an ardent young Kilkenny gentleman of eight-and-twenty, who had already distinguished himself by his philosophical writings. This was George Berkeley, afterwards Dean of Derry and Bishop of Cloyne. At the present time, the famous *Siris* of his later years was only faintly foreshadowed in the *Treatise on Human Knowledge*; and apart from the printing of a new book of Dialogues,[1] his avowed motive for crossing the Channel was, ' to make acquaintance with men of merit, rather than to engage the interests of those in power.' Two of the most prominent characters of the day, Swift and Steele, were his own countrymen; and he found the latter already disposed to welcome him. ' The first news I heard upon my coming to town was, that Mr. Steel did me the honour to desire to be acquainted with me; upon which I have been to see him, he is

---

[1] *I.e. Three Dialogues between Hylas and Philonous . . . in Opposition to Sceptics and Atheists.* They were published in May, 1713.

confined wth the Gout, and is, as I am informed, writing
a Play, since he gave over the Spectators.' [This was
probably the very play with which, as Swift said, Steele
had ' long threatened the Town,' for a few weeks later
we hear that it has been ' put off to next winter.']
Berkeley goes on to say that Steele is ' extreamly civil
and obliging,' and that he proposes no small satisfaction
in the conversation of him and his ingenious friends,
' w^{ch}, as an encouragement he tells me, are to be met
with at his house.' The next letter, besides including
some information hitherto wanting to Steele's biography, contains a passage worth quotation :—' The
value you always shew'd for the Spectator makes me
think it neither impertinent nor unwelcome News to
tell you that by his mother in Law's death he is come
into an Estate of five hundred pounds a year : the same
day his wife was brought to bed of a Son.[1] Before she
lay down the poor man told me he was in great pain,
& put to a thousand little shifts to conceal her mother's
desperate illness from her. The tender concern he
show'd on that occasion & what I have observed in another good friend of mine makes me imagine the best
men are always the best husbands. I told Mr. Steele
if he neglects to resume his writings, the world will
look on it as the effects of his growing rich. But he
says this addition to his fortune will rather encourage
him to exert himself more than ever ; and I am the
apter to believe him because there appears in his
natural temper, something very generous, and a great

---

[1] This must have been a son of whom we have no record, as
Eugene Steele was born on the 4th of March, 1712, and this letter is
dated the 23rd of February 1713.

benevolence to mankind. One instance of it is his kind and friendly behaviour to me (even tho' he has heard I am a Tory). I have dined frequently at his house in Bloomsbury Square, wch is handsome and neatly furnish'd. His table, Servants, Coach, & everything is very gentile, and in appearance above his fortune before this new acquisition. His conversation is very chearful & abounds with wit and good sense. Some body (I know not who) had given him my treatise of the Principles of Human Knowledge, and that was ye ground of his inclination to my acquaintance. For my part I should reckon it a sufficient recompence of my pains in writing it, that it gave me some share in the friendship of so worthy a man.' [1]

From this extract it is manifest that, in February, 1713,—when Berkeley wrote,—Steele's mother-in-law had died recently; and it might reasonably be supposed that the consequent increase in his income was the immediate cause of his migration to the splendours of Bloomsbury. But, as we have already shown in the preceding chapter, Mrs. Scurlock was alive some time after the move had taken place, and it cannot therefore be associated with her death, which seems simply to have followed upon some earlier and obscurer improvement in Steele's mutable circumstances. From the expression 'renewal of my employments' in one of his letters of 1712, it may indeed be that he had means we know nothing of, as the words would seem to indicate something more than his Commissionership of Stamps and his pension as Gentleman-in-Waiting, which was not an employment. In any case, Berkeley found him

---

[1] Perceval MSS., February 23, 1713.

as busy as ever with new schemes and projects. Besides the play he was writing, he was far advanced in another enterprise, of which, under the name of the 'Censorium,' we shall hear more hereafter. Berkeley describes it, in what must surely be Steele's own words, as 'a noble entertainment for persons of a refined taste.' It is to combine recitations with music calculated 'to raise those passions which are suited to the Occasion.' The room designed for the performances is in York Buildings; and he [Steele] has been at no small expense to embellish it with all imaginable decorations. 'It is by much the finest chamber I have seen, and will contain seats for a select company of two [hundred] persons of the best quality and taste, who are to be subscribers.'[1]   A later letter says 'Mr. Steele's entertainment at York Buildings only waits ye finishing of two pictures, the one of Truth, the other of Eloquence.' 'He tells me he has had some discourse with the Lord Treasurer relating to it, and talks as if he would engage my Lord Treasurer in his project, designing that it shall comprehend both Whigs and Tories.'[2]   This, it may be noted, is of itself sufficient to prove that Steele needed no intermediator to obtain access to Oxford.[3]

Besides these activities, there was the new paper, for which, in the previous year, he had invited the co-operation of Pope, and now sought to engage that of the young and gifted scholar of Trinity College, Dublin. 'You will soon hear of Mr. Steel under the Character

---

[1] Perceval MSS., March 7, 1713.   [2] *Ibid*. March 27, 1713.
[3] In May, 1711, during the progress of the *Spectator*, Harley had been created Earl of Oxford, by which name he will hereafter be referred to.

of the Guardian '—says Berkeley on the 7th of March
—' he designs it shall come out every day as the
Spectator.' The *Guardian* accordingly began its career
on the 12th. It borrowed its names from the relations
of one ' Mr. Nestor Ironside ' with a fictitious and sufficiently diversified ' Lizard family,' whose sayings and
doings were to play the chief part in its pages, and who
were brightly sketched by Steele himself in Nos. 2, 5
and 6. No. 3, against Anthony Collins and the free-
thinkers,[1] is supposed to have been the first of a series
upon this theme by Berkeley; while No. 4 upon
' Dedications ' is by Pope, who supplied some seven or
eight contributions, including his well-known ' Receipt
to make an Epick Poem,' and the discreditable puff of
himself which he palmed off upon the too-easy ' Mr.
Ironside' under the guise of a panegyric of ' pastoral
Philips.' For some time Addison gave no assistance,
only entering actively into concurrence when the
second volume was already begun. This deferred appearance is unexplained, but it may, in some measure,
have been owing to the production of *Cato*, ' a most
noble play,' Berkeley calls it, which at this time was
engaging his attention; and the Prologue and Epilogue
to which (by Pope and Garth respectively) were printed
in *Guardian* No. 33. Other contributors, as time went
on, were Tickell, Budgell, and Hughes, who had assisted
in the *Spectator*, and essays are also assigned to Parnell
and Gay. But eighty-two out of a total of one hundred
and seventy-six papers are Steele's own, and he seems

---

[1] ' There is lately published a very bold & pernicious Book
entituled a Discourse on free Thinking: I hear the Printer of it is
put into Newgate.' (Perceval MSS., January 26, 1713.)

only to have surrendered the pen to Addison as he became more and more entangled in cares of a different kind. Other things being equal, there is no appreciable falling-off in his work for the *Guardian* as compared with its two predecessors. ' Other things,' however, ' were not equal.' In the first place there are but two volumes of the *Guardian* to seven of the *Spectator*, and four of the *Tatler*. In the second place, it must have been a great disadvantage to Steele that Addison's assistance, which when it did come, was more serious than usual, should have been so long withheld. For it is the peculiarity of these two that they succeeded best in combination, and Addison, witness the *Freeholder* and the eighth volume of the *Spectator*, found it as difficult to succeed without Steele as Steele without him. Lastly, the political element, which had been practically absent from the *Spectator*, and only vaguely present in the *Tatler*, assumed a very definite aspect in the *Guardian*. The *Guardian*, as its editor boasted, may have ' demolished Dunkirk ; ' but, as will be seen, Dunkirk in its turn demolished the *Guardian*.

It is true that Steele, at the outset, made profession of impartiality in politics, although he would not, like Mr. Spectator, engage to be neutral. ' I am,' he said in his assumed character of Ironside, ' with relation to the government of the church, a tory, with regard to the state, a whig.' Further on he adds, ' I am past all the regards of this life, and have nothing to manage with any person or party, but to deliver myself as becomes an old man with one foot in the grave, and one who thinks he is passing to eternity.' But Mr. Ironside's promises were hard to fulfil, at all events in 1713. The air was filled with faction, and the stress of party was intense. To the long-protracted war—protracted, said the Tories, by the Whigs—had succeeded the inglorious peace of Utrecht, under which the French King was to uphold the Hanoverian Succession, to discountenance ' the person who since the death of King James did take upon him the title of King of Great Britain,' and to demolish the harbour and fortifications of Dunkirk. Nevertheless it was doubted, by the Whigs at all events, whether His Most Christian Majesty would keep any of these engagements. Then there were uncomfortable suspicions that the Queen herself was not indisposed to ignore the Act of Settlement, and that the Tories were secretly intriguing to secure the throne for the Chevalier de St. George. Even in the correspondence of Berkeley, preoccupied only with the search for ' men of merit,' the shadow of these uneasy rumours comes and goes. 'Mr. Addison and Mr. Steel (& so far as I can find the rest of that party) seem entirely persuaded there is a design for bringing in the Pretender ; '[1] and though he says afterwards that these apprehensions were over, and, from the friendly demeanour of Swift and Addison, seems to anticipate an approaching coalition of parties, it is clear that the feeling of security was only temporary. Berkeley's words respecting Swift, at whose Bury Street lodgings he breakfasts in company with Addison, are worth recording, because they show how loath to fall apart for political reasons alone were, even now, the familiar trio of 1708. Speaking of Steele and Addison, he notes that there has ' passed a coldness, if not a direct breach between those two gentlemen, and

[1] Perceval MSS., February 23, 1713.

Dr. Swift on the score of Politicks.' But ' Dr. Swift's
witt,' he goes on to say, ' is admir'd by both of them, &
indeed by his greatest enemies; and if I were not
afraid of disobliging my Lady [i.e. Sir John Perceval's
wife] and Mrs. Parker I should tell you that I think
him one of the best natured and agreeable men in the
world.' [1]

If an apparent peace was, however, to be preserved
with the calmer and more circumspect Addison, an open
rupture with Steele was inevitable, and it came speedily
enough. Late in 1711, Lord Nottingham—' a famous
Tory and speech-maker,' Swift calls him in the *Journal*
—had gone over to the Whigs; and since then, under
the nickname of ' Dismal,' had been the favourite butt
of ministerial pamphleteers. Even Swift himself had
condescended (upon Oxford's hint) to write a punning
ballad, ' two degrees above Grub Street,' and an imitation of Horace, against the distinguished deserter from
the Tory ranks. In April, 1713, when the *Guardian*
had reached its fortieth number, Lord Nottingham was
assailed by the *Examiner*, which, by this time, had
passed from Mrs. Manley into the hands of Oldisworth,
and the assault was not confined to him, but included
his daughter Lady Charlotte Finch, afterwards Duchess
of Somerset. 'Thus,'—said the *Examiner*,—'to instance in One of their *Late Converts*, no sooner was
Dismal among the *Whigs*, and confirm'd past Retriev-
ing, but Lady Char——e is taking Knotting in *St.
James's Chapel*, during Divine Service, in the immediate Presence both of *God* and *Her Majesty*, who were
affronted together, that the Family might appear to be

[1] Perceval MSS., March 27, 1713.

entirely come over.' Steele rightly considered this to
be a wholly unjustifiable attack, for political purposes,
upon an unoffending young lady. He expostulated
with considerable warmth, and more strength of
language than is usual to him. 'When due regard
is not had to the honour of women,'—he said with a
fine chivalry—'all human society is assaulted;' and,
whether he was prompted by Lady Charlotte's relatives
or not, there can be no doubt that in this matter he
was on the right side. The *Examiner* rejoined by
countercharges against the personalities of the *Tatler*.
In May Steele vindicated himself over his own sig-
nature; and, referring to current reports as to the
authorship of the offending paper, concluded by saying that it was nothing to him whether the *Examiner*
wrote of him in the character of 'an estranged friend
or an exasperated mistress.' By these figures of speech
it is manifest that he intended to designate Swift and
Mrs. Manley.

The 'estranged friend' was not slow in replying.
On the day after Steele's letter appeared in the
Guardian, Swift wrote, not to him but to Addison,
commenting bitterly on Steele's conduct. He referred
to the fact that the 'Author of the Examiner' (to
whom he declared himself to be altogether a stranger [1])
had, a month or two before (in March) specially
vindicated him from any participation in its pages;

---

[1] This is confirmed by the *Journal to Stella* for March 12, 1713:
'The chancellor of the exchequer sent the author of the *Examiner*
twenty guineas. He is an ingenious fellow, but the most confounded
coxcomb in the world, *so that I dare not let him see me, nor am
acquainted with him.*' [The italics are ours.]

he complained that Steele should have been better acquainted with his style and temper; and finally, reverting to his old efforts with Oxford, accused him of ingratitude. Addison, cautious always of entrance to a quarrel, handed the letter to Steele, who replied a day or two later. It is plain that he could not bring himself to believe Swift's statements, nor did he attach as much importance to Swift's interposition in his favour as Swift thought that interposition deserved. 'If you have spoken in my behalf at any time (he says), I am glad I have always treated you with respect, though (he adds candidly) I believe you an accomplice of the Examiner.' Then he concludes by congratulating him (probably sincerely) upon his recent appointment as Dean of St. Patrick's. A long letter—the original of which is unfortunately mutilated —followed from Swift. He recalls and justifies his claim to have befriended Steele, and he reasserts his ignorance of the 'supposed Author' of the *Examiner*. He had 'several times assured Mr. Addison, and fifty others, that he had not had the least hand in writing any of those papers;' and referring to a chance phrase in Steele's first *Guardian*, which he had tortured into a charge of infidelity, inquired how Steele could justify himself for endeavouring to ruin his (Swift's) credit 'as a Christian and a clergyman.' Two more letters were exchanged without mending matters. Steele seems to think that a phrase in the *Examiner* to the effect that Addison had 'bridled him in point of party' could have emanated from no one but Swift; and Swift, in words of which it is hard to contest the dignity, explicitly denies the charge. He is leaving for Ireland (he adds), and from the common accidents of life may never see Steele again. A few days after this letter, which is dated the 27th of May, 1713, he started for Dublin, to be installed in his Irish Deanery.

Opinions of this correspondence will vary as men lean to one or other of the writers. To Swift's most recent biographer, Mr. Craik, Steele is a monster of ingratitude and vanity; to the late Mr. Dilke, whose careful *Papers of a Critic* are known to every eighteenth-century student, the whole *casus belli* was trivial, and only to be explained by something which has not been disclosed. It is the old story of the falling out of friends. Each saw, or fancied he saw, in every word uttered by his adversary, some covert reference to knowledge gained in easier and more unguarded moments. It stung Swift to the quick that Steele who had known him unreservedly should touch, however indirectly, on that sore subject of infidelity: it stung Steele equally that, in politics, Swift should regard him as a puppet whose strings were pulled by Addison. Hence the insulting incredulity of the one, and the frozen fury of the other. It is possible that Steele should have accepted Swift's denial of his connection with the *Examiner*. But though, strictly speaking, Swift had ceased to write in that paper, he was still popularly associated with its utterances. Long after his contributions had ceased, Lord Lansdowne, the Secretary at War, had accused him of inserting paragraphs in it, and even within the last few weeks, as he tells us himself, it had been found necessary to announce that he was not the author. Moreover, though he

M

denied that he was personally acquainted with that author, he had certainly supplied hints for his use,[1] and as to his temper and style, nothing must have been more notorious to his intimates, past and present, than that he could write in any style and temper he pleased. If to all this there be added his known activity as a ministerial pamphleteer and inspirer of ministerial pamphlets, it is not, after all, so inconceivable that an angry adversary should find a difficulty in accepting his protestations of innocence.

But Swift, for the moment, has gone back to Ireland; and we must return to Steele, whom this episode had left more than ever inclined to the *montagne russe* of politics. His recently acquired inheritance had made him practically independent of place. 'I have resolved (he told Swift in one of the above letters) to content myself with what I can get by my own industry, and the improvement of a small estate, without being anxious whether I am ever in a Court again or not.' During the foregoing dispute the *Examiner* had openly suggested that he should be deprived of his government appointment; and already the rumour ran that his name would be omitted from the new commission for stamped paper. This, nevertheless, seems not to have been actually intended. But in the circumstances he felt he could no longer hold his office with the freedom of speech which he desired, and out of his political preoccupations had arisen a fresh ambition. Parliament would shortly be dissolved, and he would enter the new House of Commons. He accordingly resigned his Commissionership on the 4th

[1] *Journal to Stella*, January 15, 1713.

of June in a frank and characteristic letter to Oxford, which concluded as follows:—' I am going out of any particular Dependance on your Lordship, and will tell you with the freedom of an indifferent Man, that it is impossible for any Man who thinks and has any publick Spirit, not to tremble at seeing his Country, in its present Circumstances, in the Hands of so daring a Genius as yours. If Incidents should arise that should place your own Safety, and what ambitious Men call Greatness, in a Ballance against the General Good, our All depends upon your Choice under such a Temptation. You have my hearty and fervent prayers to Heaven, to avert all such Dangers from you. I thank your Lordship for the Regard and Distinction you have at sundry times show'd me, and wish you, with your Country's Safety, all Happiness and Prosperity. Share, my Lord, your good Fortune with whom you will; while it lasts you will want no Friends; but if any adverse Day happens to you, and I live to see it, you will find I think my self obliged to be your Friend and Advocate. This is talking in a strange Dialect, from a private Man to the first of a Nation; but to desire only a little, exalts a Man's Condition to a level with those who want a great deal. But I beg your Lordship's Pardon, and am with great Respect, etc.

'RICHARD STEELE.'[1]

At the same time he resigned his pension as Prince George's gentleman-in-waiting. Whatever gratitude he may have been bound to show for past favours, he could therefore be no longer accused of attacking those

[1] *Apology*, 1714, pp. 86-7.

by whom he was paid. For the next two months,
being, we must conclude, absorbed in his parliamentary campaign, he contributed but little to the *Guardian*,
where his place was taken by Addison, with Berkeley
for chief assistant; and when he again made his appearance in its pages, his theme was exclusively political.
On the 7th of July, a public thanksgiving for the
peace, at which the Whigs were conspicuously absent,
had taken place. The favour shown by the Court to the
Duc d'Aumont, the French Ambassador, had stimu-
lated the old apprehensions of danger to the Hanoverian
Succession; and there were floating rumours that some
of the conditions of the Treaty of Utrecht would be
tacitly set aside by the ministry. As regards the demolition of Dunkirk in particular, urgent efforts were
being made by its inhabitants to obtain the relaxation
of the agreement. To this end a memorial, drawn up by
M. Tugghe, the Deputy of the Dunkirk magistrates,
had been largely circulated in English, with the hope
that it might influence the popular mind. Steele, who,
like the rest of his party, saw in the maintenance of the
harbour a standing menace to England, at once expostulated, with his usual unvarnished frankness, in *Guardian*
No. 128. 'The British Nation'—he insisted—'demands the demolition of Dunkirk.' The boldness of
this declaration, thrice-repeated, immediately brought
upon him the whole pack of Tory scribblers. In their
eyes, he was a 'Villain'—a 'contemptible Wretch.' The
Examiner styled his paper a 'Seditious Libel,' and,
ignorant of his resignation of his Commissionership,
charged him with ingratitude to the Sovereign whose
bread he was eating. In a pamphlet entitled a *Letter*

from a Country Whig to Mr. Steele, the same charges were more offensively repeated. The day after this came out, Steele left for Stockbridge, for which borough he was shortly afterwards chosen Member. When he returned to London he at once replied to his assailants in a long letter, addressed ostensibly to his chief constituent, Mr. John Snow, the Bailiff of the Hampshire borough.

The Importance of Dunkirk consider'd,—for such was the title of his answer,—is now of interest more for the documents it reprinted than for the forgotten political question which it discusses. In addition to *Guardian* No. 128, Steele reproduces some quotations from the *Country Whig* and the *Examiner*, the latter of which, even at this early stage, had already suggested his expulsion from the House of Commons. He also reproduces the Tugghe Memorial, to which he replies *seriatim*; and he does not forget to lay stress upon the fact that he was no longer the servant of the Government. This pamphlet laid him open to the retort of Swift, whom the Tories had again hastily summoned from his Irish home in consequence of the breach between Oxford and Bolingbroke. Swift was still smarting under recollection of the quarrel of the previous May; and one of his earliest productions was a brief and now somewhat rare tract against his old friend, entitled the *Importance of the Guardian Considered, in a Second Letter to the Bailiff of Stockbridge*. Even Steele's admirers must admit the cruel dexterity of this performance. All Mr. Ironside's assailable features are brought into the most vivid light. The lapses of his education, the negligences of his writing, the effect upon his reputation of Addison's anonymous aid, are all by turns presented with that merciless directness and lucid self-possession in which Swift is without a rival. 'He hath no Invention [?], nor is Master of a tolerable Style;[1] his chief Talent is Humour, which he sometimes discovers both in Writing and Discourse; for after the first Bottle he is no disagreeable Companion. I never knew him taxed with Ill-nature, which hath made me wonder how Ingratitude came to be his prevailing Vice; and I am apt to think it proceeds more from some unaccountable sort of Instinct, than Premeditation. Being the most imprudent Man alive, he never follows the Advice of his Friends, but is wholly at the mercy of Fools or Knaves, or hurried away by his own Caprice; by which he hath committed more Absurdities in Oeconomy, Friendship, Love, Duty, good Manners, Politicks, Religion, and Writing, than ever fell to one Man's share.'[2]

[1] How much depends upon the point of view may be seen from the difference between Swift friendly and Swift hostile. Only a year before his final quarrel with Steele he had written in his *Proposal for Correcting the English Tongue*, 1712:—'I would willingly avoid repetition, having about a year ago communicated to the publick much of what I had to offer upon this subject, by the hands of an ingenious gentleman, who for a long time did thrice a week divert or instruct the kingdom by his papers, and is supposed to pursue the same design at present under the title of Spectator. This Author, who hath tried the force and compass of our language with so much success, agrees entirely with me in most of my sentiments relating to it; so do the greatest part of the men of wit and learning, whom I have had the happiness to converse with.' Here, it may be observed, Swift commends Steele's style and judgment, and gives him credit for the *Tatler* and *Spectator*.

[2] *Importance of the Guardian Considered*, 1713, pp. 6-7.

And then follows the story of his losing his post of Gazetteer as it has been already related in Chapter IV. Nor among the points which Swift makes, does he omit the obvious suggestion that Steele had simply resigned his Commissionership because he knew he would not be allowed to retain it. This, however, is directly traversed by Steele's own words to Oxford in the preceding June. ' I should have done this sooner' —he says—'but that I heard the Commission was passing without my Name in it, and I would not be guilty of the Arrogance of resigning what I could not hold. But having heard this since contradicted, I am obliged to give it up, as with great Humility I do by this present Writing.'[1]

What Swift did in his own unapproachable manner the ' under spur-leathers' of the party travestied and exaggerated. Twelve days after the *Importance of the Guardian*, appeared the *Character of Richard St—le, Esq.*; by 'Toby, Abel's *Kinsman*,' this being the nick-name of one Edward King, the nephew of Abel Roper of the Tory *Post Boy*. It is a clumsy and personal per-formance, reviving the old *Atalantis* scandals about Steele's chemical pursuits, debts, and so forth. But it is interesting from its references to his Welsh es-tate, his mother-in-law's recent death, and some other particulars. From the frequent advertisements of it in the *Post Boy* it appears to have been much cir-

[1] *Apology*, p. 86. Berkeley thus refers to Steele's resignation and its sequel:—' Mr. Steele having laid down his employments, because (as he says) he wou'd not be obliged to those to whom he could not be gratefull, has of late turned his head towards Politicks, & pub-lished a Pamphlet in relation to Dunkirk, wch you may perhaps have seen by this time.' (Perceval MSS., October 2, 1713.)

culated, and even pirated. A few days later came a *Second Letter from a Country Whig*, which in its turn was succeeded by a rhymed sequel to the *Character* entitled *John Tutchin's Ghost to Richard St—le.* In neither of these is there anything of especial value, but they show the activity and inveteracy of Steele's assailants.[1]

But Toby's *Character* has carried us too far in our narrative. For some time previous to the publication of the *Importance of Dunkirk consider'd*, Steele had written but little in the *Guardian*, his place being taken by Addison and Laurence Eusden. On the 23rd of September, the day after the pamphlet appeared, he published a letter respecting it, in which he says, that he has turned the many scurrilous things said against

---

[1] These and the cognate pamphlets against Steele would require a chapter to themselves. Toby's *Character*, for example, is a fertile subject for discussion. From its republication in the *Miscellaneous Works of Dr. William Wagstaffe*, 1726, it has been usually ascribed to that obscure member of the 'Staff family.' But the late Mr. Dilke (*Papers of a Critic*, 1875, i. 369-78) had grave doubts whether Wagstaffe was not a 'bogus' author, and his equivocal collection the work of various hands. He was inclined to attribute the *Character* to Swift because it showed evidence of 'personal knowledge of the man and his most private concernments.' But the tone is surely too ignoble for Swift, even when writing 'two degrees above Grub Street,' and Mr. Dilke must have forgotten that there were others—Mrs. Manley for example—who were just as well acquainted with Steele's domestic annals as Swift was. Swift may have 'furnished a hint or two'; but our own impression, fortified by certain similarities of style, is that the writer was Mrs. Manley. Yet even this is hardly necessary, for there is nothing in the pamphlet which might not be easily concocted from the scandal of the Tory coffee-houses, mingled adroitly with reminiscences of the *New Atalantis* and the just-issued *Importance of the Guardian Considered.*

him to his advantage by using them to swell his volume, and he refers to another famous anti-ministerial tract upon the subject, Toland's *Dunkirk or Dover*. With half-a-dozen papers more, the *Guardian* came to an abrupt termination on the 1st of October. Five days later appeared the *Englishman*, ' a sequel.' The *Englishman* was published by Buckley, while the *Guardian* had been issued by Tonson; and Pope explained the cessation of the latter by attributing it to a quarrel with the publisher. Steele, he alleged, stood engaged to his bookseller in articles of penalty for all the *Guardians*, but by desisting two days and altering the title to the *Englishman*, he was quit of the obligation. Pope himself published with Tonson; and he should have been well informed; but his solution is scarcely convincing, and, as critics have not failed to remark, that agreement must have been very loosely worded which could be so easily evaded. In whatever way the change was effected, it is nevertheless clear that Steele's chief desire was to obtain a fresh platform for his political enthusiasm, and, as he says, 'to rouze in this divided Nation that lost Thing called Publick Spirit.' 'I am in a thousand troubles for poor Dick,' wrote Addison from Bilton to John Hughes, who sought to engage him in a new paper of the *Spectator* type, 'and wish that his zeal for the public may not be ruinous to himself; but he has sent me word that he is determined to go on, and that any advice I can give him in this particular, will have no weight with him.'

The *Englishman*, consequently, is largely occupied with political utterances; and Dunkirk, Passive Obedience, Patriotism, and the Protestant Succession occupy

no inconsiderable portion of its pages.[1] Steele seems
upon this occasion to have been unassisted by any of
his old colleagues; and Berkeley, upon whom he might
have counted for philosophical contributions, had gone
abroad as chaplain to Lord Peterborough. But there
is reason for supposing that some of the *Englishmen*
were written by a new ally, Mr. William Moore of the
Inner Temple. There can be little doubt, too, that
Moore was mainly responsible for Steele's next pamphlet,
The Crisis. Steele himself tells us in the *Apology* that
Moore suggested it. Moore, who was an adept in constitutional law, proposed that to counteract the ' dangerous Insinuations ' thrown daily among the People,
the story of the Hanoverian Succession and its obligations should be plainly set out; and he invited Steele
' from the kind Reception the World gave to what he
published ' to lend it his name. Finally it was agreed
that Moore should furnish the facts and Steele edit
and father the text. It is probable that it is mainly
the work of Moore, and that Steele did little else than
go over it, and supply the Preface and Dedication ' to
the Clergy of the Church of England.' But he seems
to have been unusually careful to avoid the possibility
of offence. He submitted it in proof to Addison,
Hoadly and others, and he modified it in accordance
with their suggestions. After much advertisement, it
made its appearance on the 19th of January, 1714. A

---

[1] No. 26 is one of the few exceptions. It contains that famous
account of Alexander Selkirk, which, by many, is supposed to have
suggested *Robinson Crusoe.* But Defoe, like Steele, may have seen
and conversed with the moody old buccaneer, to whose memory his
Fifeshire countrymen have recently erected a statue at Largo.

few weeks later the *Englishman* came to an end, the
last number (No. 57) being issued as a *quarto* pamphlet.
In this Steele replies to the attacks made upon him by
the *Examiner*; and it contains a paragraph which shows
that, rightly or wrongly, he still associated Swift with
his assailants. After quoting one of the most un-
generous pages of Toby's *Character*, he goes on :—' I
think I know the Author of this,[1] and to show him I
know no Revenge but in the Method of heaping Coals
on his Head by Benefits, I forbear giving him what he
deserves ; for no other reason but that I know his
Sensibility of Reproach is such, as that he would be
unable to bear Life itself under half the ill Language
he has given me.' He was not wholly ignorant of the
weaker side of Swift's nature.

But whatever the extent of Swift's responsibility
for Toby's *Character*—and it seems, as we hold, to
have been indirect rather than direct—there is no
obscurity about his attitude to the *Crisis*. Even before
it appeared he made it the subject of one of those
easy Horatian paraphrases, of which he possessed the
secret, and in octosyllabics, more stinging from their
contemptuous *bonhomie*, forecast its contents, and pre-

---

[1] Other persons also seem to have connected 'Toby, Abel's *Kins-
man*,' with Swift. In the scandalous pamphlet against him entitled
Essays Divine, Moral, and Political, 1714, he is distinctly indicated
at p. 44 as the writer of the *Character*. For this reason, *inter alia*,
Mr. Dilke (*Papers of a Critic*, 1875, i. 366-9) thought the *Essays
Divine*, &c., were by Steele. But they are more probably the work
of Gilbert Burnet's youngest son, Thomas Burnet, afterwards a
Judge of Common Pleas, and author of the curious squib on
Harley called the *History of Robert Powel the Puppet-Show-Man*,
1715.

figured its author's parliamentary achievements. 'Thy genius,' he told him,

> ——'has perhaps a knack
> At trudging in a beaten track,
> But is for state affairs as fit
> As mine for politics and wit.'

'Believe me,' he says again—

> 'Believe me, what thou'st undertaken
> May bring in jeopardy thy bacon;
> For madmen, children, wits, and fools,
> Should never meddle with edge tools.'

A month after the *Crisis* had appeared, he replied to it in *The Publick Spirit of the Whigs, set forth in their generous Encouragement of the Author of the Crisis, with some Observations on the Seasonableness, Candor, Erudition and Style of that Treatise.* It is one of the most masterly, if not the most masterly, of Swift's political tracts, and no impartial critic, however prepossessed in Steele's favour, can fail to admit the destructive power of its mingled rancour and scorn. By a curious accident it experienced just that fate which later befell the *Crisis*. Its comments upon the Scotch nobility were bitterly resented in the Upper House, and both printer and bookseller were ordered into the custody of the Black Rod. A proclamation was subsequently issued in the *London Gazette* of the 20th of March for the discovery of the author, whose exposure was only evaded by the watchful ingenuity of Oxford.

Steele meanwhile had taken his seat for Stockbridge in the new parliament which met on the 16th of February, 1714. There was a large Tory majority, and his fate seems to have been a foregone conclusion. His maiden speech in support of the election of Sir Thomas Hanmer for Speaker was received with every mark of disapprobation. It is only a few lines long. Yet its reference to the part played by Hanmer in rejecting the Commerce Bill of the preceding session appears to have raised a perfect storm of opposition, which at Steele's use of the words 'I rise up to do him Honour'—a common classical recollection, already familiar in the pages of the *Spectator* [1]—swelled to a hurricane. It is possible that neither of these allusions was judicious; but it is also certain that in the mouth of any other new member they would have been indulgently received. Outside it was reported that after this *fiasco* he would never be able to speak again, and Oxford wrote to Arbuthnot that he would henceforth be the jest of the House. But there were worse things in store for the plain-spoken demolisher of Dunkirk. On the 3rd of March, as Swift had darkly hinted in the above-mentioned *Paraphrase from Horace*, a petition was lodged against his return for Stockbridge on the ground of bribery. This, being the seventeenth of its kind on the list, was felt to be too dilatory a method of proceeding; and the Ministerial agents began to call attention to his writings. Finally, on the 12th, Mr.

---

[1] Cf. *Spectator* No. 270:—'It was a pretty variation of the prospect, when any one of these fine Ladies *rose up and did honour* to herself and Friend at a distance, by curtisying.' Swift refers to this incident in one of his poems against Steele:—

> 'Especially with thee whose hasty zeal
> Against the late rejected commerce bill
> Made thee rise up, like an audacious elf,
> To do the speaker honour, not thyself.'

Auditor Foley made a formal complaint of the seditious character of certain paragraphs in the *Crisis* and *Englishman*, and Steele was ordered to attend in his place next day. This he did, and the offending paragraphs being read, were assailed with great severity by Harley (the Lord Treasurer's brother), Foley, and others of the Court party. Steele, thereupon, urged the suddenness of the attack, and asked for time to prepare his defence. After some discussion, a four-days' delay was granted. In the interim, he moved that the papers relative to Dunkirk should be laid before the House, but the motion was negatived. On the 18th he came up again. He frankly owned himself the author of the paragraphs in question, 'with the same Unreservedness with which he abjured the Pretender.' Being afterwards called upon for his defence, he replied to his assailants, paragraph by paragraph, 'speaking,' writes Queen Anne's old annalist Boyer, 'for near Three Hours to the several Heads . . . with such a Temper, Modesty, Unconcern, easy and manly Eloquence, as gave entire Satisfaction to all, who were not inveterately prepossessed against him.' On the attacks of the *Examiner* he touched with some indignation; but his only reference to the Author of the *Importance of the Guardian Considered*, and the *Publick Spirit of the Whigs*, was brief and dignified. Referring, in justification of his earlier writings, to the favourable report given by the *Tatler* of the *Project for the Advancement of Religion*, he simply added 'The Gentleman I here intended was Dr. *Swift*; this kind of Man I thought him at that time: We have not met of late, but I hope he deserves this Character still.'

During all the time that the defence lasted Addison sat by to prompt his friend, and he had Sir Robert Walpole (then plain Mr.) and General Stanhope for supporters. When he had made an end, and was withdrawn, Walpole and other leading Whigs addressed the House warmly in his favour. Young Lord Finch, too, Lady Charlotte's brother, who, like Steele himself, was a new member, rose in defence of his sister's champion. Overcome by timidity, however, he presently sat down exclaiming, ' It is strange I can't speak for this man, though I could readily fight for him.' Those near him caught up the muttered words; they were quickly repeated; and the ready outburst of encouraging applause brought the neophyte again on his feet, when, it is recorded, he made an eloquent and effective speech. But neither Lord Finch's maiden rhetoric, nor Steele's more powerful advocates, could save him from what, with pardonable energy, he terms ' the arbitrary Use of Numbers,' and ' the insolent and unmanly Sanction of a Majority.' He was expelled the House by 245 votes against 152. His fate was decided late at night; but the *Examiner* had given an account of it,—says the writer of the *Case of Richard Steele*,—twelve hours before!

Swift, in whom the spirit of retaliation seems by this time to have obliterated every other feeling, did not scruple to exult over his fallen adversary. In a second imitation of Horace, written in the person of John Dennis, and advertised, like the *Publick Spirit of the Whigs*, as ' fit to be bound up with the *Crisis*,' he invited Steele straightway to take up his abode in that Southwark sanctuary for insolvent debtors, the Mint :—

' 'Tis true, that Bloomsbury-square's a noble place :
But what are lofty buildings in thy case ?
What's a fine house embellish'd to profusion
When shoulder dabbers are in execution ? . . .
Exchange the prospects that delude thy sight,
From Highgate's steep ascent and Hampstead's height,
With verdant scenes, that, from St. George's Field,
More durable and safe enjoyments yield.' [1]

That Steele, in spite of the subscriptions to the
Crisis, was again seriously embarrassed, is perhaps to
be anticipated. He had resigned four hundred a year
to enter Parliament ; and to this loss had followed the
expenses of an election, some of the funds for which, it
was reported, had been cunningly intercepted by the
watchful 'shoulder-dabbers.' Accordingly the brief
notes of this period to his anxious wife are full of the
old vague allusions to difficulties past or pending. At
the same time help of a mysterious kind seems to have
been forthcoming, for one of the notelets mentions
3,000*l*. that is to be paid in by unknown hands for his
use. Meanwhile he turned again to periodical litera-

---

[1] Swift, of course, was not Steele's sole assailant. When the
first volume of the *Englishman* closed, in February, 1714, there came
out a curious *Letter from the facetious Dr. Andrew Tripe at Bath to
the Venerable Nestor Ironside*, still an object of solicitude to col-
lectors, and, by good judges, ascribed to Arbuthnot. In April, after
the expulsion, appeared *The Crisis upon Crisis, a Poem*, which was
succeeded in June by *A Town Eclogue ; or, A Poetical Contest
between Toby and a Minor-Poet of B—tt—n's Coffee-House*. Later
still, in August, came Lacy's *Steeleids*. These tracts sadly lack a
bibliographer ; but they yield little in the way of valuable information. Exception may be made however for *The Case of Richard
Steele, Esq.*, which contains a useful summary of the circumstances
connected with his first parliamentary experiences.

ture. Shortly before his expulsion from the House of Commons, he had begun a new paper after the *Spectator* pattern, the *Lover*. In the eleventh number he published a whimsical account of his senatorial disgrace, in which Oxford figured as Sir Anthony Crabtree and Auditor Foley as Brickdust. The *Lover*, however, in the turn things had taken, afforded too little opportunity for the more exciting topics, that, for the moment, engaged his attention. Before it was discontinued he started, in direct opposition to the *Examiner*, another and more distinctly political organ, the *Reader*. From No. 6 of this, it appears that he contemplated undertaking that enterprise, which afterwards drifted from Glover to Mallet, and was ultimately performed, only in this century, by Archdeacon Coxe,—the story of Marlborough's campaigns.[1] Besides this, he published in May the *Romish Ecclesiastical History of Late Years*, a little compilation against Popery dedicated to Lord Finch in words that did not neglect the 'Noble Motive' which first elicited that young orator's eloquence. In June followed a Letter to a Member of Parliament, probably Lord Finch again, respecting the Bill for preventing the Growth of Schism; and later, another pamphlet prompted by what he held to be further evasions of the French as regards Dunkirk. Then,—only a few days after an advertisement had

---

[1] In his *Epistle to the late Dr. Garth*, Leonard Welsted thus refers to Steele's intention :—

'Let Steele immortal Mildenheim sustain,
And trace his story in the Livian strain;
While I the subject, to his pen assign'd,
But lightly touch, and follow far behind.'

Welsted's Works, 1787, 91-2.

N

appeared in the *Daily Courant* to the effect that '*Mr.*
Steele's House on the East Side of Bloomsbury-Square,
in very good Repair, is to be Lett,'—Oxford was driven
from office, Queen Anne quitted this life at Kensington,
and the aspect of things changed materially for the ex-
member for Stockbridge.   The problem of the Protestant Succession was solved by the landing of King
George at Greenwich in September; and honours began
incontinently to rain on his courageous champion.   In
brief space Steele was made deputy Lieutenant for the
county of Middlesex, Surveyor of the Royal Stables at
Hampton Court, and (like Fielding after him) a justice
of the peace.

Not long subsequently he issued, with the motto
Fabula quanta fui! the pamphlet entitled *Mr. Steele's*
Apology for Himself and his Writings; Occasioned by
his Expulsion from the House of Commons.   It had been
advertised as forthcoming immediately after his disgrace; but it did not appear until October, 1714.   It
contains an account of his defence, with some supple-
mentary particulars, which have already been drawn
upon in the course of these pages.   The *Apology* is the
best of Steele's political efforts,—that is to say, of those
of which he was something more than the responsible
author.   But he did not excel in this branch of literature.   When the *Examiner* said that he had 'oblig'd
his Party with a very awkward *Pamphleteer* in the
room of an excellent Droll,' it was the truth told by an
enemy.   His earnestness, his popularity in another
way, his ready enthusiasm, made him the best man the
Whigs could put forward.   But he lacked many controversial qualities, such as memory, closeness of reasoning,

tact, restraint. And he was opposed to the most able and inexorable opponent who ever entered the lists of faction.

But two of Steele's publications, which belong to this period of his life, were not, in any sense, political; and with brief reference to them this chapter may be closed. One was a volume of *Poetical Miscellanies*, published at the end of 1713, with a flaming dedication to Congreve, which included some extravagant praise of that writer's little poem of *Doris*. The volume contained Pope's *Wife of Bath*, together with contributions by Gay, Tickell, Eusden, Hughes, and others. Hughes' were anonymous, as he objected to the profane proximity of Pope's Chaucer paraphrase. Of Steele's own there was nothing but a poem which he had addressed to Congreve on the *Way of the World* and the reprinted *Procession* of 1695. The other work was the curious *Ladies Library* so often referred to in the *Spectator*. The author, or compiler, was a lady unknown, and her labours drew upon Steele the expostulations of a certain Royston Meredith, who considered that she had poached upon his preserves. Steele's part in the book was confined to dispersed editorial touches and the supplying of a Preface, and three Dedications to his own friends. The first volume was inscribed to Lady Burlington; the second to the Mrs. Catherine Bovey already referred to as the suggested original of Sir Roger's ' perverse widow.' The third dedication, couched in an admirable strain of loyal and affectionate eulogy, is to Steele's own wife, who, surrounded by her family, may be supposed to be depicted in Du Guernier's frontispiece. It would be unjust not to give an extract from it, if only to show that in an age of adulatory addresses there exists at least one which is neither venal nor feigned : 'It is impossible for me to look back on many Evils and Pains which I have suffered since we came together, without a Pleasure which is not to be expressed, from the Proofs I have had in those Circumstances of your unwearied Goodness. How often has your Tenderness removed Pain from my sick Head ? How often Anguish from my afflicted Heart ? With how skilful Patience have I known you comply with the vain Projects which Pain has suggested, to have an aking Limb removed by Journeying from one side of a Room to another ; how often the next Instant travelled the same Ground again, without telling your Patient it was to no Purpose to change his Situation ? If there are such Beings as Guardian Angels, thus are they employed; I will no more believe one of them more Good, in its Inclinations, than I can conceive it more charming in its Form than my Wife.

' But I offend, and forget that what I say to you is to appear in Publick : You are so great a Lover of Home, that I know it will be irksome to You to go into the World even in an Applause. I will end this, without so much as mentioning your Little Flock, or your own amiable Figure at the Head of it : That I think them preferable to all other Children, I know is the Effect of Passion and Instinct; that I believe You the best of Wives, I know proceeds from Experience and Reason.'

CHAPTER VII.

THEATRICAL MANAGER—LAST YEARS.

WHETHER the honours conferred upon Steele by his grateful Majesty, King George, were more decorative than profitable, we are without means of deciding. If any reliance is to be placed on an expression in one of his subsequent letters, to the effect that, notwithstanding his services to the Royal family, he is not 'possessed of twenty-shillings from the favour of the Court,' it must be concluded that they made no material addition to his income. But not long after the publication of the *Ladies Library* he came in for a very definite and substantial stroke of good fortune. With the death of Queen Anne the license of Drury Lane Theatre had also expired. The patentees, at that date, were the actors Booth, Doggett, Wilks, and Colley Cibber. Under the license which had just lapsed, they had been obliged to pay a pension or annual allowance to a Tory lawyer and M.P. of the name of Collier. In his disconnected but excellent *Apology* Cibber tells the story. As the license had to be renewed, and the pension paid to somebody, ' they [the patentees] imagin'd the Merit of a *Whig* might now have as good a chance for getting into it, as that of a *Tory* had for being continued in it,' and, having no love for Collier, they hit upon the ingenious idea of applying to Steele to interest himself in their behalf, at the same time offering him the 700*l.* per annum and the position of co-partner, or Supervisor of the Theatre. His pretensions to favour at Court were for the moment considerable; but, to do them justice, they also gratefully remembered his services to the Stage in the past. 'We knew, too,' says Cibber, 'the Obligations the Stage had to his Writings; there being scarce a Comedian of Merit, in our whole Company, whom his *Tatlers* had not made better by his publick Recommendation of them. And many Days had our House been particularly fill'd, by the Influence, and Credit of his Pen. . . . We therefore beg'd him to use his Interest, for the Renewal of our License, and that he would do us the Honour of getting our Name to stand with His, in the same Commission. This, we told him, would put it still farther into his Power of supporting the Stage, in that Reputation, to which his Lucubrations had already so much contributed; and that therefore we thought no man had better Pretences to partake of its Success.' Steele, it may be guessed, was highly flattered. 'It surpriz'd him,' says Cibber, 'into an Acknowledgment, that People, who are shy of Obligations, are cautious of confessing. His Spirits took such a lively Turn upon it; that had we been all his own Sons no unexpected Act of filial Duty could have more endear'd us to him.' [1]

The boon which the patentees sought was speedily obtained. Steele made application to the King through the Duke of Marlborough, now restored to his old office

---

[1] *Apology*, 1740, pp. 289-90.

of Captain-General. His Majesty at once complied with the petition ; and the theatre, during the beginning of the season of 1714–15, was crowded with a more than usual concourse of spectators. But in the 'largess universal' of beneficence, which now radiated from the throne, the long-suspended license of Lincoln's Inn Fields was also renewed ; to be almost immediately followed by an exodus of actors from Drury Lane. One result of this was an appreciable falling off in the receipts at the latter house ; and Cibber and his colleagues seem promptly to have pointed out to Steele that, in strict fairness, his pension should be subject to the same conditions as Collier's, which was contingent upon the existence of one Theatre only, and, if a second were set up, was to be transformed from a fixed annual amount into a proportionate share of the profits. Steele behaved at this juncture with his wonted generosity. He 'stopt us short,' says Cibber, ' by assuring us, that as he came among us, by our own Invitation, he should always think himself oblig'd, to come into any Measures, for our Ease, and Service: That to be a Burthen to our Industry, would be more disagreeable to him, than it could be to us ; and as he had always taken a Delight, in his Endeavours, for our Prosperity, he should be still ready on our own Terms, to continue them.' Steele, however, suggested that it would be best for him to obtain a Patent for life in his own name, which he would then make over to them— an arrangement of which one effect would be to free them from too close a dependence upon the caprices of the Lord Chamberlain and his staff. It proved an advantage also to Steele, who, in all his dealings with his colleagues, seems to have acted in the most honourable

manner, for, instead of 700*l*., his income from the theatre
henceforth, taking one year with another, can scarcely
have been less than 1,000*l*.

The new patent for Drury Lane was received from
the Lord Chamberlain on the 19th of January, 1715.
The next day Steele set out for Boroughbridge in
Yorkshire, for which place he was going to offer himself
as member. His wife went with him as far as York.
Here she remained ' at Mr. Harrison's, over against
the Black Man in Coney Street,' to which place came
daily reports of the candidate's progress. On the 27th
he writes ' among dancing, singing, hooping, hallooing
and drinking' to tell her that he thinks he shall
succeed, and that he loves her to death. Next day he
says that he is obeying her directions exactly and
avoiding drinking, and everything else that might give
her trouble. But he seems to be still tormented by
the want of ready money. Early in February he was
elected. In the following April, after a banquet given
to the Earl of Clare, Lord-Lieutenant of Middlesex, by
his Deputies, Steele was employed to draw up a con-
gratulatory address to the King upon his peaceful
accession. This loyal effusion being duly presented,
Steele, with two of his colleagues, received the honour
of knighthood. A few weeks later the new knight
celebrated His Majesty's birthday by a *soirée*, as it
would now be called, in the great room at York Buildings which Berkeley had seen, and which, during the
chequered experiences of the last few months, could
have made but little progress. The company consisted
of more than two hundred ladies and gentlemen ; and
bating refreshments, the sumptuous character of which

appears to have been maliciously exaggerated by Steele's contemporaries,[1] the entertainment was strictly in accordance with his original programme. An ode of Horace was set to music and sung, and a poem was recited in honour of the King. Tickell wrote a Prologue, which was spoken by Miss Younger; and the preparations for supper and dancing were heralded by an Epilogue, ascribed to Addison, which pleasantly rallied some of the foibles of the good-natured host. After touching upon his early and frustrate endeavours after the philosopher's stone, it proceeds thus :—

> That Project sunk, you saw him entertain
> A notion more chimerical and vain,
> To give chaste Morals to ungovern'd youth,
> To Gamesters honesty, to Statesmen truth ;
> To make you virtuous all ; a thought more bold,
> Than that of changing Dross and Lead to Gold.
> But now to greater actions he aspir'd,
> For still his Country's good our Champion fir'd ;
> In Treaties vers'd, in Politicks grown wise,
> He look'd on DUNKIRK with suspicious eyes ;
> Into her dark foundations boldly dug,
> And overthrew in fight the fam'd SIEUR TUGGHE.
> Still on his wide unwearied view extends,
> Which I may tell, since none are here but Friends ;
> In a few months he is not without hope,
> But 'tis a secret [,] to convert the Pope.
> Of this, however, he'll inform you better
> Soon as his Holiness receives his Letter.

The last lines refer to an ironic dedication, ostensibly by Steele, but really by Bishop Hoadly, prefixed to a

---

[1] *Town Talk*, etc., 1789, p. 56.

recently published translation, by an unnamed hand, from the Italian of one Urbano Cerri, 'Secretary of the Congregation *de propaganda Fide.*' The book was entitled *An Account of the State of the Roman-Catholick Religion Throughout the World,* and was intended as a sequel to Steele's anti-papal pamphlet of the previous year. Addison probably knew perfectly well that Steele was only the putative author, so that this allusion must be added to the other shafts of friendly satire in the epilogue, which, we are told, lost nothing of their point under the admirable delivery of Wilks, who spoke it. From the account which Steele himself gives of this festival in *Town Talk* it would appear to have been intended as the prelude to many successive assemblies of the kind, of course not of the gratuitous character of the inaugural entertainment, but maintained by the two hundred subscribers ' of the best quality and taste,' of whom he had spoken to Berkeley. It is with regard to the Censorium, as it was called, that one of the most characteristic anecdotes of Steele is told. Wishing on one occasion, when it was still in course of construction, to ascertain whether the room was as well calculated to gratify the ear as the eye, he 'desired the carpenter '— says Drake—'to ascend a pulpit placed at one end of the building and speak a few sentences. The carpenter obeyed, but when mounted found himself utterly at a loss for the matter of his harangue. Sir Richard begged he would pronounce whatever first came into his head. Thus encouraged, the new-made orator began, and looking steadily at the knight, in a voice like thunder, exclaimed, ' Sir Richard Steele, here has I, and these here men, been doing your work for three months, and never seen the colour of your money. When are you to pay us ? I cannot pay my journeymen without money, and money I must have.' Sir Richard replied, that he was ' in raptures with the eloquence, but by no means admired the subject.' [1]

From the fact that in this anecdote he is called ' Sir Richard ' it might be inferred that the incident took place subsequent to the date of his knighthood. But it is more likely that it belongs to 1714, when his needs were more urgent. The Censorium must have succeeded; for Steele tells us in the following year, that the subscriptions had all been taken up.[2] It must also, in one form or another, have continued for some time to come, because Eugene Steele, who was now only three years old, is said to have acted plays in it while a school-boy.

Of Steele's doings for the next few years, we rather overhear than hear—to use a French metaphor. For the Bloomsbury mansion appears to have been substituted for one described in the addresses of his letters as ' Over-against Park-place, St. James's-street.' He also rented a little house ' by the waterside' in Paradise Row, Chelsea, for which he paid 14*l.* per annum, and he was living there in November, 1715, as the parish register records the burial ' from Sir Richard Steele's ' of one Margaret, daughter of Edward Seat, probably a servant. The *Lover* and the *Reader* after short and inconspicuous careers had both come to more or less premature ends in 1714; and he issued them together in the following year with a dedication to Garth—the ' well-natur'd Garth,' of Pope, who now, by grace of

[1] Drake's *Essays*, ed. 1814, i. 179-80.　　[2] *Town Talk*, No. 4.

King George and the touch of Marlborough's own sword, had become Sir Samuel. In July began a second volume of the *Englishman*, which ran from that month to November, and contains, among other papers, a plea for Steele's old patron Ormond, now an attainted fugitive in France. The *Englishman* was succeeded by *Town Talk*, a series of letters to a Lady in the Country,—possibly Lady Steele. It concluded with the ninth number, and early in the next year came the *Tea Table* and *Chit-Chat*, neither of which lived beyond a few numbers. In the same month of March, 1716, in which *Chit-Chat* began and ended its ephemeral existence, he published Addison's Comedy of *The Drummer*, which was produced at Drury Lane on the 10th, mainly through the instrumentality of its author's friend, the patentee. Steele supplies (perhaps unconsciously) an excellent criticism of this in his preface when he says that his ' Brother Sharers [i.e.—Cibber, Booth and Wilks] were of opinion, at the first reading of it, that it was like a picture in which the strokes were not strong enough to appear at a distance.' This is a kindly way of saying what was a fact,—that Addison's fine and finished style was wholly unable to adapt itself to the needs of theatrical perspective,—a circumstance which, coupled with his lack of dramatic talent, amply accounts for the very qualified success of the piece.

Not long after the production of the *Drummer*, Steele was appointed one of a Commission of twelve to inquire into the Estates of Traitors and Popish Recusants. Its first and most prominent object was to appropriate the lands of the Scotch noblemen and gentlemen who had taken part in the insurrection of

1715 in favour of the House of Stuart. This was a business that involved much time—we hear of it dispersedly for two or three years to come—and Steele's correspondence contains many references to his going and returning, or as often postponing the one and the other. Not much either seems to have been done in the business when all was said, for the material part was left to the Legislature. During the first year Steele does not seem to have taken any part in the invidious duties of his colleagues, though this did not prevent his religiously drawing the salary. 'Five hundred pounds "for the time the Commission was in Scotland" is already ordered me,' he tells his wife in May, 1717. Next year he did go; but only very tardily, for in September he writes—'The Commission in Scotland stands still, for want of me at Edinburgh. It is necessary there should be four there, and there are now but two; three others halt on the road, and will not go forward until I have passed by York.' Finally he goes by Wakefield, arriving in Edinburgh in November. It had been his whim to take a French master with him as a consolation in travel. His companion was a minister named Majon. 'He lies in the same room with me on the road; and the loquacity which is usual at his age, and inseparable from his nation, at once contributes to my purpose, and makes him very agreeable.'

At Edinburgh, Steele, painful and unwelcome as his mission must have been, was exceedingly well received; and the feeling of his Scottish hosts towards the popular writer as distinguished from the Whig Official —the least official, in this instance, of all officials,—is fairly expressed in the votive couplets of an unknown

'Alexander Pennicuik, gentleman,' author of a volume
of *Streams from Helicon*. Scotia, he avers, 'though
distilling tears from her crystal *lambics*,' smiles on her
illustrious visitor :—

With throbbing breast she dreads th' approaching ill,
Yet still she loves you, though you come to kill,
In midst of fears and wounds, which she doth feel, .
Kisses the hurting hand, smiles on the wounding STEELE.

Allan Ramsay, too, 'theeking pashes' at his shop,
'opposite to Niddry's Wynd head,' welcomed ''Kind
Richy Spec, the friend of a' distressed,' and probably
first made his acquaintance at this time. Steele himself
was delighted with his Scotch experiences. Writing
from Durham on his way home 'after seven days
journey from Edinburgh towards London [!],' he tells
his wife that 'You cannot imagine the civilities and
honours I had done me there [i.e.—in the Scotch
capital]; and [I] never lay better, ate or drank better,
or conversed with men of better sense.' In another fortnight he expects to be in London. He was in Scotland
again in the summer of 1718, when he took a furnished
house, and again in 1719, 1720 and 1721.

Several anecdotes cluster around these Northern
pilgrimages. Among other things Steele seems to
have cherished the 'devout imagination' that he
might effect an alliance between the Presbyterian and
Episcopal churches, and he had many and inevitably
fruitless interviews with the Scotch clergy on the
subject. To one of them, James Hart, an Edinburgh
minister, he was greatly attracted, chiefly, it would
seem, because of the contrast between the geniality of

his private life and his terrible denunciations from the pulpit. Steele christened him the 'Hangman of the Gospel.' Once, during his stay in 'Auld Reekie,' he indulged in a freak, the effect of which must have been strangely like Burns's *Jolly Beggars*. He invited all the strollers and mendicants he could find to a feast, at which, after a copious meal, they were regaled with wine and punch to their hearts' content, revealing, in their convivial freedom, so many eccentricities and 'queerities'—as Steele would have called them—of character and temperament that he declared he had learned humours enough to furnish forth an entire comedy. Another little story may find a place here. In the parish of Cummertrees in Dumfries, there is, or was, a certain tower, which formed a conspicuous object in the landscape. Riding in the neighbourhood, Steele and his friends found a shepherd on the hillside reading a book. It was his Bible. Steele asked him what he learnt in it, and the man replied, 'The way to Heaven.' 'Very well,' rejoined the other, 'we are desirous of going to the same place, and wish you would show us the way.' The shepherd turned about and said—'Weel, gentlemen, ye maun just gang by that tower.' The tower had been built in a fit of remorse for some ancient sin by an old Border Cavalier, and was known as the 'Tower of Repentance.'

Repeated attacks of gout, added to the usual absence of ready money, and the difficulties of locomotion in the days when it took three weeks to get from London to Edinburgh, account, in some measure, for the dilatory way in which Steele performed his functions on the Forfeited Estates Commission. But in 1718 there was also another reason. He was absorbed in a new project, to which his letters make frequent references. This was the plan known as the 'Fish-Pool,' an account of which he published in 1718, in collaboration with a mathematical colleague named Gillmore. For the well-boat of the Fishing Trade, they proposed to substitute a specially constructed vessel in which salmon could be brought alive from Ireland to the London markets. Steele took out a patent for this contrivance. In design it exhibited much ingenuity; but in practice it failed, as the fish battered themselves to pieces *en route*, and the scheme, with the 'very considerable estate' which had been anticipated from it, came to nothing. But Steele himself does not seem to have suffered as much as usual. The main expense, he says, in a letter of July, 1717, was to be borne by a Mr. Benson, Auditor of the Imprest, and, according to his own account, his own personal loss could not have exceeded one hundred pounds.

The correspondence with Lady Steele had at this time again grown active. In the summer of 1716, presumably, to look after the affairs of the Welsh estate, she went to Carmarthen leaving her husband and children behind her. She remained in Wales until the end of 1717. During all this period, letters, from which none of the old characteristics were absent, were frequently addressed to her by her husband. But though they had the old characteristics, they had, besides, a new subject, the children, and of these their warm-hearted father writes charmingly. How Eugene is 'a most beautiful and lusty child;' how Molly has the small-pox—as they say 'very kindly;' how Madam

Betty, the eldest (who is at school 'at Mrs. Nazereau's, Chelsea') is the gravest of matrons in her airs and civilities; how a kindly but 'Prue-like' Mrs. Keck takes him gravely to task for spending so much money upon them and yet not dressing them better,—all this is chronicled in the letters that go by nearly every post into remote Carmarthen. '*Your—Betty—Dick—Eugene —Molly's* Humble Servant'—he signs himself upon one occasion. On another he has been to see Betty at school, and the child, he says, represented to him ' in her pretty language that she seemed helpless and friendless, without anybody's taking notice of her at Christmas, when all the children but she and two more were with their relations.' So he has invited her to dinner, with one of the teachers, and they are in the room at that very moment, 'Betty and Moll very noisy and pleased together.' 'I told Betty'—he adds—'I had writ to you; and she made me open the letter again, and give her humble duty to her mother, and desire to know when she shall have the honour to see her in town.' At another time Eugene engrosses nearly the whole of the epistle :—' Your son, at the present writing, is mighty well employed in tumbling on the floor of the room and sweeping the sand with a feather. He grows a most delightful child, and very full of play and spirit. He is also a very great scholar : he can read his Primer ; and I have brought down my Virgil. He makes most shrewd remarks upon the pictures. We are very intimate friends and play-fellows. He begins to be very ragged ; and I hope I shall be pardoned if I equip him with new cloaths and frocks, or what Mrs. Evans and I shall think for his service.' Then he tells his correspondent

o

that the two girls have been with him at Paradise Row one day in June, 1717, that they were very good company, and that he had treated them to strawberries and cream, eating 'according to his fond way' more than either of them. And so, 'according to his fond way,' the letters gossip on, always hopeful, always tender, dreaming always of a forthcoming era when everything is to be forthcoming, and Her Ladyship will have put off her 'coynesses and particularities.'

Those questionable qualities do not appear to have decreased with time, or to have improved under the obstacles which Lady Steele experienced in dealing with her Welsh affairs and her Welsh relatives. Her health, too, was breaking—she has nervous terrors of thunder,—pains in the head (for which Garth prescribes water and salt), and a first fit of the gout, an ailment to which her mother had been as great a martyr as Steele himself. All these things seem to have passed into her letters, which, if one may judge from a very querulous and recriminatory example, preserved among the MSS. at Blenheim, beginning frigidly 'Sir' and ending 'Your obedient servant,' must have been largely occupied by lectures, complaints, and scoldings. Sometimes she neglects to write, or writes by another hand, or—what is especially hard to bear—writes coldly upon the blank leaf of another person's letter. But her manner must have varied with her mood, which was not always 'scornful and unkind,' and the least manifestation of this softer side of her nature brings her husband's heart into his mouth. Once when she calls him 'good Dick,' it throws him into such a transport that he declares he could almost forget his 'present most miserable lameness,' and walk down to her at Wales. 'My dear little peevish, beautiful, wise governess, God bless you,' this letter ends. In another he assures her that, lying in her place and on her pillow, he fell into tears only from thinking that his 'charming little insolent might be then awake and in pain' with headache. She tells him she wants a little flattery, and he pays her a string of compliments. Her son he says elsewhere ' is extremely pretty, and has his face sweetened with something of the Venus his mother, which is no small delight to the Vulcan who begot him.' He assures her that, though she talks of the children, they are dear to him more because they are hers than because they are his own. He loves her with 'the most ardent affection,' and ' often runs over little heats that have sometimes happened between them with tears in his eyes.' To look at her, to hear her, to touch her gives delight in a greater degree than any other creature can bestow, and to be constant to her is not virtue but good sense and wise choice. And, as before, he exhausts ingenuity in devising new modes of subscribing himself and depicting her. He is her 'languishing relict,'—her 'happy slave,'—her 'most obsequious, obedient husband.' She is his 'poor, dear, angry, pleased, witty, silly, every thing, Prue.'

Towards the end of 1717 she is meditating her return from Wales. From some of her husband's expressions it may be gathered that she is getting on worse than ever with those around her. He, on the other hand, full of belief in the future of the 'Fish Pool,' is casting about for money for his first journey to Scotland, after which time he proposes to fetch his wife home with a coach and six. But after all she seems to have come by herself. On the 4th of December she has arrived, and he is hoping for a happy meeting. There is only one letter to her after this, written to Hampton in June, 1718. The next in order, dated the 27th of December, and addressed to her cousin, Alexander Scurlock, runs briefly—'This is to let you know that my dear and honoured Wife departed this life last night.' She was buried in Westminster Abbey.

To the last she remains a contradictory shadow to the biographer—a shadow concerning whom it is difficult to make any direct averment. Both in Steele's works and correspondence there are numerous indications that she was fond of money. But such a fondness is not remarkable, or indeed unwarrantable, in a wife whose husband was always in want of it. There are other indications that she was not an affectionate mother, but there are also indications which are just as much to the contrary. At times, too, it might be supposed that she did not love her husband, and yet it is not difficult to find proof that she was sincerely attached to him. She was, in short, a married coquette, whose worst faults were fostered by Steele's extravagant admiration. Of the wit and wisdom with which he credited her we have no convincing proof, for besides the two or three letters already referred to, nothing important of her writing has been preserved with the exception of the following lines on a scrap of paper among the autographs at the British Museum :—

'Ah ! Dick Steele, that I were sure
Your love, like mine, would still endure ;

That time, nor absence, which destroys
The cares of lovers, and their joys,
May never rob me of that part
Which you have given of your heart :
Others unenvy'd may possess
Whatever they think happiness.
Grant this, O God, my great request ;
In his dear arms may I for ever rest ! '

She was tender enough to 'good Dick' in this instance. And let it be remembered that on another occasion she behaved to him with an unexpected and exceptional generosity. Steele's life, as we know, in the 'wild, unhallowed times' of his military days had not been blameless, and once, when conference had been freer and more cloudless than usual, the coach carried his ' Ruler' and himself to a boarding-school in the suburbs. Shortly afterwards appeared a young lady, for whom Steele showed unmistakable signs of affection, insomuch that his wife asked him if the child was his. He replied in the affirmative. Then said Mrs. Steele—' I beg she may be mine too,' and forthwith, under the name of Miss Ousley, she became an inmate of their house and the companion of their eldest daughter. Later in life she narrowly escaped becoming the wife of the notorious Richard Savage,—sometime her father's *protégé*,—but she was afterwards more happily united to a plain Herefordshire gentleman of the name of Aynston.

Lady Steele's death, as we have said, occurred late in 1718. In the summer of the same year Steele had paid a visit to Blenheim in company with Bishop Hoadly. By this time Marlborough had fallen into senility ; and among other things which were devised to rouse and enliven him was an amateur representation of Dryden's *All for Love*, the text of which, it is rumoured, was carefully expurgated by the vigilant Duchess. This entertainment took place during Steele's stay at the palace,—indeed, he was applied to for the prologue, but retired in favour of Hoadly. It is to Hoadly, no doubt, that we owe a couple of anecdotes of Sir Richard upon this occasion. The Antony of the moment, who, by the way, appeared girt with the sword presented to Marlborough by the Emperor, was one of the Duke's former pages, a certain Captain Fishe. Notwithstanding the purification of the play, he seems to have wooed his Cleopatra with an energy worthy of George Powell. Steele was highly delighted with this conscientious rendering of the part; and finally whispered to his companion, 'My Lord, I doubt this Fishe is flesh.' The other incident occurred when they were leaving Blenheim. Seeing the hall crowded with an army of laced coats and ruffles, Steele was appalled at the prospective drain upon his slender finances. 'Does your Lordship give money to all these fellows?' he inquired. 'No doubt,' replied Hoadly. 'Then I have not enough,' said Sir Richard; and thereupon he made them a neat little speech, complimenting them upon their critical taste, as evidenced by their judicious applause of *All for Love*, and inviting them *en masse* to Drury Lane to any play they might please to bespeak.

Early in the following year (1719), Steele's ill-starred political sympathies involved him in a misunderstanding with Addison. 'I do not ask Mr. Secretary Addison anything'—he had written to his wife not many months before, and it is probable that some constraint had already sprung up between them. In 1719, this ripened to a paper war. Lord Sunderland had proposed a measure limiting the number of peers, one result of which would have been the practical exclusion of the Commons from the honours of the Upper House. Steele, although the measure originated with his own party, felt this keenly, and immediately started the *Plebeian* to denounce the Bill. Addison replied to the *Plebeian* in the *Old Whig*, and this ' *bellum plusquam civile*,' as Johnson calls it, was continued, with increasing acrimony, through two or three numbers. As far as dignity is concerned, Steele has rather the best of the quarrel, since to his opponent's oblique personalities touching ' Grub Street pamphleteers,[1] and ' stagnated pools,' he simply rejoins by a complimentary quotation from Addison's *Cato*. Still, upon different grounds, his own conduct of the controversy was by no means irreproachable ; and in both cases it is difficult not to echo the wish that faction could have found less illustrious advocates. The worst was, that the breach thus made seems never to have been repaired ; and a few months later reconciliation was rendered impossible by Addison's death.

[1] To one misconception arising out of this controversy, it is now only necessary to refer in a footnote. It was long supposed that when, in *Old Whig*, No. 2, Addison spoke of 'Little Dickey,' he meant Steele, whereas he intended the diminutive actor Henry Norris, already mentioned as the representative of Mrs. Fardingale in the *Funeral*. The mistake, first exploded by Lord Macaulay, originated in a blunder of the *Biographia Britannica*, perpetuated by Johnson, who had not seen the *Old Whig*, which was first reprinted by Nichols, some years after Johnson's death.

On the 6th of April, the Peerage Bill was reported
in the Lords; and in December, when, after the second
reading, a motion was made for committing it, Steele,
reiterating his written arguments, was the first to speak
in opposition. Pitt, Walpole, and Sir John Pakington
(Sir Roger's prototype) followed eloquently upon the
same side, with the result that when the question was
put the measure was thrown out. There were to be
other results unfavourable to Steele. But the most interesting thing in connection with the defeated Bill is
the fact that it prompted a *rapprochement* between Steele
and his old opponent the Earl of Oxford. Oxford's fall,
it will be remembered, had preceded the death of Queen
Anne. In the year following that event, he had been
impeached by the Commons, and consigned to the Tower,
where he lay two years, being only tardily acquitted
and released in July, 1717. He had now resumed his
seat in Parliament, and in this matter of the Peerage
Bill was on the side of Steele, who, in December, 1719,
addressed a long letter to him on the subject. Steele's
review of the Bill it is now needless to recall; but his
opening sentences are characteristic of his chivalrous
and forgiving nature. After defending his former
writings as the outpourings of a too zealous patriotism,
he makes a frank apology for all he had spoken or
written to Oxford's disadvantage 'foreign to the argument and cause which he was then labouring to support.'
' You will please to believe,' he goes on—and the words
have an unmistakable ring of manly sincerity—' I could
not have been so insensible as not to be touched with
the generosity of part of your conduct towards me, or
have omitted to acknowledge it accordingly, if I had not

thought that your very Virtue was dangerous; and that it was (as the world then stood) absolutely necessary to depreciate so adventurous a Genius surrounded with so much power as your Lordship then had. I transgressed, my Lord, against you when you could make twelve Peers in a day; I ask your pardon, when you are a private Nobleman; and as I told you, when I resigned the Stamp-office, I wished you all prosperity, consistent with the public good; so I now congratulate you upon the pleasure you must needs have, in looking back upon the true fortitude with which you have passed through the dangers arising from the rage of the people, and the envy of the rest of the world. If to have rightly judged of men's passions and prejudices, vices and virtues, interests and inclinations, and to have waited with skill and courage for proper seasons and incidents to make use of them, for a man's safety and honour, can administer pleasure to a Man of Sense and Spirit, your Lordship has abundant cause of satisfaction.'

This is the noblest fashion of flattery, and almost inevitably suggests a comparison. There was a great writer at this moment in Ireland,—now, as he told Bolingbroke, 'six years older and twenty years duller,' —but nevertheless slowly elaborating his masterpiece, *Gulliver's Travels.* Swift's intellectual gifts were far superior to Steele's; but Steele doing honour to the unhonoured Oxford is a pleasant picture beside the savage joy of Swift over the disgraced and fallen Marl-borough.

Successful as Steele's latest incursion into politics had been in attaining its object, it produced its usual consequences to himself. His opposition to the Peerage Bill aroused the anger of the Duke of Newcastle, then Lord Chamberlain, and his patent for Drury Lane was revoked. In anticipation of this blow, as well as to vindicate himself and his brother-managers, and defend the stage generally, he established the *Theatre*, by 'Sir John Edgar,' which brought upon him, among other things, a ferocious attack from the wolfish old critic, John Dennis, a man whom he had formerly befriended, but who was now smarting under some neglect by the Drury Lane potentates of his tragedy of *Coriolanus*.[1] Steele's reply to this onslaught is a mixture of satire, dignity, good-humour and raillery, some of which last must have been rather over his adversary's head. But, in addition to a few useful biographical particulars, already drawn upon in this memoir, it contains a memorable passage respecting its author's friendship with Addison. In Cibber's dedication to Steele, a few months before, of his tragedy of *Ximenes*, resenting the undue commendation of Addison which had been one of the weapons of Steele's political opponents, he fell into the opposite extreme of likening Steele to an eagle and Addison to a wren carried upon his back.[2] Dennis charged Steele with tacit complicity in this absurd piece of bad taste. After admitting that, on the contrary, it had given him pain, Steele, in the character of Edgar, comments as follows :—' It could not be imagined, that, to diminish a worthy man, as soon as he was no more to be seen, could add to him, who had always raised, and almost worshipped him, when living. There

[1] *Characters and Conduct of Sir John Edgar*, 1720.
[2] V. *All for Love*, Act ii. sc. 1.

never was a more strict friendship than between those Gent.emen; nor had they ever any difference but what proceeded from their different way of pursuing the same thing. The one with patience, foresight and temperate address, always waited and stemmed the torrent; while the other often plunged himself into it, and was as often taken out by the temper of him who stood weeping on the brink for his safety, whom he could not dissuade from leaping into it. Thus these two men lived for some years past shunning each other, but still preserving the most passionate concern for their mutual welfare. But when they met, they were as unreserved as boys, and talked of the greatest affairs, upon which they saw where they differed, without pressing (what they knew impossible) to convert each other.' Towards the close of the same paper he again refers with a touch of self-reproachful sadness to his wife, and to Addison, both now dead and gone:—'There is not now in his [Steele's] sight that excellent man, whom Heaven made his friend and superior, to be, at a certain place, in pain for what he should say or do. I will go on in his further encouragement: the best Woman that ever Man had cannot now lament and pine at his neglect of himself.' The *Theatre*, from No. 12 of which these passages are taken, came to an end in April, 1720. The only other works which belong to this period are *The Spinster*, a pamphlet-plea for the Woollen Trade as against Linens and Calicoes, now interesting chiefly for the minute details which it gives respecting the cost of a Fine Lady's dress; and two tracts, entitled respectively *The Crisis of Property* and *A Nation a Family*, in which he

warmly combats the South Sea Mania. The withdrawal
of his License largely occupies his correspondence; and,
with exception of some dispersed memoranda, relating
to a visit to Edinburgh in the summer of 1720, it pre-
sents but little biographical interest. One letter, however, may be quoted: it is the last specimen of its kind
we shall give. It is addressed to his eldest daughter
Elizabeth, a girl of eleven, while at school, and apparently under the surveillance of that friendly Mrs.
Keck to whom reference has already been made:—

'MY DEAR CHILD,—I have yours of the 30th of the
last month, and from your diligence and Improvement
conceive hopes of your being as excellent a person as
your mother; You have great opportunityes of becoming
such a one by observing the maximes and Sentiments
of Her Bosome Friend Mrs. Keck, who has condescended to take upon Her the care of you and your
Sister, for which you are always to pay Her the same
respect as if She were your Mother.

'I have observed that your Sister has for the first
time Written the *Initiall* or first letters of Her name,
tell Her I am highly delighted to see Her subscription
in such Fair letters, and how many fine things those
two letters stand for when she Writes them M: S: is
Milk and Sugar, Mirth and Safety, Musick and Songs,
Meat and Sause, as well as Molly and Spot and Mary
and Steele.

'You See I take pleasure in conversing with you by
Prattling any thing to divert you; I hope We shall
next month have an happy Meeting, when I will entertain you with some thing that may be as good for

the Father as the Children, and consequently please us all.

'I am Madam,
'Y^r Affectionate Father &
'Most H^{mble} Servant
'Richard Steele.
'Mrs. Steele,
'Edinburgh Octr 7th 1720.'

Steele's changing fortunes changed once more in 1721. Walpole, his ancient ally, became Chancellor of the Exchequer; and he was speedily reinstated as Governor of the Royal Company of Comedians. Later in the same year he published a second edition of Addison's *Drummer*, with a prefatory letter or dedication to Congreve commenting upon what he considered to be certain unjust aspersions made by Tickell in his recently published edition of Addison's works, in which the *Drummer* was not included. Most of the passages in this very valuable document which relate to Steele himself have already been used, or reproduced in these pages; those respecting Addison belong rather to his biography than Steele's. It is sufficient to say that Steele manifests once more his chivalrous admiration for his old friend. One little passage, however, may be here cited, because it confirms what has been stated in an earlier chapter. If Steele 'owned what others writ,' the result was not always to his advantage. 'What'—he says, replying to Tickell's insinuation that he had concealed Addison's authorship of certain pieces —' what I never did declare was Mr. Addison's, I had his direct injunctions to hide; against the natural warmth and passion of my own temper towards my friends. Many of the Writings now published as his I have been very patiently traduced and calumniated for; as they were pleasantries and oblique strokes upon certain of the wittiest men of the Age: who will now restore me to their good will in proportion to the abatement of [the] Wit which they thought I employed against them.' [1]

In March, 1722, Steele was elected M.P. for Wendover, Bucks, vanquishing Sir Roger Hill by a majority of seventy-one. Nothing of importance seems to have occurred to him during the next few months, when, it may be presumed, he was engaged in preparing for the production of his last play—*The Conscious Lovers*. From an advertisement in the papers in October, it would seem that the first title was *The Unfashionable Lovers*. It was acted at Drury Lane in November. The chief female part—that of Indiana—was taken by Mrs. Oldfield; and the chief male parts by Wilks, Booth and Cibber. Despite the attempts of Dennis to prejudice the public against it, the play was a considerable success, being acted twenty-six nights; and when published in the following month, was dedicated to the King, who, it is said, sent the author 500*l*.

The plot of the *Conscious Lovers* is to be found in the *Andria* of Terence. It is probable that, as Steele allows in his preface, the excellent acting was the main cause of the favour it found with the audience. At all events, one is more inclined in this instance to agree with the author's own canon, that a play is to be seen and not read, than in any of his former pieces—the *Lying Lover* not excepted. Like the *Lying Lover*, the

---

[1] Dedication of the *Drummer*, 1722.

Conscious Lovers is burdened with a serious scene directed against duelling, which the *Biographia Dramatica* informs us would probably have constituted the final word on that text, 'had not the subject been since more amply and completely treated by the admirable author of *Sir Charles Grandison,* in the affair between that truly accomplished gentleman and Sir Hargrave Pollexfen,'—a sentence which suggests the retort that Richardson, who built Lovelace out of Rowe's Lothario, is just as likely to have been indebted to the Bevil and Myrtle of the *Conscious Lovers.* There is also a scene between a father and a long-lost daughter which completed the transformation of the piece from a comedy to a *drame sérieux.* But its construction and evolution are far more skilful than any of its author's earlier efforts;[1] and one can imagine that in such a scene as the following Cibber and Mrs. Younger must have surpassed themselves. The part of Phillis, indeed, became a great favourite with those queens of comedy, Mrs. Abington and Mrs. Margaret Woffington :—

Tom . . . . Ah! too well I remember when, and how, and on what Occasion I was first surpriz'd. It was on the first of *April,* one thousand seven hundred and fifteen, I came into Mr. *Sealand's* Service ; I was then a Hobble-de-Hoy, and you a pretty little tight Girl, a favourite Handmaid of the Housekeeper.—At that Time, we neither of us knew what was in us : I remember, I was order'd to get out of the Window, one pair of Stairs, to rub the Sashes

---

[1] Cibber, no doubt, is responsible for something of this. Steele's Preface says distinctly that his colleague superintended the production of the play with great care, and that he 'altered the Disposition of the Scenes.'

clean,—the Person employ'd, on the innerside, was your
Charming self, whom I had never seen before.

Phil. I think, I remember the silly Accident : What
made ye, you Oaf, ready to fall down into the Street ?

Tom. You know not, I warrant you—You could not
guess what surpriz'd me. You took no Delight, when you
immediately grew wanton, in your Conquest, and put your
Lips close, and breath'd upon the Glass, and when my
Lips approach'd, a dirty Cloth you rubbed against my Face,
and hid your beauteous Form ; when I again drew near,
you spit, and rubb'd and smil'd at my Undoing.

Phil. What silly Thoughts you Men have !

Tom. We were *Pyramus* and *Thisbe*—but ten times
harder was my Fate ; *Pyramus* could peep only through a
Wall, I saw her, saw my *Thisbe* in all her Beauty, but as
much kept from her as if a hundred Walls between, for
there was more, there was her will against me—Would she
but yet relent ! Oh, Phillis ! Phillis ! shorten my Torment
and declare you pity me.

Phil. I believe, it's very sufferable ; the Pain is not so
exquisite, but that you may bear it, a little longer.[1]

This 'flippant scene of low love'—as Steele himself styles it in *Guardian* No. 87—must have been
calqué sur le vif, for the first draught of it appears in
the above periodical as an actual experience. There
are one or two other passages which reveal Steele's
characteristic touch. Such, for example, is the little
preachment which Bevil Junior addresses to Indiana
upon politeness to our inferiors ; such, again, the
defence by Mr. Sealand of the status of the merchant,
a defence in which one recognises the hand that penned
Sir Andrew Freeport's utterances upon the dignity of

---

[1] *The Conscious Lovers*, 1723, Act iii. pp. 40-41.

trade. Still more like Steele is a passing reference to Addison. 'These moral Writers practice Virtue after Death'—says young Bevil in Act i. 'This charming Vision of *Mirza*! Such an Author consulted in a Morning, sets the Spirits for the Vicissitudes of the Day better than the Glass does a Man's Person.' But if Indiana, and her impossible relations to her lover, could ever have been made credible, it must have been by the magic of Mrs. Oldfield's acting; and the improbabilities which Highmore the painter, even in the height of the play's popularity, pointed out to its author, are more manifest than ever to the reader of to-day. The *Conscious Lovers* fully deserves the praise which honest Parson Adams gives to its morality, but in adding that it contains 'some things almost solemn enough for a sermon' he writes its epitaph as a comedy.

Its success with Steele's contemporaries seems, however, to have diverted his energies once more into the line of dramatic composition; and in the summer of 1723 it was announced that he would present the Town with another play in the winter. This was probably the *School of Action*, several scenes of which, with fragments of another piece called the *Gentleman*, were published by Nichols in 1809. In the latter Steele seems to have intended to make use of that paper in the *Spectator* about servants which afterwards served as the basis for Townley's farce of *High Life below Stairs*. But long before the winter he was obliged to go to Bath for his health. He had been ill when the *Conscious Lovers* was in rehearsal; and he was ill again now, in mind as well as in body. His money difficulties had reached a point when, for the sake of his children, some effort must be made to solve them finally. While at Bath he heard of the death of his only remaining son Eugene—a bright and promising boy, but of an exceedingly delicate constitution, which had not been improved by precocious recitations at the 'Censorium.' It is doubtful whether Steele ever again returned to London. In April he was living at Hereford, where his friend Hoadly was now Bishop, and he lodged at the house of a mercer who acted as agent for the Welsh estate. While at Hereford a definite scheme for the gradual extinction of his debts out of his income from the Playhouse seems to have been agreed upon. It is printed by Nichols, and confirms the statement of Dr. John Hoadly that his retirement from London was dictated rather by 'a principle of doing justice to his creditors' than by the 'perils of a hundred gaols' to which Swift attributes it.[1] Deducting those debts that could be immediately discharged, the rest amounted to about three thousand five hundred pounds. As there is no mention in the above scheme of any sums derived from his late wife's property, it must be assumed that what remained of it was settled upon the children. But as the scheme contemplated the disappearance of the whole debt in four years, and as Steele lived five years longer, we may fairly conclude that his creditors were paid.

[1] 'Thus *Steele*, who own'd what others writ,
And flourish'd by imputed Wit,
From Perils of a hundred Jayls,
Withdrew to starve and dye in *Wales*.'
A Satire on Dr. Delany, 1730, p. 8.

The whole matter of his money affairs, however, is exceedingly obscure, and the information upon the subject conflicting. When his affairs were in the hands of trustees, he, or they for him, sold his share in the Playhouse, one result of which was a lawsuit with his old colleagues. This, in 1726, was decided against him. During the remainder of his life, he seems to have lived partly at Hereford, partly at Carmarthen. He was at both places in 1725. After this he had a stroke of paralysis, which greatly impaired his understanding; and he was carried to Carmarthen. 'I was told,' says Victor, 'he retained his cheerful sweetness of temper to the last; and would often be carried out in a summer's evening, where the country lads and lasses were assembled at their rural sports,—and, with his pencil, give an order on his agent, the mercer, for a new gown to the best dancer.'[1] He died on the 1st of September, 1729, at a house, now no longer in existence, which he occupied in King Street, Carmarthen; and he was buried on the 4th, by his own desire, in St. Peter's Church, where in 1876 a brass mural tablet was erected to his memory. There is an earlier monument to him at Llangunnor.

His daughter Mary—the 'M. S.' of the letter quoted some pages back—only survived him for a few months, dying in 1730. Elizabeth, the eldest and sole remaining child, seems to have inherited her mother's beauty with something of her father's wit and improvidence. She had several suitors, two of whom fought a duel on her account. In May, 1732, she

---

[1] Victor's *Original Letters, Dramatic Pieces, and Poems*, 1776, i. 330.

married the Honble. John Trevor, then a Welsh judge, and afterwards the third Lord Trevor of Bromham in Bedfordshire. About the same time, one of Mr. Trevor's sisters married the Earl of Sunderland; and thus Steele's daughter became connected by marriage with the family of that great Captain whom her father had so loved and honoured.

CHAPTER VIII.

CONCLUSION.

THERE are several portraits of Sir Richard Steele. To three of them he himself makes reference in his reply to one of Dennis's papers, which contains a coarse verbal-caricature of him in the Rowlandson or Bunbury manner—a 'caricature,' says Mr. Thackeray, which has 'a dreadful resemblance to the original.' This, it may humbly be submitted, is true of all caricatures of merit; but it need not therefore be accepted as the *vera effigies*. Dennis, here and elsewhere, laid stress upon Steele's short face, his black peruke, and his dusky countenance. The short face Sir Richard could scarcely have contested, as he pleads guilty to it in the *Spectator*. But the wig, he contends, was in this instance brown; and he evades the 'dusky countenance.' He was, in fact, what was called in those days 'a black man;' and he goes on to say, with respect to this 'insinuation against his beauty,' that he has ordered new editions of his face after Kneller, Thornhill and Richardson to disabuse mankind.[1] The first, he tells us, has painted him 'resolute;' the second '.thoughtful;' the third 'indolent.' All these

---

[1] *Theatre*, No. 11.

pictures, we believe, are still in existence. The Rich-ardson, the earliest in point of date, and an unusually fine specimen of the painter's art, is in the National Portrait Gallery. It gives us the Steele of 1712—the Steele of the *Spectator*. He here appears as a portly, good-humoured man, 'of a ruddy countenance,' with broad dark eyebrows, very bright brown eyes, and a mass of curling brown hair that hides his ears. He wears a collarless coat, and a plain cravat. The Kneller, the 'resolute' one, was painted for the Kit-Cat Club in 1714, and engraved by Faber and Houbraken. A beautiful little copy of it, by Vertue, generally forms the frontispiece to the collected plays. This portrait exhibits Steele in the voluminous 'full-bottomed dress-periwig,' in which he rode abroad, or penned homilies against luxury and extravagance. There is a squareness about the face, and an Irish vivacity in the dark eyes, which makes one think it must have been more like Steele than the other. The Thornhill, at Cobham Hall, is perhaps better known than either the Kneller or the Richardson. Familiar as the original of the circular print that figures in so many of Nichols's publications, it depicts him in the disarray of a dressing gown and tasselled cap. When it was painted in 1717 he was forty-six. Nichols mentions another portrait by Michael Dahl, taken when he was Commissioner in Scotland; and there is a reputed Kneller, from the collection of the Earl of Oxford, at Stationers' Hall. Dennis seems to have regarded Sir Richard's reply to his personal remarks as proof positive of his vanity. But Dennis did not understand raillery, and Steele was not vain of his appearance. 'My person,' he says in his charming paper on Estcourt, 'is very little of my Care; and it is indifferent to me what is said of my Shape, my Air, my Manner, my Speech, or my Address.' . . . 'I am arrived at the Happiness of thinking nothing a Diminution to me, but what argues a Depravity of my Will.'

As regards Steele's character, its picture has been drawn by two masters in the art, of whom every man of letters must desire to speak with becoming respect. But neither the graphic pen of Lord Macaulay, nor the caressing periods of Mr. Thackeray's famous lecture, can be said to have done full or final justice to the subject. In the former case especially, it is impossible not to feel that the attractions of antithesis, and the desire of providing a foil to Addison, added, it may be, to some obscure repugnance, have warped and distorted the representation. Hence the case against Steele is everywhere sedulously heightened. For example, wine, with Addison, only ' breaks the spell which lies on his fine intellect,' but Steele, on the contrary, 'drinks himself into a fever.' Again, the exaggeration of epigram rises at times to absolute misstatement. To speak of Steele's ' dicing himself into a spunging house' is a strange accusation against the man who spent his literary lifetime in fighting sharpers and gamesters, and concerning whose experimental knowledge of gambling there is no evidence whatever. That Addison neither obtained Steele's place for him, nor 'corrected his plays' in the sense in which the phrase is used, nor did one or two things for his friend that Lord Macaulay ascribes to his good offices, are matters of minor detail. But the partial attitude of the whole picture is curiously illustrated by the grudging way in which, when Steele

is incontestably right, his critic admits the fact. He
was right, Lord Macaulay allows, in the debate on the
Peerage Bill. Yet he was right, we are to believe, only
by accident. 'It seems to us that the premises of both
the controversialists were unsound ; that on those premises Addison reasoned well and Steele ill, and that
consequently Addison brought out a false conclusion
while Steele blundered on the truth.' There is the less
reason, however, for debating this question, because it
has been discussed minutely in an essay by Mr. John
Forster, which, subject to some recent rectifications, is
a worthy tribute to Steele. But it must not be forgotten, on the other hand, that Lord Macaulay's leaning
to Addison led him to expose the stupid story of ' Little
Dickey.' And, though some of Steele's more ardent
champions seek to ignore the fact, it should also be
remembered that the work of an incomparable history-
painter is not vitiated by his imperfect sympathy with
a single figure.

Against Mr. Thackeray's sketch the charge of imperfect sympathy cannot be made with equal force. His
picture of Steele, graced with all the charm of his
matchless style, and set in the most picturesque
eighteenth-century framework, has one incalculable
advantage, after which the painstaking biographer,
testing, searching, correcting, comparing, however
minutely and laboriously, may pant in vain. It is
alive. It is a real Steele that he puts before us,—as
real a Steele as he who in *Esmond* likens Lady Castle-
wood to Niobe and Sigismunda, or explains the battle
of Blenheim to Mr. Addison in his garret at the
Haymarket. But its strength is also its weakness, for

the Steele of the biographer is sacrificed to the Steele
of the novelist. For example, Mr. Thackeray draws
in his lecture a most delightful, and, as he admits,
imaginary picture of Steele's school-days. This, regarded as fiction, is perfectly legitimate. Regarded
as biography, it is impossible not to see that it is based
upon the old belief that Steele was some three or four
years younger than Addison, whereas he was some
weeks his senior. Probably, too, it would have modified Mr. Thackeray's account if he had known that
the damning of the *Lying Lover* was not the cause of
Steele's ceasing to write for the stage; and when he
speaks of his hand being too careless to gripe the golden
opportunity of the Hanoverian Succession, it would
have been more accurate to say that there was no
golden opportunity to gripe. That he was never a
cornet in the Horse Guards, and never, according to
the latest information, could have been reviewed by
King William in that capacity, are trifles that need
not be insisted on. The real drawback of the whole
presentment, admirable as it is, lies in the fact that
it seems to have been conceived under the domina-
tion of that disastrous ' poor Dick ' of Addison. Doing
justice to Steele's generosity, kindliness, amiability, it
leaves upon us the impression that he was weaker,
frailer, more fallible than the evidence warrants. So
strong, however, is the hold which Mr. Thackeray's
Steele has taken upon the popular fancy, that it would
now be difficult to displace it. It is very vivid, very
human, and in most essentials could scarcely be dis-
proved. Nor does the present writer propose to attempt
that graceless and ungrateful task. But in supplement

to the foregoing pages—pages in which Steele has been
allowed, as far as possible, to exhibit himself to the reader
—it is needful to linger for a few moments upon one or
two points of his character and career which have only
been referred to incidentally.

One of the most recurrent topics in the story of his
life is his habitual want of money, and it is not a
worshipful one. For a 'Christian Hero' and Captain
of Fusileers—for 'the pink and pride of chivalry to
turn pale before a writ,' as Mr. Thackeray puts it, is
certainly undignified. Nevertheless, while admitting
the impeachment, it cannot but be remembered that
there were also some extenuating circumstances. Improvidence, not prodigality, was Steele's error; and it
was fostered by the conditions of his education and the
uncertainty of his means. In his childhood he had
been a dependent, owing his 'being,' as he says, to the
charity of relatives. Until his first marriage in 1705,[1]
when he was thirty-four, he must have been a distinctly needy man. His pay as an ensign and captain
could not have been large; he apparently received little
or nothing from Lord Cutts in the way of money; and
his first three plays brought him no substantial returns.
No post that he afterwards held was long retained. His
small salary as Gentleman-Waiter, with the subsequent
pension, only lasted about seven years. His Gazetteership he held for three years; his Commissionership of
Stamps endured no longer; and it was but for a few
months that he enjoyed these offices together. Of his

---

[1] See pp. 50–1. It is most likely that the marriage took place
before August in this year, when Steele, writing to Lord Cutts, refers
to his prospects in the West Indies.

Barbadoes property we have no trustworthy particulars; but it seems to have been greatly over-estimated. Probably his second wife's property was also less than is supposed,—it is stated indifferently as four, five, and six hundred a year,—and after her death, it presumably went to his children. His most definite income was derived from Drury Lane; but this, during a year, was intermitted; and by that time he had long been embarrassed. There remain his allowances as a Commissioner in Scotland, his secret service money, his literary and other occasional gains. These, in the aggregate, amounted to a large sum. But as a source of settled income they must have been profoundly uncertain. Government payments were not then made with the regularity and precision of the present day; and all Steele's receipts, from whatever source, seem to have been liable to peculiar duties, discounts and drawbacks. To a prudent man this kind of revenue would be discomforting; to an imprudent man, generous by nature, and lavish with the open-handedness of those who have long been impoverished, it was disastrous. The marvel is, that with his idiosyncrasy, and his ever-projecting brain, Steele's liabilities were not, in the end, more considerable. His fellow-countryman, Goldsmith, without a family, managed to leave a debt of two thousand pounds behind him. Steele owed nearly double this sum, but he had discharged it before he died.

More than one anecdote is told in connection with what Johnson rotundly styles his 'imprudence of generosity, or vanity of profusion.' For one of these Johnson is himself the popular authority, and it is repeated in Boswell. Steele, as we know, had borrowed

1,000*l.* of Addison, which he had repaid.[1] At some
later period he borrowed another 100*l.*, which Addison,
so the story goes, reclaimed by an execution, a course
which has been variously criticised. In a brilliantly
improvised passage, concocted from one of Steele's
letters to his wife and the account of the banquet at
the Censorium, Lord Macaulay accepts and defends
Addison's procedure. 'Few private transactions which
took place a hundred and twenty years ago'—he says—
'are proved by stronger evidence;' and it must be
admitted that the story was freely circulated. Johnson
said it was 'known to all who were acquainted with
the literary history of the period,' which, seeing the
confusion a small fact has imported into his own story
of the sale of the *Vicar of Wakefield*, can scarcely be
regarded as conclusive. But when Malone questioned
him specially as to his authority, he said he had received the story from Savage, to whom Steele had
related it with tears in his eyes. Better security than
that of Savage, with whom Steele had quarrelled, might
reasonably be asked for. But the story was confirmed
to Johnson by Benjamin Victor the dramatist, who had
it from Wilks, Steele's own colleague. Burke, too, told
Boswell that he had heard it from Lady Dorothea
Primrose, of whom it was alleged (though inexorable
Mr. Croker questioned the fact) that she had lived long
enough to know Steele personally; and Hawkins too
had heard it from a person, who heard it from Hooke
of the Roman History, who, in his turn, heard it from
Pope. The most direct account of the incident is contained in a letter to Garrick from Johnson's informant

[1] See Chapter III. p. 76.

Victor, who received it a second time from Steele himself. Victor's version was to the effect, that on the forfeiture of the bond for the money, Addison's attorney enforced it by a sale, and that the surplus was remitted to Steele with a ' genteel ' letter (' genteel ' in those days still meant ' gentlemanly ') warning him against a way of living which must end in his inevitable ruin. Steele, Victor alleges, confirmed this story. ' He told me, it was literally true—and that he received it [? the letter] as he believed it was meant by his friend, *to do him service.*[1] But the anecdote naturally pleases neither the advocates of Steele nor the advocates of Addison ; and were it not for Victor's narrative, the most convenient solution would be that suggested by Dr. Thomas Sheridan, who regarded Addison's execution as simply put in to screen Steele's goods from other creditors. In any case no breach seems to have been made between the friends on this account.

The story of the bond, as we have seen, was related by various persons. But there are some other anecdotes which seem to rest exclusively on the authority of Savage, and must bear all the disadvantages of that dubious origin.[2] Once, he told Johnson, Sir Richard, in order to keep out of the way of his creditors, carried

---

[1] Victor's *Original Letters*, etc., 1776, i. 329. Victor, it may be added, says the amount was 1,000*l.* But he wrote his letter in 1762, long after his interview with Steele, which he places in 1725.

[2] ' It was always dangerous to trust him [Savage],'—says Johnson,—' because he considered himself as discharged by the first quarrel from all ties of honour or gratitude, and would betray those secrets which in the warmth of confidence had been imparted to him.' Again, ' when he loved any man, he suppressed all his faults ; and, when he had been offended by him, concealed all his virtues.' (*Life of Savage.*)

him (Savage) in his coach to a petty tavern near Hyde
Park Corner, kept him hard at work all day writing to
his dictation, and finally sent him out to sell the MS. to
pay for the dinner which they had eaten. Upon another
occasion, said Savage, being embarrassed by a number
of bailiffs, when he was about to give a party, Steele
hit upon the brilliant expedient of putting them into
his livery, and so managed successfully to carry out his
entertainment. A *quasi*-colour is given to the story
by the fact that it seems to be referred to in *Examiner*
No. 11, which attacks Steele as Mr. *Tatler*. 'I have
heard of a certain Illustrious Person, who having a
Guard du Corps, that forc'd their Attendance upon him,
put them into a Livery, and maintain'd them as his
Servants : Thus answering that famous Question, *Quis
custodiet ipsos Custodes?* For he, I think, might properly be said to keep his Keepers, in *English* at least, if
not in *Latin*.' Finally, a third of Savage's stories (or
fables) relates how he, Steele, and Ambrose Phillips,
issuing one evening from a tavern in Gerrard Street,
were warned by a friendly tradesman that there were
bailiffs on the watch. Instantly all the three companions rushed off different ways as if smitten by a
sudden panic. These *ana* appear in most lives of
Steele, and cannot well be omitted from any account of
him. But for biographical purposes no great importance
need be attached to them, as they are based upon un-
satisfactory evidence.

Closely connected with the careless good-fellowship
which they betoken, is another infirmity of Steele,
upon which, perhaps, too much stress has been laid.
His kindly gregarious nature easily seduced him into

convivial excesses, which in his sober moments no one deplored more than himself, and his regrets and resolutions often find their place in his missives to his wife. But it does not seem that he was in any sense a drunkard, still less that ·he was what is called a hard drinker. Such evidence as exists rather tends to show that, like many impulsive and excitable persons, he was easily affected by wine. In any case, his frailty in this way can scarcely be regarded as exceptional. In days when Harley went reeling into the presence of Queen Anne, when Bolingbroke 'drank like a fish,' when Swift left the Catonic Addison 'half-fuddled,' and was himself 'sick all night' after supper at Lord Mountjoy's, it is absurd to hold Steele, who was warmer-hearted than any of them, up to special reprobation because he tells his wife in a private letter that he has 'been a little intemperate, and discomposed with it.' It would be sufficient to leave this subject here. But the following extract from a letter of Dr. Hoadly, printed by Nichols, is so characteristic of Steele's good and bad qualities that it deserves reproduction :—

'My father, when Bishop of Bangor, was, by invitation, present at one of the Whig meetings held at the Trumpet in Shoe Lane [? Shire Lane] where Sir Richard, in his zeal, rather exposed himself, having the double duty of the day upon him, as well to celebrate the immortal memory of King William, it being the 4th of November, as to drink his friend Addison up to conversation-pitch, whose phlegmatic constitution was hardly warmed for society by that time Steele was not fit for it. Two remarkable circumstances happened. *John* SLY,[1] the hatter, of facetious

---

[1] John Sly, 'Haberdasher of Hats and Tobacconist,' is often mentioned in the *Spectator*. He died in 1729

memory, was in the house ; and, when pretty mellow, took it into his head to come into the company upon his knees, with a tankard of ale in his hand, to drink off to the *immortal memory*, and to retire in the same manner. Steele, sitting next my Father, whispered him, *Do laugh; it is humanity to laugh.* Sir Richard in the evening, being too much in the same condition, was put into a chair and sent home. Nothing would serve him but being carried to the Bishop of Bangor's, late as it was. However, the chair-men carried him home, and got him up stairs, when his great complaisance would wait on them downstairs, which he did, and then was got quietly to bed.'

Next day came a letter to Hoadly containing the following apologetic couplet :—

'Virtue with so much ease on Bangor sits,
    All faults he pardons, though he none commits.'

This anecdote, with its sequel, goes far to illustrate that strange medley, Steele's character. All his lifetime he seems to have presented the spectacle of a weak will contending with an honest purpose ; and to have prompted in the critical that endless and inevitable comparison of his precepts and his practice which had assailed him in his capacity of 'Christian Hero.' The reconciliation of religion and breeding,—the enabling men 'to go to Heaven with a very good mien'—which he strove to effect in his writings, however edifying on paper, became, when exemplified in his own person, a doctrine of uncertain sound, resulting in a rather la-mentable failure to make the best of both worlds. By his words, by those 'ordinary rules of right reason,' to which he is so fond of appealing, he is constantly on the right side; by his actions he is as persistently on the wrong. Yet he was not in the least an hypocrite. Mawworm or Tartuffe might affirm that they had written those pious entries in his diary, or composed those prayers which appear among his papers; but they would hardly have penned or prepared them, as he did, to be seen and read by no one. His love and reverence for virtue were, as Pope said, real. But his quick enthusiasm and his impressible temperament often betrayed him into actions and landed him in dilemmas which meaner men would have easily avoided. Most of his faults are to be traced to this cause. But along with those faults he had conspicuous merits. With all his inconsistency, he is strangely consistent in some things. In his first book, in his plays, in his essays, he has always one end in view,—the improvement of human nature and the reformation of society. In politics, when so many were changing sides, he never wavered in his principles; nor, at a time when the tone of political morality was notoriously low, does he seem ever to have sacrificed his opinions to his interests. He was unswerving in his loyalty to his friends; he was the most loving of fathers; and, in days when marriage was a lighter tie than now, his devotion to his wife may be called romantic. There have been wiser, stronger, greater men. But many a strong man would have been stronger for a touch of Steele's indulgent sympathy; many a great man has wanted his genuine largeness of heart; many a wise man might learn something· from his deep and wide humanity. His virtues redeemed his frailties. He was thoroughly amiable, kindly, and generous. *Faute d'archanges il faut aimer des créatures imparfaites.*

Of his work it may be said generally that his essays

Q

alone survive.   Upon the strength of his slender contribution to the *Poetical Miscellanies*, and a few prologues
and occasional verses, it would be impossible to set up
a claim for him as a poet, to which dignity, indeed,
he never pretended.[1]   His political pamphlets served
the purposes of the hour, and, except to the minute
student of parliamentary history, or the all-sifting
biographer, are now unreadable.   If they had never
formed part of his works at all, it would have been no
loss, or rather it would have been a loss that the absence
of much of the scandal and obloquy they brought upon
him would have amply atoned for.   Let us assume for
a moment that Addison, by championing the Whigs,
had exposed himself to such an attack as *Toby's Character*.   How all the Grub Street of Manleys and Oldis-
worths would have aired its venal virtue over his
putting an execution into a friend's house,—over his
fondness for flattery, his oratorical shortcomings, his
splendid, unhappy marriage!   But Addison was wise in
his generation, and kept his head clear of that ' cloud
of poisonous flies.'   Steele, more eager, more reckless in
' backing of his friends,' blundered hopelessly into it;
and his reputation has suffered accordingly.   It is well
to remember how much that he would otherwise have
escaped in the way of mere tittle-tattle and depreciation
is due to that luckless excursion into faction.

   With regard to his plays little need be said in addition to what is contained in an earlier chapter.   To-day,
if not, like his political tracts, actually dead, they are

---

[1] *Anticipation of the Posthumous Character of Sir Richard Steele*,
by Dr. Thomas Rundle, afterwards Bishop of Derry.   *Epist. Corr.*
1809, ii. p. 690.

but faintly animate. They were not brilliant successes in his own time, and they have never passed into the repertory of the stage. The fact that their author so willingly leaned upon the plot of a predecessor indicates his weak point;—the lack of that constructive stagecraft which still seems to be one of the rarest gifts of Englishmen. Another difficulty with which he struggled manfully was his praiseworthy but debatable desire to import direct moral teaching into his work. Whether this can or should be done, and whether Steele's attempt to do it was chargeable with the blame of initiating the pestilent Sentimental Drama of subsequent years,—the ‘mawkish drab of spurious breed,’[1] who, in Garrick's words, was to supplant the Comic Muse,—are questions which it is needless to discuss here. It is sufficient to note that in Steele's case the fusion of the pulpit and the stage was not satisfactorily accomplished. In the dialogue, too, it may be admitted with Chalmers that he is ‘sometimes tedious.’ ‘He wants the quick repartee of Congreve; and, though possessed of humour, falls into the style rather of an essay than a drama.’ Still it was impossible that so lively a humourist, and so penetrating an observer, could fail entirely. As already pointed out, his comedies contain several original sketches of character, some of which have furnished hints to other hands, while, in all of them, there are episodes —witness the little idyll of Tom and Phillis in the last chapter—which, it is safe to say, nobody but Mr. Bickerstaff could have invented.

As a prose writer Steele does not rank with the great masters of English style. He claimed indeed in

---

[1] Prologue to *She Stoops to Conquer*, 1773.

his capacity as a *Tatler* to use 'common speech,' to be even incorrect[1] if need were, and it may be added he sometimes abused this license, in a way that laid him open to the merciless criticism of Swift and others, much of whose material is derived from the dissection of his parts of speech. Writing hastily in all sorts of places to which the printer had traced him, scribbling off an essay from his bed or at a coffee-house table, bound at all hazards to supply the needful amount of 'copy' for which the press was waiting, it must be obvious that his method was the reverse of that of his fastidious colleague and contributor, who would often stop the press to insert a conjunction or preposition. Hence his style is frequently involved, and sometimes disfigured by words of which the sense seems but half-remembered. It is only when his subject stirs him strongly that he attains to real elevation and dignity of diction. Now and then, the warmth of his feeling reaches its flashing-point; and the result is some supremely happy phrase, such as the well-known 'To love her is a liberal Education,' which he applies to the Lady Elizabeth Hastings.[2] As might be expected from his emotional nature, his pathetic side is especially strong; but it is strong with all the defects of that nature,—that is to say, it is rather poignant and intense than fine or suggestive. He is not in the least ashamed of his tears; and when, with Master Stephen, he mounts his stool to be melancholy, he is for no half-measures in grief. He delights in highly-wrought situations, which he breaks off abruptly at the critical moment like the story of Clarinda and Chloe.[3] Sometimes, as in the

[1] *Tatler*, No. 5.   [2] *Ibid.*, No. 49.   [3] *Ibid.*, No. 94.

case of the bridegroom who shoots his bride by accident,[1] he heightens the tragedy by a playful prelude. He is at his best when he is depending wholly upon his personal memories, as in the familiar paper upon his father's death. The character of his humour, too, is strongly influenced by his personal *differentia*. It has little of practised art or perceptive delicacy; but it is uniformly kindly, genial, indulgent, recognising always that to 'step aside is human.' An object is never so ludicrous but he has somewhere a subordinate stroke to show that though he is laughing, there is nothing malicious in his mirth. Nay, so much compassion has he for the frailties of his fellow-creatures, that he often seems to be satirising himself more than others, and smiling—a little ruefully perhaps—at his own weaknesses rather than at theirs. His humour, in short, has the prevailing characteristics of his genius,—it is spontaneous and genuine, but often loose and ill-considered in expression. Still it is so cheerful and good-natured, so frank and manly, that one is often tempted to echo the declaration of Leigh Hunt—'I prefer open-hearted Steele with all his faults to Addison with all his essays.'

Steele's manner was, in truth, the reverse of Addison's. In the one the man of the world predominated— in the other the man of letters. While Addison allows his impressions to crystallise round some recollection from Castiglione or Heylyn, Steele, with his eye on the object, sketches what he sees among his fellows. He is sensitive about his claim to 'scholarship;' but his range of reading is restricted, and his real book is

[1] *Tatler*, No. 82.

human nature. He is an excellent critic of a common-sense type, and when he speaks of an author or picture it is with intelligent sympathy rather than with science. Concerning the stage he is a thoroughly trustworthy authority, because he knew the boards and the actors, and cared little for the unities. His habits of life pre-cluded him from research and the slow elaboration of masterpieces; and much of his work must have been the mere *tour de force* of a quick apprehension or a ready pen. He teems with ideas and suggestions arising from his daily experiences; but they are the result rather of his observations than of his reflections. None of his little stories are originated by himself, but are simply the result of a quick imagination playing about an incident which he has heard yesterday, or read to-day. *Valentine and Unnion, Inkle and Yarico,* the *Cornish Lovers,* the *Murder of Mrs. Eustace* are all of this kind, and even the charming episode of *Brunetta and Phillis,* which had been thought to be suggested by a passage in Pepys, now proves to be a graceful paraphrase of a real Barbadian tragedy.[1] It was this actuality of sug-gestion, coupled with his native bias towards the hor-tatory and didactic, which prompted so many 'moral essays' among his papers. One sees that to string together a series of precepts, or rather to fuse them in the warmth of a quick-kindled enthusiasm, was easier to him, and more suited to his opportunities, than to build up his work by lingering touches. His utter-ances on Charity, Benevolence, Praise, Flattery, Dis-

---

[1] *West Indian Quarterly,* 1885, i. pt. iii., which contains an interesting article by Mr. N. Darnell Davis on 'The *Spectator's* Essays relating to the West Indies.'

tinction, Ambition, and the like, are admirable lay-sermons, full of a noble and earnest sincerity. But his native vein is the study of humanity, and upon this he delights to exhaust the resources of his genial humour, his wit, his raillery and his playfulness. The world about him, not always a very reputable world, but one of considerable extent and variety,—this is what he shows us, this is what he laughs with and at, this is what he strives to conquer by the light artillery of ridicule. Of his domestic pieces, we have already given sufficient indication, and we have also sufficiently exhibited his skill in character-drawing. We shall conclude by a couple of sketches, one playfully satirical, the other wholly playful. Both are pictures of women, of whom Steele wrote with an insight, an admiration, an honesty and a chivalry which should for ever entitle him to the gratitude of the 'Beautiful Sex.' The first is a picture of a coquette from *Tatler* No. 27 :—

'As a Rake among Men is the Man who lives in the constant Abuse of his Reason, so a Coquet among Women is one who lives in continual Mis-application of her Beauty. The chief of all whom I have the Honour to be acquainted with, is pretty Mrs. *Toss*: She is ever in Practice of something which disfigures her, and takes from her Charms ; tho' all she does tends to a contrary Effect. She has naturally a very agreeable Voice and Utterance, which she has chang'd for the prettiest Lisp imaginable. She sees, what she has a Mind to see, at half a Mile Distance ; but poring with her Eyes half shut at every one she passes by, she believes much more becoming. The *Cupid* on her Fan and she have their Eyes full on each other, all the Time in which they are not both in Motion. Whenever her Eye is turn'd from that dear Object, you may have a Glance and

your Bow, if she is in Humour, return'd as civily as you
make it ; but that must not be in the Presence of a Man
of greater Quality : For Mrs. *Toss* is so thoroughly well
bred, that the chief Person present has all her Regards.
And she, who giggles at Divine Service, and laughs at her
very Mother, can compose her self at the Approach of a
Man of a good Estate.'

The second is from *Tatler* No. 34. After relating
how Damia and Clidamira ('I assure you Women of
Distinction') have appealed to him to decide upon their
rival claims to be '*very* pretty,' he continues :—

'To put 'em to the Tryal, Look ye, said I, I must not
rashly give my Judgment in Matters of this Importance ;
pray let me see you dance : I play upon the Kit. They
immediately fell back to the lower End of the Room. You
may be sure they curt'sy'd low enough to me : But they
began. Never were Two in the World so equally match'd,
and both Scholars to my Name-sake *Isaac*.[1] Never was
Man in so dangerous a Condition as my self, when they
began to expand their Charms. Oh ! Ladies, Ladies, cry'd
I, not half that Air, you'll fire the House. Both smil'd ;
for by the by, there's no carrying a Metaphor too far, when
a Lady's Charms are spoke of. Some body, I think, has
call'd a fine Woman dancing, a Brandish'd Torch of
Beauty.[2] These Rivals mov'd with such an agreeable
Freedom, that you would believe their Gesture was the

---

[1] A famous dancing-master :—

    'And *Isaac's* Rigadoon shall live as long
    As Raphael's painting, or as Virgil's song.'

[2] This reference, which seems to have escaped the annotators
is evidently to Waller's song beginning—

    'Behold the brand of beauty tost !
    See, how the motion doth dilate the flame !

necessary Effects of the Musick, and not the Product of Skill and Practice. Now *Clidamira* came on with a Crowd of Graces, and demanded my Judgment with so sweet an Air— But she had no sooner carried it, but *Damia* made her utterly forgot by a gentle sinking, and a Rigadoon Step. The Contest held a full half Hour ; and I protest, I saw no manner of Difference in their Perfections, till they came up together, and expected my Sentence. Look ye Ladies, said I, I see no Difference in the least in your Performance; but you *Clidamira* seem to be so well satisfied that I shall determine for you, that I must give it to *Damia*, who stands with so much Diffidence and Fear, after showing an equal Merit to what she pretends to. Therefore, *Clidamira*, you are a pretty ; but *Damia*, you are a *very* pretty Lady. For, said I, Beauty loses its Force, if not accompanied with Modesty. She that has an humble Opinion of her self, will have every body's Applause, because she does not expect it; while the vain Creature loses Approbation, through too great a Sense of deserving it.'

' The Entertainment to be concluded with a Dance,' say the Queen Anne playbills. It is with a dance that we end our study of Queen Anne's essayist.

INDEX.

PRINTED BY
SPOTTISWOODE AND CO., NEW-STREET SQUARE
LONDON

GENERAL LISTS OF WORKS

PUBLISHED BY

Messrs. LONGMANS, GREEN, & CO.

39 PATERNOSTER ROW, LONDON, E.C.

————oo:ö:oo————

HISTORY, POLITICS, HISTORICAL MEMOIRS, &c.

Arnold's Lectures on Modern History. 8vo. 7s. 6d.
Bagwell's Ireland under the Tudors. Vols. 1 and 2. 2 vols. 8vo. 32s.
Beaconsfield's (Lord) Speeches, edited by Kebbel. 2 vols. 8vo. 32s.
Boultbee's History of the Church of England, Pre-Reformation Period. 8vo. 15s.
Bramston & Leroy's Historic Winchester. Crown 8vo. 6s.
Buckle's History of Civilisation. 3 vols. crown 8vo. 24s.
Chesney's Waterloo Lectures. 8vo. 10s. 6d.
Cox's (Sir G. W.) General History of Greece. Crown 8vo. Maps, 7s. 6d.
—   —   Lives of Greek Statesmen. Two Series. Fcp. 8vo. 2s. 6d. each.
Creighton's History of the Papacy during the Reformation. 2 vols. 8vo. 32s.
De Tocqueville's Democracy in America, translated by Reeve. 2 vols. crown 8vo. 16s.
Doyle's English in America. 8vo. 18s.
Epochs of Ancient History :—
     Beesly's Gracchi, Marius, and Sulla, 2s. 6d.
     Capes's Age of the Antonines, 2s. 6d.
     —   Early Roman Empire, 2s. 6d.
     Cox's Athenian Empire, 2s. 6d.
     — Greeks and Persians, 2s. 6d.
     Curteis's Rise of the Macedonian Empire, 2s. 6d.
     Ihne's Rome to its Capture by the Gauls, 2s. 6d.
     Merivale's Roman Triumvirates, 2s. 6d.
     Sankey's Spartan and Theban Supremacies, 2s. 6d.
     Smith's Rome and Carthage, the Punic Wars, 2s. 6d.
Epochs of Modern History :—
     Church's Beginning of the Middle Ages, 2s. 6d.
     Cox's Crusades, 2s. 6d.
     Creighton's Age of Elizabeth, 2s. 6d.
     Gairdner's Houses of Lancaster and York, 2s. 6d.
     Gardiner's Puritan Revolution, 2s. 6d.
     —   Thirty Years' War, 2s. 6d.
     —   (Mrs.) French Revolution, 1789-1795, 2s. 6d.
     Hale's Fall of the Stuarts, 2s. 6d.
     Johnson's Normans in Europe, 2s. 6d.
     Longman's Frederick the Great and the Seven Years' War, 2s. 6d.
     Ludlow's War of American Independence, 2s. 6d.
     M'Carthy's Epoch of Reform, 1830-1850, 2s. 6d.
     Morris's Age of Queen Anne, 2s. 6d.
     —   The Early Hanoverians, 2s. 6d.
     Seebohm's Protestant Revolution, 2s. 6d.
     Stubbs's Early Plantagenets, 2s. 6d.
     Warburton's Edward III., 2s. 6d.
Epochs of Church History :—
     Perry's The Reformation in England, 2s. 6d.
     Tucker's The English Church in other Lands, 2s. 6d.
Freeman's Historical Geography of Europe. 2 vols. 8vo. 31s. 6d.

London : LONGMANS, GREEN, & CO.

Froude's English in Ireland in the 18th Century. 3 vols. crown 8vo. 18s.
— History of England. Popular Edition. 12 vols. crown 8vo. 3s. 6d. each.
Gardiner's History of England from the Accession of James I. to the Outbreak of the Civil War. 10 vols. crown 8vo. 60s.
— Outline of English History, B.C. 55–A.D. 1880. Fcp. 8vo. 2s. 6d.
Grant's (Sir Alex.) The Story of the University of Edinburgh. 2 vols. 8vo. 36s.
Greville's Journal of the Reigns of George IV. & William IV. 3 vols. 8vo. 36s.
— — — Reign of Queen Victoria, 1837–1852. 3 vols. 8vo. 36s.
Hickson's Ireland in the Seventeenth Century. 2 vols. 8vo. 28s.
Lecky's History of England in the Eighteenth Century. Vols. 1 & 2, 1700–1760, 8vo. 36s. Vols. 3 & 4, 1760–1784, 8vo. 36s.
— History of European Morals. 2 vols. crown 8vo. 16s.
— — — Rationalism in Europe. 2 vols. crown 8vo. 16s.
— Leaders of Public Opinion in Ireland. Crown 8vo. 7s. 6d.
Longman's Lectures on the History of England. 8vo. 15s.
— Life and Times of Edward III. 2 vols. 8vo. 28s.
Macaulay's Complete Works. Library Edition. 8 vols. 8vo. £5. 5s.
— — — Cabinet Edition. 16 vols. crown 8vo. £4. 16s.
— History of England :—

Student's Edition. 2 vols. cr. 8vo.12s.	Cabinet Edition. 8 vols. post 8vo. 48s.
People's Edition. 4 vols. cr. 8vo.16s.	Library Edition. 5 vols. 8vo. £4.

Macaulay's Critical and Historical Essays, with Lays of Ancient Rome In One Volume :—

Authorised Edition. Cr. 8vo. 2s. 6d. or 3s. 6d. gilt edges.	Popular Edition. Cr. 8vo. 2s. 6d.

Macaulay's Critical and Historical Essays :—

Student's Edition. 1 vol. cr. 8vo. 6s.	Cabinet Edition. 4 vols. post 8vo. 24s.
People's Edition. 2 vols. cr. 8vo. 8s.	Library Edition. 3 vols. 8vo. 36s.

Macaulay's Speeches corrected by Himself. Crown 8vo. 3s. 6d.
Malmesbury's (Earl of) Memoirs of an Ex-Minister. Crown 8vo. 7s. 6d.
Maxwell's (Sir W. S.) Don John of Austria. Library Edition, with numerous Illustrations. 2 vols. royal 8vo. 42s.
May's Constitutional History of England, 1760–1870. 3 vols. crown 8vo. 18s.
— Democracy in Europe. 2 vols. 8vo. 32s.
Merivale's Fall of the Roman Republic. 12mo. 7s. 6d.
— General History of Rome, B.C. 753–A.D. 476. Crown 8vo. 7s. 6d.
— History of the Romans under the Empire. 8 vols. post 8vo. 48s.
Nelson's (Lord) Letters and Despatches. Edited by J. K. Laughton. 8vo. 16s.
Pears' The Fall of Constantinople. 8vo. 16s.
Seebohm's Oxford Reformers—Colet, Erasmus, & More. 8vo. 14s.
Short's History of the Church of England. Crown 8vo. 7s. 6d.
Smith's Carthage and the Carthaginians. Crown 8vo. 10s. 6d.
Taylor's Manual of the History of India. Crown 8vo. 7s. 6d.
Walpole's History of England, 1815–1841. 3 vols. 8vo. £2. 14s.
Wylie's History of England under Henry IV. Vol. 1, crown 8vo. 10s. 6d.

BIOGRAPHICAL WORKS.

Armstrong's (E. J.) Life and Letters. Edited by G. F. Armstrong. Fcp. 8vo. 7s. 6d.
Bacon's Life and Letters, by Spedding. 7 vols. 8vo. £4. 4s.
Bagehot's Biographical Studies. 1 vol. 8vo. 12s.

London : LONGMANS, GREEN, & CO.

Carlyle's Life, by J. A. Froude. Vols. 1 & 2, 1795–1835, 8vo. 32*s.* Vols. 3 & 4, 1834–1881, 8vo. 32*s.*
— (Mrs.) Letters and Memorials. 3 vols. 8vo. 36*s.*
De Witt (John), Life of, by A. C. Pontalis. Translated. 2 vols. 8vo. 36*s.*
English Worthies. Edited by Andrew Lang. Crown 8vo. 2*s.* 6*d.* each.
    Charles Darwin. By Grant Allen. | Marlborough. By George Saintsbury.
        Shaftesbury (The First Earl). By H. D. Traill.
        Admiral Blake. By David Hanney.
Fox (Charles James). The Early History. By Sir G. O. Trevelyan, Bart. Crown 8vo. 6*s.*
Grimston's (Hon. R.) Life, by F. Gale. Crown 8vo. 10*s.* 6*d.*
Hamilton's (Sir W. R.) Life, by Graves. Vols. 1 and 2, 8vo. 15*s.* each.
Havelock's Life, by Marshman. Crown 8vo. 3*s.* 6*d.*
Hullah's (John) Life. By his Wife. Crown 8vo. 6*s.*
Macaulay's (Lord) Life and Letters. By his Nephew, Sir G. O. Trevelyan, Bart., M.P. Popular Edition, 1 vol. crown 8vo. 6*s.* Cabinet Edition, 2 vols. post 8vo. 12*s.* Library Edition, 2 vols. 8vo. 36*s.*
Mendelssohn's Letters. Translated by Lady Wallace. 2 vols. cr. 8vo. 5*s.* each.
Mill (James) Biography of, by Prof. Bain. Crown 8vo. 5*s.*
— (John Stuart) Recollections of, by Prof. Bain. Crown 8vo. 2*s.* 6*d.*
—   Autobiography. 8vo. 7*s.* 6*d.*
Mozley's Reminiscences of Oriel College. 2 vols. crown 8vo. 18*s.*
—   —   — Towns, Villages, and Schools. 2 vols. cr. 8vo. 18*s.*
Müller's (Max) Biographical Essays. Crown 8vo. 7*s.* 6*d.*
Newman's Apologia pro Vitâ Suâ. Crown 8vo. 6*s.*
Pasolini's (Count) Memoir, by his Son. 8vo. 16*s.*
Pasteur (Louis) His Life and Labours. Crown 8vo. 7*s.* 6*d.*
Shakespeare's Life (Outlines of), by Halliwell-Phillipps. 2 vols. royal 8vo. 10*s.* 6*d.*
Southey's Correspondence with Caroline Bowles. 8vo. 14*s.*
Stephen's Essays in Ecclesiastical Biography. Crown 8vo. 7*s.* 6*d.*
Taylor's (Sir Henry) Autobiography. 2 vols. 8vo. 32*s.*
Telfer's The Strange Career of the Chevalier D'Eon de Beaumont. 8vo. 12*s.*
Wellington's Life, by Gleig. Crown 8vo. 6*s.*

MENTAL AND POLITICAL PHILOSOPHY, FINANCE, &c.

Amos's View of the Science of Jurisprudence. 8vo. 18*s.*
— Primer of the English Constitution. Crown 8vo. 6*s.*
Bacon's Essays, with Annotations by Whately. 8vo. 10*s.* 6*d.*
— Works, edited by Spedding. 7 vols. 8vo. 73*s.* 6*d.*
Bagehot's Economic Studies, edited by Hutton. 8vo. 10*s.* 6*d.*
— The Postulates of English Political Economy. Crown 8vo. 2*s.* 6*d.*
Bain's Logic, Deductive and Inductive. Crown 8vo. 10*s.* 6*d.*
        PART I. Deduction, 4*s.* | PART II. Induction, 6*s.* 6*d.*
— Mental and Moral Science. Crown 8vo. 10*s.* 6*d.*
— The Senses and the Intellect. 8vo. 15*s.*
— The Emotions and the Will. 8vo. 15*s.*
— Practical Essays. Crown 8vo. 4*s.* 6*d.*
Buckle's (H. T.) Miscellaneous and Posthumous Works. 2 vols. crown 8vo. 21*s.*
Crozier's Civilization and Progress. 8vo. 14*s.*
Crump's A Short Enquiry into the Formation of English Political Opinion. 8vo. 7*s.* 6*d.*
Dowell's A History of Taxation and Taxes in England. 4 vols. 8vo. 48*s.*

London : LONGMANS, GREEN, & CO.

Green's (Thomas Hill) Works. (3 vols.) Vols. 1 & 2, Philosophical Works. 8vo. 16s. each.
Hume's Essays, edited by Green & Grose. 2 vols. 8vo. 28s.
— Treatise of Human Nature, edited by Green & Grose. 2 vols. 8vo. 28s.
Lang's Custom and Myth : Studies of Early Usage and Belief. Crown 8vo. 7s. 6d.
Leslie's Essays in Political and Moral Philosophy. 8vo. 10s. 6d.
Lewes's History of Philosophy. 2 vols. 8vo. 32s.
Lubbock's Origin of Civilisation. 8vo. 18s.
Macleod's Principles of Economical Philosophy. In 2 vols. Vol. 1, 8vo. 15s. Vol. 2, Part I. 12s.
— The Elements of Economics. (2 vols.) Vol. 1, cr. 8vo. 7s. 6d. Vol. 2, Part I. cr. 8vo. 7s. 6d.
— The Elements of Banking. Crown 8vo. 5s.
— The Theory and Practice of Banking. Vol. 1, 8vo. 12s. Vol. 2, 14s.
— Elements of Political Economy. 8vo. 16s.
— Economics for Beginners. 8vo. 2s. 6d.
— Lectures on Credit and Banking. 8vo. 5s.
Mill's (James) Analysis of the Phenomena of the Human Mind. 2 vols. 8vo. 28s.
Mill (John Stuart) on Representative Government. Crown 8vo. 2s.
— — on Liberty. Crown 8vo. 1s. 4d.
— — Essays on Unsettled Questions of Political Economy. 8vo. 6s. 6d.
— — Examination of Hamilton's Philosophy. 8vo. 16s.
— — Logic. 2 vols. 8vo. 25s. People's Edition, 1 vol. cr. 8vo. 5s.
— — Principles of Political Economy. 2 vols. 8vo. 30s. People's Edition, 1 vol. crown 8vo. 5s.
— — Subjection of Women. Crown 8vo. 6s.
— — Utilitarianism. 8vo. 5s.
— — Three Essays on Religion, &c. 8vo. 5s.
Miller's (Mrs. Fenwick) Readings in Social Economy. Crown 8vo. 2s.
Mulhall's History of Prices since 1850. Crown 8vo. 6s.
Sandars's Institutes of Justinian, with English Notes. 8vo. 18s.
Seebohm's English Village Community. 8vo. 16s.
Sully's Outlines of Psychology. 8vo. 12s. 6d.
— Teacher's Handbook of Psychology. Crown 8vo. 6s. 6d.
Swinburne's Picture Logic. Post 8vo. 5s.
Thompson's A System of Psychology. 2 vols. 8vo. 36s.
Thomson's Outline of Necessary Laws of Thought. Crown 8vo. 6s.
Twiss's Law of Nations in Time of War. 8vo. 21s.
— — in Time of Peace. 8vo. 15s.
Webb's The Veil of Isis. 8vo. 10s. 6d.
Whately's Elements of Logic. Crown 8vo. 4s. 6d.
— — — Rhetoric. Crown 8vo. 4s. 6d.
Wylie's Labour, Leisure, and Luxury. Crown 8vo. 6s.
Zeller's History of Eclecticism in Greek Philosophy. Crown 8vo. 10s. 6d.
— Plato and the Older Academy. Crown 8vo. 18s.
— Pre-Socratic Schools. 2 vols. crown 8vo. 30s.
— Socrates and the Socratic Schools. Crown 8vo. 10s. 6d.
— Stoics, Epicureans, and Sceptics. Crown 8vo. 15s.
— Outlines of the History of Greek Philosophy. Crown 8vo. 10s. 6d.

London : LONGMANS, GREEN, & CO.

MISCELLANEOUS WORKS.

A. K. H. B., The Essays and Contributions of. Crown 8vo.
    Autumn Holidays of a Country Parson. 3s. 6d.
    Changed Aspects of Unchanged Truths. 3s. 6d.
    Common-Place Philosopher in Town and Country. 3s. 6d.
    Critical Essays of a Country Parson. 3s. 6d.
    Counsel and Comfort spoken from a City Pulpit. 3s. 6d.
    Graver Thoughts of a Country Parson. Three Series. 3s. 6d. each.
    Landscapes, Churches, and Moralities. 3s. 6d.
    Leisure Hours in Town. 3s. 6d. Lessons of Middle Age. 3s. 6d.
    Our Little Life. Essays Consolatory and Domestic. Two Series. 3s. 6d.
    Present-day Thoughts. 3s. 6d.   [each.
    Recreations of a Country Parson. Three Series. 3s. 6d. each.
    Seaside Musings on Sundays and Week-Days. 3s. 6d.
    Sunday Afternoons in the Parish Church of a University City. 3s. 6d.
Armstrong's (Ed. J.) Essays and Sketches. Fcp. 8vo. 5s.
Arnold's (Dr. Thomas) Miscellaneous Works. 8vo. 7s. 6d.
Bagehot's Literary Studies, edited by Hutton. 2 vols. 8vo. 28s.
Beaconsfield (Lord), The Wit and Wisdom of. Crown 8vo. 1s. boards; 1s. 6d. cl.
— (The) Birthday Book. 18mo. 2s. 6d. cloth; 4s. 6d. bound.
Evans's Bronze Implements of Great Britain. 8vo. 25s.
Farrar's Language and Languages. Crown 8vo. 6s.
French's Nineteen Centuries of Drink in England. Crown 8vo. 10s. 6d.
Froude's Short Studies on Great Subjects. 4 vols. crown 8vo. 24s.
Lang's Letters to Dead Authors. Fcp. 8vo. 6s. 6d.
Macaulay's Miscellaneous Writings. 2 vols. 8vo. 21s. 1 vol. crown 8vo. 4s. 6d.
— Miscellaneous Writings and Speeches. Crown 8vo. 6s.
— Miscellaneous Writings, Speeches, Lays of Ancient Rome, &c. Cabinet Edition. 4 vols. crown 8vo. 24s.
— Writings, Selections from. Crown 8vo. 6s.
Müller's (Max) Lectures on the Science of Language. 2 vols. crown 8vo. 16s.
— — Lectures on India. 8vo. 12s. 6d.
Smith (Sydney) The Wit and Wisdom of. Crown 8vo. 1s. boards; 1s. 6d. cloth.
Wilkinson's The Friendly Society Movement. Crown 8vo. 2s. 6d.

ASTRONOMY.

Herschel's Outlines of Astronomy. Square crown 8vo. 12s.
Nelson's Work on the Moon. Medium 8vo. 31s. 6d.
Proctor's Larger Star Atlas. Folio, 15s. or Maps only, 12s. 6d.
— New Star Atlas. Crown 8vo. 5s.
— Light Science for Leisure Hours. 3 Series. Crown 8vo. 5s. each.
— The Moon. Crown 8vo. 10s. 6d.
— Other Worlds than Ours. Crown 8vo. 5s.
— The Sun. Crown 8vo. 14s.
— Studies of Venus-Transits. 8vo. 5s.
— Orbs Around Us. Crown 8vo. 5s.
— Universe of Stars. 8vo. 10s. 6d.
Webb's Celestial Objects for Common Telescopes. Crown 8vo. 9s.
— The Sun and his Phenomena. Fcp. 8vo. 1s.

THE 'KNOWLEDGE' LIBRARY.

Edited by RICHARD A. PROCTOR.

How to Play Whist. Crown 8vo. 5s.
Home Whist. 16mo. 1s.
The Borderland of Science. Cr. 8vo. 6s.
Nature Studies. Crown 8vo. 6s.
Leisure Readings. Crown 8vo. 6s.
The Stars in their Seasons. Imp. 8vo. 5s.
Myths and Marvels of Astronomy. Crown 8vo. 6s.

Pleasant Ways in Science. Cr. 8vo. 6s.
Star Primer. Crown 4to. 2s. 6d.
The Seasons Pictured. Demy 4to. 5s.
Strength and Happiness. Cr. 8vo. 5s.
Rough Ways made Smooth. Cr. 8vo. 5s.
The Expanse of Heaven. Cr. 8vo. 5s.
Our Place among Infinities. Cr. 8vo. 5s.

London : LONGMANS, GREEN, & CO.

CLASSICAL LANGUAGES AND LITERATURE.

Æschylus, The Eumenides of.   Text, with Metrical English Translation, by J. F. Davies. 8vo. 7s.

Aristophanes' The Acharnians, translated by R. Y. Tyrrell. Crown 8vo. 2s. 6d.

Aristotle's The Ethics, Text and Notes, by Sir Alex. Grant, Bart. 2 vols. 8vo. 32s.

—   The Nicomachean Ethics, translated by Williams, crown 8vo. 7s. 6d.

—   The Politics, Books I. III. IV. (VII.) with Translation, &c. by Bolland and Lang. Crown 8vo. 7s. 6d.

Becker's *Charicles* and *Gallus*, by Metcalfe. Post 8vo. 7s. 6d. each.

Cicero's Correspondence, Text and Notes, by R. Y. Tyrrell. Vols. 1 & 2, 8vo. 12s. each.

Homer's Iliad, Homometrically translated by Cayley. 8vo. 12s. 6d.

—   — Greek Text, with Verse Translation, by W. C. Green. Vol. 1' Books I.-XII. Crown 8vo. 6s.

Mahaffy's Classical Greek Literature. Crown 8vo. Vol. 1, The Poets, 7s. 6d. Vol. 2, The Prose Writers, 7s. 6d.

Plato's Parmenides, with Notes, &c. by J. Maguire. 8vo. 7s. 6d.

Sophocles' Tragœdiæ Superstites, by Linwood. 8vo. 16s.

Virgil's Works, Latin Text, with Commentary, by Kennedy. Crown 8vo. 10s. 6d.

—   Æneid, translated into English Verse, by Conington.   Crown 8vo. 9s.

—   —   —   —   —   — by W. J. Thornhill. Cr. 8vo. 7s. 6d.

—   Poems,   —   —   —   Prose, by Conington. Crown 8vo. 9s.

Witt's Myths of Hellas, translated by F. M. Younghusband. Crown 8vo. 3s. 6d.

— The Trojan War,   —   —   Fcp. 8vo. 2s.

— The Wanderings of Ulysses,   —   Crown 8vo. 3s. 6d.

NATURAL HISTORY, BOTANY, & GARDENING.

Allen's Flowers and their Pedigrees. Crown 8vo. Woodcuts, 5s.

Decaisne and Le Maout's General System of Botany. Imperial 8vo. 31s. 6d.

Dixon's Rural Bird Life. Crown 8vo. Illustrations, 5s.

Hartwig's Aerial World, 8vo. 10s. 6d.

—   Polar World, 8vo. 10s. 6d.

—   Sea and its Living Wonders. 8vo. 10s. 6d.

—   Subterranean World, 8vo. 10s. 6d.

—   Tropical World, 8vo. 10s. 6d.

Lindley's Treasury of Botany. Fcp. 8vo. 6s.

Loudon's Encyclopædia of Gardening. 8vo. 21s.

—   —   Plants. 8vo. 42s.

Rivers's Orchard House. Crown 8vo. 5s.

— Rose Amateur's Guide. Fcp. 8vo. 4s. 6d.

— Miniature Fruit Garden. Fcp. 8vo. 4s.

Stanley's Familiar History of British Birds. Crown 8vo. 6s.

Wood's Bible Animals. With 112 Vignettes. 8vo. 10s. 6d.

— Common British Insects. Crown 8vo. 3s. 6d.

— Homes Without Hands, 8vo. 10s. 6d.

— Insects Abroad, 8vo. 10s. 6d.

— Horse and Man. 8vo. 14s.

— Insects at Home. With 700 Illustrations. 8vo. 10s. 6d.

— Out of Doors. Crown 8vo. 5s.

— Petland Revisited. Crown 8vo. 7s. 6d.

— Strange Dwellings. Crown 8vo. 5s. Popular Edition, 4to. 6d.

London: LONGMANS, GREEN, & CO.

THE FINE ARTS AND ILLUSTRATED EDITIONS.

Dresser's Arts and Art Manufactures of Japan. Square crown 8vo. 31s. 6d.
Eastlake's Household Taste in Furniture, &c. Square crown 8vo. 14s.
Jameson's Sacred and Legendary Art. 6 vols. square 8vo.
    Legends of the Madonna. 1 vol. 21s.
    — — — Monastic Orders 1 vol. 21s.
    — — — Saints and Martyrs. 2 vols. 31s. 6d.
    — — — Saviour. Completed by Lady Eastlake. 2 vols. 42s.
Macaulay's Lays of Ancient Rome, illustrated by Scharf. Fcp. 4to. 10s. 6d.
The same, with *Ivry* and the *Armada*, illustrated by Weguelin. Crown 8vo. 3s. 6d.
Moore's Lalla Rookh, illustrated by Tenniel. Square crown 8vo. 10s. 6d.
New Testament (The) illustrated with Woodcuts after Paintings by the Early
    Masters. 4to. 21s. cloth, or 42s. morocco.
Perry on Greek and Roman Sculpture. With 280 Illustrations engraved on
    Wood. Square crown 8vo. 31s. 6d.

CHEMISTRY, ENGINEERING, & GENERAL SCIENCE.

Arnott's Elements of Physics or Natural Philosophy. Crown 8vo. 12s. 6d.
Bourne's Catechism of the Steam Engine. Crown 8vo. 7s. 6d.
   — Examples of Steam, Air, and Gas Engines. 4to. 70s.
   — Handbook of the Steam Engine. Fcp. 8vo. 9s.
   — Recent Improvements in the Steam Engine. Fcp. 8vo. 6s.
   — Treatise on the Steam Engine. 4to. 42s.
Buckton's Our Dwellings, Healthy and Unhealthy. Crown 8vo. 3s. 6d.
Crookes's Select Methods in Chemical Analysis. 8vo. 24s.
Culley's Handbook of Practical Telegraphy. 8vo. 16s.
Fairbairn's Useful Information for Engineers. 3 vols. crown 8vo. 31s. 6d.
   — Mills and Millwork. 1 vol. 8vo. 25s.
Ganot's Elementary Treatise on Physics, by Atkinson. Large crown 8vo. 15s.
   — Natural Philosophy, by Atkinson. Crown 8vo. 7s. 6d.
Grove's Correlation of Physical Forces. 8vo. 15s.
Haughton's Six Lectures on Physical Geography. 8vo. 15s.
Helmholtz on the Sensations of Tone. Royal 8vo. 28s.
Helmholtz's Lectures on Scientific Subjects. 2 vols. crown 8vo. 7s. 6d. each.
Hudson and Gosse's The Rotifera or 'Wheel Animalcules.' With 30 Coloured
    Plates. 6 parts. 4to. 10s. 6d. each.
Hullah's Lectures on the History of Modern Music. 8vo. 8s. 6d.
   — Transition Period of Musical History. 8vo. 10s. 6d.
Jackson's Aid to Engineering Solution. Royal 8vo. 21s.
Jago's Inorganic Chemistry, Theoretical and Practical. Fcp. 8vo. 2s.
Kerl's Metallurgy, adapted by Crookes and Röhrig. 3 vols. 8vo. £4, 19s.
Kolbe's Short Text-Book of Inorganic Chemistry. Crown 8vo. 7s. 6d.
Lloyd's Treatise on Magnetism. 8vo. 10s. 6d.
Macalister's Zoology and Morphology of Vertebrate Animals. 8vo. 10s. 6d.
Macfarren's Lectures on Harmony. 8vo. 12s.

London: LONGMANS, GREEN, & CO.

Miller's Elements of Chemistry, Theoretical and Practical. 3 vols. 8vo. Part I. Chemical Physics, 16s. Part II. Inorganic Chemistry, 24s. Part III. Organic Chemistry, price 31s. 6d.

Mitchell's Manual of Practical Assaying. 8vo. 31s. 6d.

Northcott's Lathes and Turning. 8vo. 18s.

Owen's Comparative Anatomy and Physiology of the Vertebrate Animals. 3 vols. 8vo. 73s. 6d.

Piesse's Art of Perfumery. Square crown 8vo. 21s.

Reynolds's Experimental Chemistry. Fcp. 8vo. Part I. 1s. 6d. Part II. 2s. 6d. Part III. 3s. 6d.

Schellen's Spectrum Analysis. 8vo. 31s. 6d.

Sennett's Treatise on the Marine Steam Engine. 8vo. 21s.

Smith's Air and Rain. 8vo. 24s.

Stoney's The Theory of the Stresses on Girders, &c. Royal 8vo. 36s.

Swinton's Electric Lighting : Its Principles and Practice. Crown 8vo. 5s.

Tilden's Practical Chemistry. Fcp. 8vo. 1s. 6d.

Tyndall's Faraday as a Discoverer. Crown 8vo. 3s. 6d.

—   Floating Matter of the Air. Crown 8vo. 7s. 6d.

—   Fragments of Science. 2 vols. post 8vo. 16s.

—   Heat a Mode of Motion. Crown 8vo. 12s.

—   Lectures on Light delivered in America. Crown 8vo. 5s.

—   Lessons on Electricity. Crown 8vo. 2s. 6d.

—   Notes on Electrical Phenomena. Crown 8vo. 1s. sewed, 1s. 6d. cloth.

—   Notes of Lectures on Light. Crown 8vo. 1s. sewed, 1s. 6d. cloth.

—   Sound, with Frontispiece and 203 Woodcuts. Crown 8vo. 10s. 6d.

Watts's Dictionary of Chemistry. 9 vols. medium 8vo. £15. 2s. 6d.

Wilson's Manual of Health-Science. Crown 8vo. 2s. 6d.

THEOLOGICAL AND RELIGIOUS WORKS.

Arnold's (Rev. Dr. Thomas) Sermons. 6 vols. crown 8vo. 5s. each.

Boultbee's Commentary on the 39 Articles. Crown 8vo. 6s.

Browne's (Bishop) Exposition of the 39 Articles. 8vo. 16s.

Bullinger's Critical Lexicon and Concordance to the English and Greek New Testament. Royal 8vo. 15s.

Colenso on the Pentateuch and Book of Joshua. Crown 8vo. 6s.

Conder's Handbook of the Bible. Post 8vo. 7s. 6d.

Conybeare & Howson's Life and Letters of St. Paul :—

     Library Edition, with Maps, Plates, and Woodcuts. 2 vols. square crown 8vo. 21s.

     Student's Edition, revised and condensed, with 46 Illustrations and Maps. 1 vol. crown 8vo. 7s. 6d.

Cox's (Homersham) The First Century of Christianity. 8vo. 12s.

Davidson's Introduction to the Study of the New Testament. 2 vols. 8vo. 30s.

Edersheim's Life and Times of Jesus the Messiah. 2 vols. 8vo. 24s.

—   Prophecy and History in relation to the Messiah. 8vo. 12s.

Ellicott's (Bishop) Commentary on St. Paul's Epistles. 8vo. Galatians, 8s. 6d. Ephesians, 8s. 6d. Pastoral Epistles, 10s. 6d. Philippians, Colossians and Philemon, 10s. 6d. Thessalonians, 7s. 6d.

—   Lectures on the Life of our Lord. 8vo. 12s.

Ewald's Antiquities of Israel, translated by Solly. 8vo. 12s. 6d.

—   History of Israel, translated by Carpenter & Smith. Vols. 1–7, 8vo. £5.

London : LONGMANS, GREEN, & CO.

Hobart's Medical Language of St. Luke. 8vo. 16s.

Hopkins's Christ the Consoler. Fcp. 8vo. 2s. 6d.

Jukes's New Man and the Eternal Life. Crown 8vo. 6s.

— Second Death and the Restitution of all Things. Crown 8vo. 3s. 6d.

— Types of Genesis. Crown 8vo. 7s. 6d.

— The Mystery of the Kingdom. Crown 8vo. 3s. 6d.

Lenormant's New Translation of the Book of Genesis. Translated into English. 8vo. 10s. 6d.

Lyra Germanica : Hymns translated by Miss Winkworth. Fcp. 8vo. 5s.

Macdonald's (G.) Unspoken Sermons. Two Series, Crown 8vo. 3s. 6d. each.

— The Miracles of our Lord. Crown 8vo. 3s. 6d.

Manning's Temporal Mission of the Holy Ghost. Crown 8vo. 8s. 6d.

Martineau's Endeavours after the Christian Life. Crown 8vo. 7s. 6d.

— Hymns of Praise and Prayer. Crown 8vo. 4s. 6d. 32mo. 1s. 6d.

— Sermons, Hours of Thought on Sacred Things. 2 vols. 7s. 6d. each.

Monsell's Spiritual Songs for Sundays and Holidays. Fcp. 8vo. 5s. 18mo. 2s.

Müller's (Max) Origin and Growth of Religion. Crown 8vo. 7s. 6d.

— . — Science of Religion. Crown 8vo. 7s. 6d.

Newman's Apologia pro Vitâ Suâ. Crown 8vo. 6s.

— The Idea of a University Defined and Illustrated. Crown 8vo. 7s.

— Historical Sketches. 3 vols. crown 8vo. 6s. each.

— Discussions and Arguments on Various Subjects. Crown 8vo. 6s.

— An Essay on the Development of Christian Doctrine. Crown 8vo. 6s.

— Certain Difficulties Felt by Anglicans in Catholic Teaching Considered. Vol. 1, crown 8vo. 7s. 6d. Vol. 2, crown 8vo. 5s. 6d.

— The Via Media of the Anglican Church, Illustrated in Lectures, &c. 2 vols. crown 8vo. 6s. each

— Essays, Critical and Historical. 2 vols. crown 8vo. 12s.

— Essays on Biblical and on Ecclesiastical Miracles. Crown 8vo. 6s.

— An Essay in Aid of a Grammar of Assent. 7s. 6d.

Overton's Life in the English Church (1660–1714). 8vo. 14s.

Rogers's Eclipse of Faith. Fcp. 8vo. 5s.

— Defence of the Eclipse of Faith. Fcp. 8vo. 3s. 6d.

Sewell's (Miss) Night Lessons from Scripture. 32mo. 3s. 6d.

— — Passing Thoughts on Religion. Fcp. 8vo. 3s. 6d.

— — Preparation for the Holy Communion. 32mo. 3s.

Smith's Voyage and Shipwreck of St. Paul. Crown 8vo. 7s. 6d.

Supernatural Religion. Complete Edition. 3 vols. 8vo. 36s.

Taylor's (Jeremy) Entire Works. With Life by Bishop Heber. Edited by the Rev. C. P. Eden. 10 vols. 8vo. £5. 5s.

Tulloch's Movements of Religious Thought in Britain during the Nineteenth Century. Crown 8vo. 10s. 6d.

TRAVELS, ADVENTURES, &c.

Aldridge's Ranch Notes in Kansas, Colorada, &c. Crown 8vo. 5s.

Alpine Club (The) Map of Switzerland. In Four Sheets. 42s.

Baker's Eight Years in Ceylon. Crown 8vo. 5s.

— Rifle and Hound in Ceylon. Crown 8vo. 5s.

Ball's Alpine Guide. 3 vols. post 8vo. with Maps and Illustrations :—I. Western Alps, 6s. 6d. II. Central Alps, 7s. 6d. III. Eastern Alps, 10s. 6d.

Ball on Alpine Travelling, and on the Geology of the Alps, 1s.

London: LONGMANS, GREEN, & CO.

Bent's The Cyclades, or Life among the Insular Greeks. Crown 8vo. 12s. 6d.
Brassey's Sunshine and Storm in the East. Crown 8vo. 7s. 6d.
— Voyage in the Yacht 'Sunbeam.' Crown 8vo. 7s. 6d. School Edition,
fcp. 8vo. 2s. Popular Edition, 4to. 6d.
— In the Trades, the Tropics, and the 'Roaring Forties.' Édition de
Luxe, 8vo. £3. 13s. 6d. Library Edition, 8vo. 21s.
Crawford's Across the Pampas and the Andes. Crown 8vo. 7s. 6d.
Dent's Above the Snow Line. Crown 8vo. 7s. 6d.
Froude's Oceana ; or, England and her Colonies. Crown 8vo. 2s. boards ; 2s. 6d.
cloth.
Hassall's San Remo Climatically considered. Crown 8vo. 5s.
Howitt's Visits to Remarkable Places. Crown 8vo. 7s. 6d.
Maritime Alps (The) and their Seaboard. By the Author of ' Vèra.' 8vo. 21s.
Three in Norway. By Two of Them. Crown 8vo. Illustrations, 6s.

WORKS OF FICTION.

Beaconsfield's (The Earl of) Novels and Tales. Hughenden Edition, with 2
Portraits on Steel and 11 Vignettes on Wood. 11 vols. crown 8vo. £2. 2s.
Cheap Edition, 11 vols. crown 8vo. 1s. each, boards ; 1s. 6d. each, cloth.

Lothair.	Contarini Fleming.
Sybil.	Alroy, Ixion, &c.
Coningsby.	The Young Duke, &c.
Tancred.	Vivian Grey.
Venetia.	Endymion.
Henrietta Temple.	

Black Poodle (The) and other Tales. By the Author of ' Vice Versâ.' Cr. 8vo. 6s.
Brabourne's (Lord) Friends and Foes from Fairyland. Crown 8vo. 6s.
Harte (Bret) On the Frontier. Three Stories. 16mo. 1s.
— — By Shore and Sedge. Three Stories. 16mo. 1s.
In the Olden Time. By the Author of ' Mademoiselle Mori.' Crown 8vo. 6s.
Melville's (Whyte) Novels. 8 vols. fcp. 8vo. 1s. each, boards ; 1s. 6d. each, cloth.

Digby Grand.	Good for Nothing.
General Bounce.	Holmby House.
Kate Coventry.	The Interpreter.
The Gladiators.	The Queen's Maries.

The Modern Novelist's Library. Crown 8vo. price 2s. each, boards, or 2s. 6d.
each, cloth.

By Bret Harte.	By Various Writers.
In the Carquinez Woods.	The Atelier du Lys.
	Atherstone Priory.
By Mrs. Oliphant.	The Burgomaster's Family.
In Trust, the Story of a Lady	Elsa and her Vulture.
and her Lover.	Mademoiselle Mori.
By James Payn.	The Six Sisters of the Valleys.
Thicker than Water.	Unawares.

Oliphant's (Mrs.) Madam. Crown 8vo. 3s. 6d.
Payn's (James) The Luck of the Darrells. Crown 8vo. 3s. 6d.
Reader's Fairy Prince Follow-my-Lead. Crown 8vo. 5s.
Sewell's (Miss) Stories and Tales. Crown 8vo. 1s. each, boards ; 1s. 6d. cloth ;
2s. 6d. cloth extra, gilt edges.

Amy Herbert. Cleve Hall.	A Glimpse of the World.
The Earl's Daughter.	Katharine Ashton.
Experience of Life.	Laneton Parsonage.
Gertrude. Ivors.	Margaret Percival. Ursula.

London : LONGMANS, GREEN, & CO.

Stevenson's (R. L.) The Dynamiter. Fcp. 8vo. 1*s*. sewed ; 1*s*. 6*d*. cloth.
— — Strange Case of Dr. Jekyll and Mr. Hyde. Fcp. 8vo. 1*s*. sewed ; 1*s*. 6*d*. cloth.
Sturgis' My Friend and I. Crown 8vo. 5*s*.
Trollope's (Anthony) Novels. Fcp. 8vo. 1*s*. each, boards ; 1*s*. 6*d*. cloth.
The Warden | Barchester Towers.

POETRY AND THE DRAMA.

Armstrong's (Ed. J.) Poetical Works. Fcp. 8vo. 5*s*.
— (G. F.) Poetical Works :—

Poems, Lyrical and Dramatic. Fcp. 8vo. 6*s*.
Ugone : a Tragedy. Fcp. 8vo. 6*s*.
A Garland from Greece. Fcp. 8vo. 9*s*.

King Saul. Fcp. 8vo. 5*s*.
King David. Fcp. 8vo. 6*s*.
King Solomon. Fcp. 8vo. 6*s*.
Stories of Wicklow. Fcp. 8vo. 9*s*.

Bailey's Festus, a Poem. Crown 8vo. 12*s*. 6*d*.
Bowen's Harrow Songs and other Verses. Fcp. 8vo. 2*s*. 6*d*. ; or printed on hand-made paper, 5*s*.
Bowdler's Family Shakespeare. Medium 8vo. 14*s*. 6 vols. fcp. 8vo. 21*s*.
Dante's Divine Comedy, translated by James Innes Minchin. Crown 8vo. 15*s*.
Goethe's Faust, translated by Birds. Large crown 8vo. 12*s*. 6*d*.
— — translated by Webb. 8vo. 12*s*. 6*d*.
— — edited by Selss. Crown 8vo. 5*s*.
Ingelow's Poems. Vols. 1 and 2, fcp. 8vo. 12*s*. Vol. 3 fcp. 8vo. 5*s*.
Macaulay's Lays of Ancient Rome, with Ivry and the Armada. Illustrated by Weguelin. Crown 8vo. 3*s*. 6*d*. gilt edges.
The same, Popular Edition. Illustrated by Scharf. Fcp. 4to. 6*d*. swd , 1*s*. cloth.
Pennell's (Cholmondeley) 'From Grave to Gay.' A Volume of Selections. Fcp. 8vo. 6*s*.
Reader's Voices from Flowerland, a Birthday Book, 2*s*. 6*d*. cloth, 3*s*. 6*d*. roan.
Shakespeare's Hamlet, annotated by George Macdonald, LL.D. 8vo. 12*s*.
Southey's Poetical Works. Medium 8vo. 14*s*.
Stevenson's A Child's Garden of Verses. Fcp. 8vo. 5*s*.
Virgil's Æneid, translated by Conington. Crown 8vo. 9*s*.
— Poems, translated into English Prose. Crown 8vo. 9*s*.

AGRICULTURE, HORSES, DOGS, AND CATTLE.

Dunster's How to Make the Land Pay. Crown 8vo. 5*s*.
Fitzwygram's Horses and Stables. 8vo. 5*s*.
Horses and Roads. By Free-Lance. Crown 8vo. 6*s*.
Lloyd's The Science of Agriculture. 8vo. 12*s*.
Loudon's Encyclopædia of Agriculture. 21*s*.
Miles's Horse's Foot, and How to Keep it Sound. Imperial 8vo. 12*s*. 6*d*.
— Plain Treatise on Horse-Shoeing. Post 8vo. 2*s*. 6*d*.
— Remarks on Horses' Teeth. Post 8vo. 1*s*. 6*d*.
— Stables and Stable-Fittings. Imperial 8vo. 15*s*.
Nevile's Farms and Farming. Crown 8vo. 6*s*.
— Horses and Riding. Crown 8vo. 6*s*.
Steel's Diseases of the Ox, a Manual of Bovine Pathology. 8vo. 15*s*.
Stonehenge's Dog in Health and Disease. Square crown 8vo. 7*s*. 6*d*.
— Greyhound. Square crown 8vo. 15*s*.
Taylor's Agricultural Note Book. Fcp. 8vo. 2*s*. 6*d*.
Ville on Artificial Manures, by Crookes. 8vo. 21*s*.
Youatt's Work on the Dog. 8vo. 6*s*.
— — — — Horse. 8vo. 7*s*. 6*d*.

London : LONGMANS, GREEN, & CO.

SPORTS AND PASTIMES.

The Badminton Library of Sports and Pastimes. Edited by the Duke of Beaufort and A. E. T. Watson. With numerous Illustrations. Crown 8vo. 10s. 6d. each.

Hunting, by the Duke of Beaufort, &c.
Fishing, by H. Cholmondeley-Pennell, &c. 2 vols.
Racing, by the Earl of Suffolk, &c.
Shooting, by Lord Walsingham, &c. 2 vols.

Campbell-Walker's Correct Card, or How to Play at Whist. Fcp. 8vo. 2s. 6d.
Dead Shot (The) by Marksman. Crown 8vo. 10s. 6d.
Francis's Treatise on Fishing in all its Branches. Post 8vo. 15s.
Jefferies' The Red Deer. Crown 8vo. 4s. 6d.
Longman's Chess Openings. Fcp. 8vo. 2s. 6d.
Peel's A Highland Gathering. Illustrated. Crown 8vo. 10s. 6d.
Pole's Theory of the Modern Scientific Game of Whist. Fcp. 8vo. 2s. 6d.
Proctor's How to Play Whist. Crown 8vo. 5s.
Ronalds's Fly-Fisher's Entomology. 8vo. 14s.
Verney's Chess Eccentricities. Crown 8vo. 10s. 6d.
Wilcocks's Sea-Fisherman. Post 8vo. 6s.
Year's Sport (The) for 1885. 8vo. 21s.

ENCYCLOPÆDIAS, DICTIONARIES, AND BOOKS OF REFERENCE.

Acton's Modern Cookery for Private Families. Fcp. 8vo. 4s. 6d.
Ayre's Treasury of Bible Knowledge. Fcp. 8vo. 6s.
Brande's Dictionary of Science, Literature, and Art. 3 vols. medium 8vo. 63s.
Cabinet Lawyer (The), a Popular Digest of the Laws of England. Fcp. 8vo. 9s.
Cates's Dictionary of General Biography. Medium 8vo. 28s.
Doyle's The Official Baronage of England. Vols. I.–III. 3 vols. 4to. £5. 5s.; Large Paper Edition, £15. 15s.
Gwilt's Encyclopædia of Architecture. 8vo. 52s. 6d.
Keith Johnston's Dictionary of Geography, or General Gazetteer. 8vo. 42s.
M'Culloch's Dictionary of Commerce and Commercial Navigation. 8vo. 63s.
Maunder's Biographical Treasury. Fcp. 8vo. 6s.
— Historical Treasury. Fcp. 8vo. 6s.
— Scientific and Literary Treasury. Fcp. 8vo. 6s.
— Treasury of Bible Knowledge, edited by Ayre. Fcp. 8vo. 6s.
— Treasury of Botany, edited by Lindley & Moore. Two Parts, 12s.
— Treasury of Geography. Fcp. 8vo. 6s.
— Treasury of Knowledge and Library of Reference. Fcp. 8vo. 6s.
— Treasury of Natural History. Fcp. 8vo. 6s.
Quain's Dictionary of Medicine. Medium 8vo. 31s. 6d., or in 2 vols. 34s.
Reeve's Cookery and Housekeeping. Crown 8vo. 7s. 6d.
Rich's Dictionary of Roman and Greek Antiquities. Crown 8vo. 7s. 6d.
Roget's Thesaurus of English Words and Phrases. Crown 8vo. 10s. 6d.
Ure's Dictionary of Arts, Manufactures, and Mines. 4 vols. medium 8vo. £7. 7s.
Willich's Popular Tables, by Marriott. Crown 8vo. 10s.

London : LONGMANS, GREEN, & CO.

A SELECTION

OF

EDUCATIONAL WORKS.

---◆◇◆---

TEXT-BOOKS OF SCIENCE

Abney's Treatise on Photography. Fcp. 8vo. 3s. 6d.
Anderson's Strength of Materials. 3s. 6d.
Armstrong's Organic Chemistry. 3s. 6d.
Ball's Elements of Astronomy. 6s.
Barry's Railway Appliances. 3s. 6d.
Bauerman's Systematic Mineralogy. 6s.
  — Descriptive Mineralogy. 6s.
Bloxam and Huntington's Metals. 5s.
Glazebrook's Physical Optics. 6s.
Glazebrook and Shaw's Practical Physics. 6s.
Gore's Art of Electro-Metallurgy. 6s.
Griffin's Algebra and Trigonometry. 3s. 6d. Notes and Solutions, 3s. 6d.
Jenkin's Electricity and Magnetism. 3s. 6d.
Maxwell's Theory of Heat. 3s. 6d.
Merrifield's Technical Arithmetic and Mensuration. 3s. 6d. Key, 3s. 6d.
Miller's Inorganic Chemistry. 3s. 6d.
Preece and Sivewright's Telegraphy. 5s.
Rutley's Study of Rocks, a Text-Book of Petrology. 4s. 6d.
Shelley's Workshop Appliances. 4s. 6d.
Thomé's Structural and Physiological Botany. 6s.
Thorpe's Quantitative Chemical Analysis. 4s. 6d.
Thorpe and Muir's Qualitative Analysis. 3s. 6d.
Tilden's Chemical Philosophy. 3s. 6d. With Answers to Problems. 4s. 6d.
Unwin's Elements of Machine Design. 6s.
Watson's Plane and Solid Geometry. 3s. 6d.

THE GREEK LANGUAGE.

Bloomfield's College and School Greek Testament. Fcp. 8vo. 5s.
Bolland & Lang's Politics of Aristotle. Post 8vo. 7s. 6d.
Collis's Chief Tenses of the Greek Irregular Verbs. 8vo. 1s.
  — Pontes Græci, Stepping-Stone to Greek Grammar. 12mo. 3s. 6d.
  — Praxis Græca, Etymology. 12mo. 2s. 6d.
  — Greek Verse-Book, Praxis Iambica. 12mo. 4s. 6d.
Farrar's Brief Greek Syntax and Accidence. 12mo. 4s. 6d.
  — Greek Grammar Rules for Harrow School. 12mo. 1s. 6d.
Hewitt's Greek Examination-Papers. 12mo. 1s. 6d.
Isbister's Xenophon's Anabasis, Books I. to III. with Notes. 12mo. 3s. 6d.
Jerram's Graecè Reddenda. Crown 8vo. 1s. 6d.

London : LONGMANS, GREEN, & CO.

Kennedy's Greek Grammar. 12mo. 4s. 6d.
Liddell & Scott's English-Greek Lexicon. 4to. 36s.; Square 12mo. 7s. 6d.
Linwood's Sophocles, Greek Text, Latin Notes. 4th Edition. 8vo. 16s.
Mahaffy's Classical Greek Literature. Crown 8vo. Poets, 7s. 6d. Prose Writers, 7s. 6d.
Morris's Greek Lessons. Square 18mo. Part I. 2s. 6d.; Part II. 1s.
Parry's Elementary Greek Grammar. 12mo. 3s. 6d.
Plato's Republic, Book I. Greek Text, English Notes by Hardy. Crown 8vo. 3s.
Sheppard and Evans's Notes on Thucydides. Crown 8vo. 7s. 6d.
Thucydides, Book IV. with Notes by Barton and Chavasse. Crown 8vo. 5s.
Valpy's Greek Delectus, improved by White. 12mo. 2s. 6d. Key, 2s. 6d.
White's Xenophon's Expedition of Cyrus, with English Notes. 12mo. 7s. 6d.
Wilkins's Manual of Greek Prose Composition. Crown 8vo. 5s. Key, 5s.
—   Exercises in Greek Prose Composition. Crown 8vo. 4s. 6d. Key, 2s. 6d.
—   New Greek Delectus. Crown 8vo. 3s. 6d. Key, 2s. 6d.
—   Progressive Greek Delectus. 12mo. 4s. Key, 2s. 6d.
—   Progressive Greek Anthology. 12mo. 5s.
—   Scriptores Attici, Excerpts with English Notes. Crown 8vo. 7s. 6d.
—   Speeches from Thucydides translated. Post 8vo. 6s.
Yonge's English-Greek Lexicon. 4to. 21s.; Square 12mo. 8s. 6d.

THE LATIN LANGUAGE.

Bradley's Latin Prose Exercises. 12mo. 3s. 6d. Key, 5s.
—   Continuous Lessons in Latin Prose. 12mo. 5s. Key, 5s. 6d.
—   Cornelius Nepos, improved by White. 12mo. 3s. 6d.
—   Eutropius, improved by White. 12mo. 2s. 6d.
—   Ovid's Metamorphoses, improved by White. 12mo. 4s. 6d.
—   Select Fables of Phædrus, improved by White. 12mo. 2s. 6d.
Collis's Chief Tenses of Latin Irregular Verbs. 8vo. 1s.
—   Pontes Latini, Stepping-Stone to Latin Grammar. 12mo. 3s. 6d.
Hewitt's Latin Examination-Papers. 12mo. 1s. 6d.
Isbister's Cæsar, Books I.-VII. 12mo. 4s.; or with Reading Lessons, 4s. 6d.
—   Cæsar's Commentaries, Books I.-V. 12mo. 3s. 6d.
—   First Book of Cæsar's Gallic War. 12mo. 1s. 6d.
Jeffcott & Tossell's Helps for Latin Students. Fcp. 8vo. 2s.
Jerram's Latiné Reddenda. Crown 8vo. 1s. 6d.
Kennedy's Child's Latin Primer, or First Latin Lessons. 12mo. 2s.
—   Child's Latin Accidence. 12mo. 1s.
—   Elementary Latin Grammar. 12mo. 3s. 6d.
—   Elementary Latin Reading Book, or Tirocinium Latinum. 12mo. 2s.
—   Latin Prose, Palæstra Stili Latini. 12mo. 6s.
—   Subsidia Primaria, Exercise Books to the Public School Latin Primer.
     I. Accidence and Simple Construction, 2s. 6d. II. Syntax, 3s. 6d.
—   Key to the Exercises in Subsidia Primaria, Parts I. and II. price 5s.
—   Subsidia Primaria, III. the Latin Compound Sentence. 12mo. 1s.
—   Curriculum Stili Latini. 12mo. 4s. 6d. Key, 7s. 6d.
—   Palæstra Latina, or Second Latin Reading Book. 12mo. 5s.

London: LONGMANS, GREEN, & CO.

Millington's Latin Prose Composition. Crown 8vo. 3s. 6d.
— Selections from Latin Prose. Crown 8vo. 2s. 6d.
Moody's Eton Latin Grammar. 12mo. 2s. 6d. The Accidence separately, 1s.
Morris's Elementa Latina. Fcp. 8vo. 1s. 6d. Key, 2s. 6d.
Parry's Origines Romanæ, from Livy, with English Notes. Crown 8vo. 4s.
The Public School Latin Primer. 12mo. 2s. 6d.
— — — — Grammar, by Rev. Dr. Kennedy. Post 8vo. 7s. 6d.
Prendergast's Mastery Series, Manual of Latin. 12mo. 2s. 6d.
Rapier's Introduction to Composition of Latin Verse. 12mo. 3s. 6d. Key, 2s. 6d.
Sheppard and Turner's Aids to Classical Study. 12mo. 5s. Key, 6s.
Valpy's Latin Delectus, improved by White. 12mo. 2s. 6d. Key, 3s. 6d.
Virgil's Æneid, translated into English Verse by Conington. Crown 8vo. 9s.
— Works, edited by Kennedy. Crown 8vo. 10s. 6d.
— — translated into English Prose by Conington. Crown 8vo. 9s.
Walford's Progressive Exercises in Latin Elegiac Verse. 12mo. 2s. 6d. Key, 5s.
White and Riddle's Large Latin-English Dictionary. 1 vol. 4to. 21s.
White's Concise Latin-Eng. Dictionary for University Students. Royal 8vo. 12s.
— Junior Students' Eng.-Lat. & Lat.-Eng. Dictionary. Square 12mo. 5s.
Separately { The Latin-English Dictionary, price 3s.
{ The English-Latin Dictionary, price 3s.
Yonge's Latin Gradus. Post 8vo. 9s.; or with Appendix, 12s.

WHITE'S GRAMMAR-SCHOOL GREEK TEXTS.

Æsop (Fables) & Palæphatus (Myths). 32mo. 1s.
Homer, Iliad, Book I. 1s.
— Odyssey, Book I. 1s.
Lucian, Select Dialogues. 1s.
Xenophon, Anabasis, Books I. III. IV. V. & VI. 1s. 6d. each; Book II. 1s.; Book VII. 2s.

Xenophon, Book I. without Vocabulary. 3d.
St. Matthew's and St. Luke's Gospels. 2s. 6d. each.
St. Mark's and St. John's Gospels. 1s. 6d. each.
The Acts of the Apostles. 2s. 6d.
St. Paul's Epistle to the Romans. 1s. 6d.

The Four Gospels in Greek, with Greek-English Lexicon. Edited by John T. White, D.D. Oxon. Square 32mo. price 5s.

WHITE'S GRAMMAR-SCHOOL LATIN TEXTS.

Cæsar, Gallic War, Books I. & II. V. & VI. 1s. each. Book I. without Vocabulary, 3d.
Cæsar, Gallic War, Books III. & IV. 9d. each.
Cæsar, Gallic War, Book VII. 1s. 6d.
Cicero, Cato Major (Old Age). 1s. 6d.
Cicero, Lælius (Friendship). 1s. 6d.
Eutropius, Roman History, Books I. & II. 1s. Books III. & IV. 1s.
Horace, Odes, Books I. II. & IV. 1s. each.
Horace, Odes, Book III. 1s. 6d.
Horace, Epodes and Carmen Seculare. 1s.

Nepos, Miltiades, Simon, Pausanias, Aristides. 9d.
Ovid. Selections from Epistles and Fasti. 1s.
Ovid, Select Myths from Metamorphoses. 9d.
Phædrus, Select Easy Fables. 9d.
Phædrus, Fables, Books I. & II. 1s.
Sallust, Bellum Catilinarium. 1s. 6d.
Virgil, Georgics, Book IV. 1s.
Virgil, Æneid, Books I. to VI. 1s. each. Book I. without Vocabulary, 3d.
Virgil, Æneid, Books VII. VIII. X. XI. XII. 1s. 6d. each.

London: LONGMANS, GREEN, & CO.

THE FRENCH LANGUAGE.

Albités's How to Speak French. Fcp. 8vo. 5s. 6d.
—   Instantaneous French Exercises. Fcp. 2s. Key, 2s.
Cassal's French Genders. Crown 8vo. 3s. 6d.
Cassal & Karcher's Graduated French Translation Book.   Part I. 3s. 6d.
    Part II. 5s. Key to Part I. by Professor Cassal, price 5s.
Contanseau's Practical French and English Dictionary. Post 8vo. 3s. 6d.
—   Pocket French and English Dictionary. Square 18mo. 1s. 6d.
—   Premières Lectures. 12mo. 2s. 6d.
—   First Step in French. 12mo. 2s. 6d. Key, 3s.
—   French Accidence. 12mo. 2s. 6d.
—   — Grammar. 12mo. 4s. Key, 3s.
Contanseau's Middle-Class French Course. Fcp. 8vo. :—

Accidence, 8d.	French Translation-Book, 8d.
Syntax, 8d.	Easy French Delectus, 8d.
French Conversation-Book, 8d.	First French Reader, 8d.
First French Exercise-Book, 8d.	Second French Reader, 8d.
Second French Exercise-Book, 8d.	French and English Dialogues, 8d.

Contanseau's Guide to French Translation. 12mo. 3s. 6d. Key, 3s. 6d.
—   Prosateurs et Poètes Français. 12mo. 5s.
—   Précis de la Littérature Française. 12mo. 3s. 6d.
—   Abrégé de l'Histoire de France. 12mo. 2s. 6d.
Féval's Chouans et Bleus, with Notes by C. Sankey, M.A. Fcp. 8vo. 2s. 6d.
Jerram's Sentences for Translation into French. Cr. 8vo. 1s. Key, 2s. 6d.
Prendergast's Mastery Series, French. 12mo. 2s. 6d.
Souvestre's Philosophe sous les Toits, by Stièvenard. Square 18mo. 1s. 6d.
Stepping-Stone to French Pronunciation. 18mo. 1s.
Stièvenard's Lectures Françaises from Modern Authors. 12mo. 4s. 6d.
—   Rules and Exercises on the French Language. 12mo. 3s. 6d.
Tarver's Eton French Grammar. 12mo. 6s. 6d.

THE GERMAN LANGUAGE.

Blackley's Practical German and English Dictionary. Post 8vo. 3s. 6d.
Buchheim's German Poetry, for Repetition. 18mo. 1s. 6d.
Collis's Card of German Irregular Verbs. 8vo. 2s.
Fischer-Fischart's Elementary German Grammar. Fcp. 8vo. 2s. 6d.
Just's German Grammar. 12mo. 1s. 6d.
— German Reading Book. 12mo. 3s. 6d.
Longman's Pocket German and English Dictionary. Square 18mo. 2s. 6d.
Naftel's Elementary German Course for Public Schools. Fcp. 8vo.

German Accidence. 9d.	German Prose Composition Book. 9d.
German Syntax. 9d.	First German Reader. 9d.
First German Exercise-Book. 9d.	Second German Reader. 9d.
Second German Exercise-Book. 9d.	

Prendergast's Mastery Series, German. 12mo. 2s. 6d.
Quick's Essentials of German. Crown 8vo. 3s. 6d.
Selss's School Edition of Goethe's Faust. Crown 8vo. 5s.
— Outline of German Literature. Crown 8vo. 4s. 6d.
Wirth's German Chit-Chat. Crown 8vo. 2s. 6d.

London : LONGMANS, GREEN, & CO.

Spottiswoode & Co. Printers, New-street Square, London.

Lightning Source UK Ltd.
Milton Keynes UK
UKHW012214301118
333276UK00011B/1218/P